◆ *Lonelier than God*

Lonelier than God

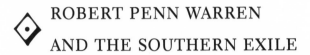 ROBERT PENN WARREN
AND THE SOUTHERN EXILE

Randy Hendricks

THE UNIVERSITY OF GEORGIA PRESS
Athens & London

Acknowledgments for previously published works appear
on pages xii–xiii, which constitute an extension of
the copyright page.

© 2000 by the University of Georgia Press
Athens, Georgia 30602
All rights reserved
Designed by Walton Harris
Set in 10/14 Electra by G&S Typesetters, Inc.
Printed and bound by McNaughton & Gunn

The paper in this book meets the guidelines for
permanence and durability of the Committee on
Production Guidelines for book longevity of the
Council on Library Resources.

Printed in the United States of America

04   03   02   01   00   C   5   4   3   2   1

Library of Congress Cataloging-in-Publication Data

Hendricks, Randy, 1956–   .
Lonelier than God: Robert Penn Warren
and the Southern exile /
Randy Hendricks.
    p.   cm.
Includes bibliographical references (p.   ) and index.
ISBN 0-8203-2178-8 (alk. paper)
1. Warren, Robert Penn, 1905–   — Criticism and
interpretation.   2. Alienation (Social psychology) in
literature.   3. Southern States — In literature.
4. Loneliness in literature.   5. Exiles in literature.
I. Title.
PS3545.A748Z687   2000
813'.52 — dc21   99-40179
                                                      CIP

British Library Cataloging-in-Publication Data available

For Amanda and Derek
and in memory of Deborah

CONTENTS

◆ PREFACE

The years 1997–98 will prove to have been seminal years for scholars and readers of Robert Penn Warren. First came the publication of the much anticipated biography by Joseph Blotner and more recently *The Collected Poems of Robert Penn Warren*, edited by John Burt. Both have provided valuable information that offers new ways to interpret the significance of Warren's career. A master biographer's detailed record of time, place, and event shows the relation of these to the work. A master editor's scholarly edition of what many take to be the most substantial portion of that work presents the poems as they appeared in Warren's volumes over the course of his career, a record perhaps even more valuable for tracing his development as a poet.

To be sure, Warren was not neglected before these books were published. Since the appearance of James Justus's *The Achievement of Robert Penn Warren* in 1981, numerous articles have been published; important book-length studies by William Bedford Clark, Victor Strandberg, Randolph Runyon, Hugh Ruppersburg, Calvin Bedient, and Burt have shaped a substantial body of Warren criticism; and these have led more recently to new directions of inquiry, including the first full-length work of feminist criticism of Warren, by Lucy Ferriss. The volumes by Blotner and Burt now promise a long season of bloom for further critical and scholarly interest.

My own effort here is perhaps best described as a complement to this body of criticism and scholarly research, offering, through a close examination of one important element in Warren, a new chapter in this growing body. It is not a work in the wake of Blotner and Burt, as it was conceived and written by and large before their appearance. Although it would be absurd to claim for it the magnitude and scope of either, it does, by homing in on the idea of the exile, locate itself on a hub in Warren's work from which spokes reach out to touch a cluster of larger themes; from this position it offers a new view of his development as poet, fiction writer, and social and literary critic. I have not in the process reduced Warren's writing to the theme of exile so much as I have taken the exile motif as exemplary of this cluster of problems—American, Southern, modern, eternal.

Warren's use of the exile figure is important on two fronts. First, it is a key to his relation to a significant body of twentieth-century Southern literature, representing, in fact, a culmination of an important movement in modern Southern literature which takes exile as a major postheroic theme. Second, as a dynamic figure within his own work the figure of the exile becomes an index to his growth as an artist and the relation of that growth to his regional sensibilities. As a writer whose career encompasses most of the century, Warren himself provides an important index to Southern literary history: his high modern sense of art, which for him is associated with a frozen Southern past, changes to a more personal and idiosyncratic sense of art, which is associated with a fluctuating sense of history.

Yet concentration on the exile in Warren's work blurs lines that are usually drawn between early and late Warren and Warren as poet, novelist, and critic. It becomes much more difficult to think of him as a New Critic or, even more absurdly, a neo-Confederate. It becomes much clearer that as our assessment of his significance continues, he will have to be reckoned as a major figure of the last half of the twentieth century, one who will strongly influence any consideration of whatever such slippery terms as "contemporary," "postmodern," and "Southern" will come to mean in the future.

◆ ACKNOWLEDGMENTS

Over the course of the last ten years a number of people have been instrumental in the advancement of this book toward its present form. I thank in particular William Shurr, Allison Ensor, Michael Lofaro, and Bruce Wheeler, all of the University of Tennessee, who read the work in earlier forms and commented in ways that led me ever forward in my thinking. I also thank Marjorie Pryse, formerly of the University of Tennessee and now of the State University of New York, Buffalo. More than any other, and probably more than she knows, Dr. Pryse through her writing and her teaching helped shape my formal knowledge of regionalist theory. William Bedford Clark and James Perkins showed enthusiasm for this project when it was sorely needed.

My greatest scholarly debt I owe to Robert Drake. Dr. Drake scared me twenty years ago when he actually expected me to know things in his fiction-writing class. In the years since, he has become my most valuable reader, mentor, and conversationalist.

Portions of chapters 1, 2, and 6 were previously published in different forms in the *West Georgia College Review*, the *South Atlantic Review*, and the *Mississippi Quarterly* respectively.

Kimily Willingham has been little short of a savior in preparing the manuscript. My editors at the University of Georgia Press — Nancy Grayson Holmes, Karen Orchard, Kristine M. Blakeslee, Jennifer Comeau, and David DesJardines — have guided me with patient and expert hands. Patricia Sterling did an excellent job of copyediting the manuscript.

Finally, I owe a debt as well to my family: to my children, Amanda and Derek, who showed patience when I closed the door in order to write; and to my late wife, Deborah, who kept the faith for twenty years and who learned that this book had been approved for publication just weeks before she died. Her smile at the news was payment enough for the work.

Excerpts from *All the King's Men*, copyright 1946 and renewed 1974 by Robert Penn Warren, reprinted by permission of Harcourt, Inc.

Excerpts from "Death of a Traveling Salesman" from *A Curtain of Green and Other Stories*, copyright © 1941 and renewed 1969 by Eudora Welty, reprinted by permission of Harcourt, Inc.

Excerpts from *Democracy and Poetry* by Robert Penn Warren, Cambridge, Mass: Harvard University Press, copyright © 1975 by Robert Penn Warren, reprinted by permission of the publishers.

Excerpts from *Jefferson Davis Gets His Citizenship Back* copyright © 1980 by Robert Penn Warren. Reprinted with permission of the University Press of Kentucky.

Excerpts from "The Life You Save May Be Your Own" from *A Good Man Is Hard to Find and Other Stories* by Flannery O'Connor, copyright 1953 by Flannery O'Connor, renewed 1981 by Regina O'Connor, reprinted by permission of Harcourt, Inc.

Excerpts from *Portrait of a Father* copyright © 1980 by Robert Penn Warren. Reprinted with permission of The University Press of Kentucky.

◇ *Lonelier than God*

CHAPTER ONE

The Wanderer Confronts Home

A Narrative Pattern

The right to exist as a man assumes
the right to knowledge.

ROBERT PENN WARREN, "Knowledge and the Image of Man"

◆ Anyone who reads Robert Penn Warren's literary oeuvre, or
even a large chunk of it, will notice that it is peopled with wanderers. More accurately, it is heavily weighted with the recurrence of
a single wanderer—in different guises, to be sure, but almost always
rendered to reveal a central conflict between an intrusive familial or
regional identity on the one hand and an "American" or metropoli-
tan identity that courts his anonymity on the other. Warren's wanderer is at least one response to the poet's sense that people living in
the modern age must try to live responsibly *against* a technological
society that exacts the price of the self, an identity Warren defined as
"the felt principle of significant unity" in his foreword to *Democracy
and Poetry* (xii). This definition, as he goes on to explain, emphasizes
first his belief that people live by created images of themselves, by
their imaginations, and second his belief that it is necessary for human beings to see themselves involved in a constant symbiotic relationship with others and with the past (xiii). To lose such a sense of
identity is to lose the ability to make the imaginative connections
necessary to sustain an image of the self as simultaneously a responsible individual and a part of a larger whole. It is to become a
wanderer.

Sustained over the six decades of Warren's career, the wandering figure evolves in a way that is both a gauge of his developing concerns as a writer and an index to the enormous area over which he tested his vision of what constitutes a viable selfhood. Equally important is the fact that Warren's evolving treatment of the wanderer reveals how he worked to find a satisfactory form for his wanderer theme throughout his career, particularly in its later stages. A study of the evolution of the wanderer and of that figure's relation to a theme cannot be separated finally from a study of Warren's developing sense of form and, more specifically, his special understanding and use of irony.

Before I launch into that analysis, however, it will be useful here at the beginning to look at the cultural and literary background of Warren's wanderer theme. By doing so one may see the fuller significance of his handling of it and, I believe, something more about the depth of his accomplishment as a writer. The wanderer theme is inextricably bound with Warren's Southern consciousness, both as a man and as a writer for whom Southern consciousness was problematic, multidimensional, and dynamic.

One can grasp something of this complexity by looking at two significant modern literary treatments of Southern consciousness written seventy years apart. The first records a conversation between Barbara Garnet and John March in George Washington Cable's 1894 novel *John March*:

"But, Mr. March, what is it in the South we Southerners love so? Mr. Fair [a Northerner] asked me this morning and when I couldn't explain he laughed. Of course I didn't confess my hu-mil-i-a-tion; I intimated that it was simply something a North-ern-er can't un-der-stand. Wasn't that right?"

"Certainly! They *can't* understand it! They seem to think the South we love is a certain region and everything and everybody within its borders."

"I have a mighty dim idea where its Northern border is sit-u-a-ted."

"Why, so we all have! Our South isn't a matter of boundaries, or skies, or landscapes. Don't you and I find it all here now, simply because we've both got the true feeling—the one heart-beat for it?"

Barbara's only answer was a stronger heart-beat.

"It's not," resumed March, "a South of climate, like a Yankee's Florida. It's a certain ungeographical South-within-the-South—as portable and intangible—as—"

"As our souls in our bodies," interposed Barbara.

"You've said it exactly! It's a sort o' something—social, civil, political, economic—"

"Romantic?"

"Yes, romantic! Something that makes—"

"No land like Dixie in all the wide world over!"

"Good!" cried John. "Good!" (326–27)

In the second passage, Southerner Brad Tolliver explains the South to film director Yasha Jones in Warren's 1963 novel *Flood:*

"Hell, the whole South is lonesome. It is as lonesome as coon hunting, which has always been a favorite sport, and that is lonesomer than anything except frog-gigging on a dark night in a deep pond and your skiff leaking, and some folks prefer it that way.

"Hell, the South is the country where a man gets drunk just so he can feel even lonesomer and then comes to town and picks a fight for companionship. The Confederate States were founded on lonesomeness. They were all so lonesome they built a pen around themselves so they could be lonesome together. The only reason the Confederate army held together as long as it did against overwhelming odds was that everybody felt that it would just be too damned lonesome to go home and be lonesome by yourself.

"The South. . . . Folks say 'the South,' but the word doesn't mean a damned thing. It is a term without a referent. No—it means something, but it does not mean what folks think it means. It means a profound experience, communally shared—yeah. But you know what that shared experience is that makes the word *South?*"

"No."

"It is lonesomeness," Brad said. "It is angry lonesomeness. Angry lonesomeness makes Southerners say the word *South* like an idiot Tibetan monk turning a broke-down prayer wheel on which he has forgot to hang any prayers.

"Hell, no Southerner believes that there is any South. He just believes that if he keeps on saying the word he will lose some of the angry lonesomeness. The only folks in the South who are not lonesome are the colored folks. They may be angry but they are not lonesome. You know what?"

"What?" Yasha Jones obligingly asked.

"That . . . is the heart of the race problem. It is not guilt. That is crap. It is simply that your Southerner is deeply and ambiguously disturbed to have folks around him who are not as lonesome as he is. Especially if they are black folks. . . . Fiddlersburg is a praying town, just like the South is a praying country. But it is not because they believe in God. They do not not believe in God. What they believe in is the black hole in the sky God left when he went away." (165–66)

Lewis P. Simpson has very astutely contrasted this passage with the famous passage from William Faulkner's 1948 novel *Intruder in the Dust* in which Gavin Stevens defines for his nephew Charles Mallison the significance of the Battle of Gettysburg to Southern consciousness; he says that every fourteen-year-old Southern boy has available whenever he wants it the moment when that battle has not yet begun and everything hangs in the balance, has available, in other words, the great *if* of Southern history. Warren's passage, according to Simpson, records a shift in the Southern literary imagination from a tension between "the moral order of memory and history" to a tension between "a gnostic society and the existential self" (90). For Faulkner the Southern imagination is characterized by its tendency to freeze the past—to see it as one great meadow, as he put it in "A Rose for Emily," in which all events are perceived as having occurred simultaneously (129). Warren has written about his own conversion

from a similar view of the Southern past in *Who Speaks for the Negro?*
The "unchangable" South had changed for him when during the
Depression he saw the desperate need to claw out of the misery that
had plagued the region since just after the Civil War (12). The passage is testimonial evidence of Warren's significance as a writer who
records a shift in collective consciousness.

I believe that by looking at the excerpt from *Flood* in relation to
Cable's earlier depiction of Southern consciousness, however, one
can see something more about the terms of that shift. Brad's speech
does not echo and reverse the passage from Faulkner's novel so much
as it does the dialogue between Barbara and John in Cable's. For example, Brad's statement that "no Southerner believes that there is any
South" may be a darker treatment of Barbara's "mighty dim idea" of
where the South's northern border is located and John's "portable and
intangible" South-within-the-South. In fact, one might almost read
Brad's words as an ironic response to the dialogue from the earlier
novel. Reading the two passages intertextually and paraphrasing a
statement from Warren's essay "Pure and Impure Poetry" may reveal
Brad here as a kind of cynical Mercutio outside the garden wall as
the lovers inside relish a private world that reflects their inner feeling
(*New and Selected Essays* 6). What is available even to postbellum
Southerners such as Barbara Garnet and John March, which is not
available to Brad Tolliver, is really a religious faith — not Christianity
per se, though certainly associated with it, but rather the conviction
of an intangible reality that confirms their communal and cultural
reality and that sanctions the love dawning at this moment in John's
fumbling for words and Barbara's more rapid heartbeat. It is the very
conviction that Brad Tolliver would say they do not really have but
cling to in order to lose their lonesomeness — an interpretation not
altogether off the mark, considering that the passage begins with Barbara's anxiety over an inability to communicate the idea of the South
to an outsider, an anxiety she hopes to alleviate by turning to her
fellow communicant, John.

There is yet another reason to consider *Flood* alongside *John*

March. Both are, in a sense, "Reconstruction" novels. Cable's novel depicts the changes brought about during the post–Civil War rise in land speculation in the South, and Warren's is set during what might be called the second Reconstruction of the South, which began with Roosevelt's New Deal and continued through the 1960s. Brad's hometown of Fiddlersburg is about to be flooded by a new government-built reservoir. Against a backdrop that forces them to see themselves in new relations, the characters in both novels struggle with the concept of regional identity, and one may do well at this point to remember that Cable's relation to the South was similar to Warren's: both lived the second half of their lives in the North with at least some feeling of having been exiled. Yet an important distinction must be made here. Whereas John March learns something of a broader world through his dealing with Northern speculators, scalawags, and freedmen in a bildungsroman pattern, Brad Tolliver, already knowledgeable about the broader world, returns to his hometown at the novel's beginning to try to discover his relation to home. Thus *Flood* can be related to a number of twentieth-century Southern narratives that begin where traditional narratives end—with a return. This narrative pattern is as significant in twentieth-century Southern writing as heroic narratives were to the antebellum and Reconstruction eras. In fact, what may actually have happened is a transfiguration of one type—the Southern cavalier or backwoodsman hero—into another—the Southern exile.

That Cable was already in 1894 dealing with Southern consciousness in terms of an inward struggle and difficulty in articulation—though his characters come up finally with a Romantic or religious notion of their identity—distinguishes him from a contemporary such as Thomas Nelson Page. In fact, Cable's narrative represents a stage in the development of literary treatments of Southern consciousness toward a literature that is increasingly modern, or unheroic if the heroic is, as Michael Kreyling has defined it, "an inherent and instantaneously acknowledged capacity to render the provisional nature of any situation or condition into part of a consecrated pattern" (4). In fact, the struggle of John March to articulate his Southernness is a sign of development or, again, transfiguration in a literature that establishes a countermyth to the heroic ideal of the Old South — but does not undermine that myth so much as it attempts to find new terms and new figures on which the myth (which is necessary at some level for life to be lived in any cultural sense) may be made available to a modern consciousness. The creation of strong, antitraditional Southern women in the fiction of Southern women writers such as Kate Chopin, Ellen Glasgow, Katherine Anne Porter, and, for that matter, Margaret Mitchell is a major part of that development. So is the fiction of the African American writer Charles Chesnutt, whose collection of stories titled *The Conjure Woman* is a complex response to both Page's and George Washington Harris's use of former slaves as narrators and whose novel *The House behind the Cedars* is an early "Return" narrative. If both William Alexander Percy and his nephew Walker continued to follow the vein of the heroic narrative pattern even in an age when the hero is extraneous because "tradition means nothing if it does not mean continuity over time" (Kreyling 155), other white male Southern writers have used more covert narrative methods, perhaps borrowed more covert strategies, as they find themselves in the dubious position of being attacked for a tradition that was seriously depleted when they inherited it.

As rich and suggestive as this field might prove, to explore its full import goes well beyond my scope. I discuss this significant portion of Southern literary history ever so sketchily in order to locate the wanderer theme and the Return narrative in a larger context. There is yet another context important to consider here. Judith Fetterley, Marjorie Pryse, and other feminist critics have argued that the fiction of nineteenth-century American women regionalist writers reverses a predominant male nationalistic pattern of bildungsroman or picaresque by beginning narratives not with a journey but with a return. We have long underestimated the significance of this implicit critique of a male narrative paradigm, according to Pryse, by failing to distinguish it from the local-color school, when in fact the psychological depth and command of language with which some of these women wrote about a specific locale constitute some of the earliest and most mature examples of the native realism America produced. The genre culminated at the end of the century with Sarah Orne Jewett's masterpiece *The Country of the Pointed Firs*, the first chapter of which is titled "The Return." Something of the same "counternarrative" may be seen in the regionalism of Emily Dickinson, especially when set against the nationalism of Walt Whitman. One must also note, however, that the counternarrative is hardly gender-exclusive and regional altogether. Warren himself saw the implied critique of the nationalist impulse in the poetry of Herman Melville, and of course Warren and others, particularly Donald Davidson, were making similar arguments about the distinctiveness of American literary regionalism as early as the 1930s. Still, I would argue that a narrative pattern very similar to the one Pryse sees in nineteenth-century women regionalist writers also occurs in the writing of twentieth-century Southerners, men and women, who write of exile in wanderer stories that may or may not deal with the exile's outward journey but do almost invariably deal in one fashion or another with the exile's return.

Modern Southern writers have, in fact, produced a large number of wandering figures representing a wide range of occupations and social classes: laborers, salesmen, scholars, preachers, and criminals come readily to mind, as well as actual vagabonds. Within this diversity, however, certain common features make it possible to speak of *a* figure of the Southern wanderer. Warren's wife, Eleanor Clark, once said to him, and one imagines she said it with some exasperation, "You're just like Jews, you southerners." Warren later said to an interviewer, "I think there's some truth in that. . . . There's a certain insideness of the outsider" (qtd. in Walker 257). Both assertions can help readers understand something about an abundance of modern Southern narratives that focus on the exile from a traditional South-

ern community. Commonly in such narratives the wandering protagonist is ironically isolated because he has rejected the traditional
community, perhaps after first having been himself rejected by that
community but just as often in order to resist the community's efforts
to draw him in. He rejects the closeness, the insideness, the closed-
ness of a community isolated from modern American society.

A common method for dramatizing this alienation of the wanderer
has been to involve the figure in the lives of characters who are
equally isolated from American mass society but also insulated from
any pain of isolation by being embedded in an agrarian culture (or
a similarly stable community) whose emphasized values are usually
continuity and fertility. These are the bedrock values, as Michael
Kreyling has shown, of the traditional Southern heroic narrative, but
they are discovered here in unlikely places. The irony at the core of
this situation is that the wanderer, though usually the more worldly
and articulate character, is seduced as a result of contact with the
more isolated characters. The meeting is a reproach to the wanderer,
for it forces him to confront his personal past, which is what he has
been fleeing all along. And I should add here that the pattern per-
sists even though it is handled with a great variation in tone among
different writers. The Southern wanderer reverses the quest of the
traditional Southern hero. Rather than performing actions that are
the coalescence of communal ideals or an intransient reality, he gives
over all extrinsic meaning and seeks to exclude evidence of any
meaning, as Simpson points out, beyond the conflict between deterministic forces and his own solipsism. His is a negative quest that
proves as difficult as the hero's search for a meaningful action, and
the result is often affirmation *through* irony. Consideration of a few
examples will help establish the pattern and some of its variations.

Eudora Welty's first published story, "Death of a Traveling Salesman," is a good case in point. Its structure is based seemingly on a
simple dichotomous view of past and present, city and country. The
wanderer, R. J. Bowman, an itinerant shoe salesman embracing modern American culture and its material rewards, is discomposed in part

because of a recent bout with influenza and the strange palpitations of his weakened heart but also by the circumstance of being cast suddenly into a culture very different from the one he has adopted for his professional life. After wrecking his car, Bowman seeks help at a tenant farmhouse from a man named Sonny and his wife (whose symbolic significance is emphasized by the fact that she is referred to simply as "the woman" throughout the story).

The effect of this conflict of industrial and agrarian cultures is the ironic ineffectuality of the more sophisticated character. Bowman first mistakes the couple for a mother and son and is shocked to learn that they are actually married and, what's more, that the woman is pregnant. He becomes even more uncomfortable when Sonny responds to his offer to pay him for getting his car back on the road by saying, "We don't take money for such" (127); the salesman doesn't normally function in a world where there are such confusing concepts as unliquefiable services. His professional life has been marked by his putting up at progressively larger hotels where, of course, service is bought. Finally, when he offers them matches, both Sonny and his wife unconsciously exclude Bowman from their community by preferring to "bory some fire" from Redmond, the landowner — one of their own people (127). With this stroke Welty makes it clear that the wall between Bowman and the couple is not simply a class barrier and that *place* means something more intangible and intricate than geographic region.

As he is confronting this strangeness, however, Bowman is also conscious of a link between the life inside the small house and his own past through memories that this experience awakens, memories particularly of his grandmother, all of which have to do with comfort. She was a comfortable soul who had a large feather bed that Bowman recalls with longing (119). A more direct link between the woman in the tenant house and the grandmother is occasioned by the similarity Bowman sees between a "red-and-yellow pieced quilt" on the woman's bed and a painting done by his grandmother in girlhood, a depiction of Rome burning. Such items would normally suggest distinction, but in Bowman's disorientation they suggest human continuity (122–23). The nostalgia and the unexpected comforts of this strange house — the fire, the plain meal, the couch in the dark living room, and Sonny's bootleg whiskey tasting like the fire from the hearth — are powerfully seductive. But for Bowman "[T]here was something like guilt in such stillness and silence" (125).

Guilt for what? For not being on the road as a good salesman should be? Or for having gone on the road in the first place? Bowman does not articulate an answer, but the guilt he feels is definitely linked with the kind of life he is confronting in the tenant farmhouse, hence with his grandmother and his own past. His career has been an upwardly mobile flight from permanence, and the fruitful marriage in this small house is a painful rebuke to that life. His alienation is self-imposed, and it is enhanced by his profession. It is, furthermore, symbolized by his recurring irrational fear that the woman might be able to hear the wild beating of his failing heart. And even though many of Bowman's impressions may be hallucinations, their symbolic value seems clear. Welty treats him as a pathetic figure ultimately, bringing him to the brink of recognition and then having him die as he attempts to preserve his adopted, mobile way of life. He leaves all the cash he has under the lamp on the table and tries to return to his restored automobile, the major symbol of his chosen profession.

Flannery O'Connor's "The Life You Save May Be Your Own" is another example of a short story that develops this pattern of a wanderer's guilt-evoking confrontation with strangers who suggest his past. In fact, there are some very particular similarities between this and Welty's story. Central again is a defunct automobile, which the wanderer must restore to continue what amounts to his flight. Another parallel is that O'Connor's Mr. Shiftlet, a one-armed itinerant carpenter, comes much as Bowman does to an isolated farm where he is eventually forced to confront his own past. Although O'Connor's comic treatment of the tension between mobile and stable ways of life is, at least at the level of characterization, more ironic than

Welty's—the seduction is intentional and mutual in O'Connor's story rather than accidental and one-sided as in Welty's—the pattern of juxtaposing them seems the common narrative over which each author writes her individual story.

Bowman's movement away from his past is measured by his putting up at better and better hotels; Shiftlet's career is more diverse, though still thoroughly modern and unagrarian. During his first meeting with the landowner Mrs. Crater, a woman "ravenous for a son-in-law" who wants Shiftlet to marry her retarded daughter, Lucynell (150), Shiftlet delivers his résumé (a vita similar to that of another of O'Connor's wanderers, the Misfit in "A Good Man Is Hard to Find"): "He had been a gospel singer, a foreman on the railroad, an assistant in an undertaking parlor, and he come over the radio for three months with Uncle Roy and his Red Creek Wranglers. He said he had fought and bled in the Arm Service of his country and visited every foreign land and that everywhere he had seen people that didn't care if they did a thing one way or another. He said he hadn't been raised that-away" (148).

Shiftlet's repeated references to the way he was raised constitute a dramatic irony in the exchange with Mrs. Crater, since the reader knows that his true goal is to obtain the automobile parked in Mrs. Crater's shed. In fact, though, there are several instances of verity behind the surface ironies of the story. Despite the fact that she is using her property to bait Lucynell and attract Shiftlet, it is obvious that Mrs. Crater genuinely loves her daughter. And despite the fact that his main objective is to get Mrs. Crater's automobile, there is a kind of fertility in the union between Shiftlet and Lucynell as he teaches her to say the first word she has ever spoken. The final irony is the realization on Shiftlet's part that the past—the way he had been raised, if you will—has had its lasting effect. The realization engulfs Shiftlet after he abandons Lucynell in a restaurant, absconds with the resurrected automobile, and picks up a hitchhiker, a fellow wanderer who has just left home.

A reader of both stories might well remember Bowman's guilt

when Shiftlet says to the young hitchhiker, "My mother was an angel of Gawd. He took her from heaven and giver to me and I left her." To this the boy replies, "My old woman is a flea bag and yours is a stinking pole cat!" (156). By introducing the hitchhiker in this late scene, O'Connor is able to suggest Shiftlet's past without having to narrate his break with home explicitly. It is easy enough to make the connection between the boy and a younger Shiftlet. Having, like the boy, rejected his past, Shiftlet confronts the permanence of a life, perhaps an awful one, with Mrs. Crater and Lucynell on the old woman's "plantation"; although he never seriously contemplates staying, the confrontation causes a fusion of past and present and an awakening of guilt similar to Bowman's. Ultimately, there is also the same sort of desperation to flee. The story ends with Shiftlet in the automobile, alone again, racing a "galloping shower" into a city with the suggestive name of Mobile (156). Both O'Connor and Welty accelerate the pace of the wanderers' flight at the end of their stories in passages that show them getting really nowhere.

The pattern that accounts entirely for the structures of Welty's and O'Connor's stories—juxtaposing modern culture with a presumably anachronistic agrarian ex-culture through the consciousness of a wanderer—has also been incorporated into the more elaborate structures of the novel. William Faulkner's *Light in August* achieves a broad juxtaposition of modern and agrarian cultures by setting the story of pregnant and unworldly, though not helpless, Lena Grove against the story of Joe Christmas. Though she herself is on the road, Lena Grove seems more a fusion of romantic quester and lily of the field than an aimless wanderer. Her experience recalls eighteenth-century narratives that develop the idea of a benevolent relationship between host and traveler—a community of strangers. To some minds Joe Christmas, by contrast, is *the* outsider in modern fiction, the man whose tragedy is that he does not know who or what he is racially and who chooses to create a self that pricks all elements of Southern society rather than simply "pass," which he could rather easily have done.

Even within the experience of Christmas alone Faulkner uses a variation on the seductive pattern I am trying to document here. Offered both permanence and a chance of fertility with Joanna Burden, Joe rejects her because, like Bowman's, his psyche demands less complex human associations, relations unmarred by love, kindness, and pity—qualities that Christmas categorizes with his byword as the "muck" of the world. Instead of cash and personal salesmanship, which Bowman and to some extent Shiftlet depend on, Christmas relies on violence to keep his human relations "clean." Early on, his life becomes a pattern of rejecting shows of kindness. He is more comfortable psychologically with McEachern, the harsh, puritan disciplinarian who adopts him, than with McEachern's wife, because the regular and harsh punishments of the man are easier to understand than the attempted kindness of the woman. This pattern of rejection is repeated in the novel with Joanna Burden, another outsider because of her family's involvement first in the abolition movement and later in Reconstruction (her father having been killed by no less a version of the Southern hero than John Sartoris). As long as he has only sexual relations with her, even though her loving takes strange forms, Joe can be Joanna's lover. When she brings such "muck" into the relationship as the desire to have a child, however, and then later unsettles him by praying for him, the terms of their living together begin to violate Joe's carefully preserved image of what he is. That image is seen most clearly in a passage describing the temptation and then his rejection of Joanna's offer of marriage: *"Why not? It would mean ease, security, for the rest of your life. You would never have to move again. And you might as well be married to her as this* thinking, 'No. If I give in now, I will deny all the thirty years that I have lived to make me what I chose to be" (232).

Like Macbeth, Joe is doomed at least in part by his own self-creation. In the aftermath of his killing Joanna, he is tragic as he dies with an unfired pistol in his hand, seemingly accepting the inevitable outcome of his self-creation. To die passively seems to be his only recourse, just as earlier the only recourse he could see to remain alive and to remain the self he had chosen to be was to refuse Joanna Burden. Though Christmas kills her technically in self-defense, the conclusion is so foregone that he was thinking of the act in the past tense before it happened. Faulkner makes it quite clear that this act of physical self-defense is only an extension of the actually more desperate act of refusing Joanna in order to remain what he "chose to be." Joe's desperation has its parallels in Bowman's leaving all his cash behind him in Welty's story and in Shiftlet's racing into Mobile at the end of O'Connor's.

One could easily discuss other variations on this narrative pattern in Southern fiction. In Walker Percy's *The Moviegoer*, Binx Bolling, the Percy character who most closely resembles the type of the wanderer I am concerned with here, negotiates between the clean world of brokerage and the more troublesome *traditions* represented by his Aunt Emily, his obligations to his cousin Kate, and the more earthy world of his mother's family at the fish camp. In a more recent work, Leroy Moffitt's discovery that he has left the "insides" out of his marriage as well as out of history initiates a panic in the climax of Bobbie Ann Mason's "Shiloh" which makes him heir to Bowman and Shiftlet. Black Southern writers, who may have had little stake in perpetuating the Southern heroic narrative, have nevertheless written versions of the wanderer narrative. In addition to Chesnutt there is Ralph Ellison, whose narrator in *Invisible Man* is constantly made to remember his legacy by dreams or other reminders of the grandfather even as he takes the wanderer's customary Franklinesque journey away from home (Franklinesque at least in the beginning). Alice Walker uses a version of the narrative pattern in her popular story "Everyday Use" and accomplishes much by shifting the point of view from the wanderer to the stay-at-home mother.

Certainly, closer examination might reveal important differences based on race and gender or distinctions between modern and postmodern writers. I defer such discussion for now, for with the pattern loosely defined I want to consider why—among writers of such diverse backgrounds, temperaments, styles, concerns, and now even literary periods—this pattern is so prominent.

Of several possible explanations, I begin with the most obvious one: that the pattern is, of course, an American pattern of experience written about by Ernest Hemingway and F. Scott Fitzgerald as well as Faulkner. But certainly there is the additional influence of historical reality for Southern writers who have witnessed and as often as not been a part of this century's mass exodus from the rural South. With nine million Southerners having migrated out of the region and even more having moved from the farm to towns and cities by 1960, the Southern countryside became, as historian Jack Temple Kirby has said, "enclosed and depopulated as dramatically as . . . rural England toward the end of the eighteenth century" (xv). Kirby's study of migration patterns also underlines the fact that among the nine million who left the region the racial split was almost fifty-fifty (320). Another interpreter of the modern South writing on this phenomenon, Lewis M. Killian, has defined white Southerners as a *minority* in the European regional rather than in the American racial sense and has documented life in the "hillbilly ghettos" of the North, where Southern identity tended to persist after migration and, in fact, to be something of a scourge (91). Rather than diffusing their Southern identity by individually moving north for jobs, many Southern whites followed a pattern of family or clan migration similar to that of many blacks and retained thereby something of a communal identity through their very otherness. John Shelton Reed has followed this theory of an ethnic analogy in his studies of the persistence of a Southern subculture within a mass society. (The analogy is an interesting complement—perhaps a corrective—for W. J. Cash's savage ideal, and I return to it later.)

The narrative pattern may be understood as well as part of a larger literary milieu. As they were casting off the Southern heroic narrative in self-defense and youthful rebellion, Southerners as much as any other group of modern writers were being influenced by the mythic method pioneered by James Joyce, T. S. Eliot, W. B. Yeats, Eugene O'Neill, and, of course, Faulkner. They were indeed taking a backward glance at their own regional history, in Allen Tate's phrase, as they entered the modern world (545), but also apparent in their stories are biblical and classical models—the Prodigal Son and Odysseus—as well as medieval and modern Christian legends. Certainly wanderlust and homesickness are not peculiarly Southern.

What Southern writers have done with the recurrence of this narrative pattern, however, is to tell, in a sense, a single story. It is the story of the problem of *home* for the modern Southerner, who has at least the idea, perhaps the illusion, that he used to have a home but is homeless now because of some change, perhaps some catastrophe. Without illogically reducing the meaning of the nebulous term *South*, one can see in just the selection of stories I have already referred to that home has some terrible associations for the wanderer—poverty, racism, ignorance, and zealous fundamentalism. There is also the sense of what John Crowe Ransom described as a phenomenon of the postbellum South: that some people "were grotesque in their efforts to make an art out of living when they were not decently making the living" ("Reconstructed" 16). But the writers also show that love, when it exists, is inextricably and complexly interwoven with these unflattering conditions and manners. They have in common the perception of this dubious relation to the rural past, and their stories dramatize its reproach and horror to the wanderer. The *idea* of the rural past is the siren song against which the wanderer must stop his ears or bind himself and keep the oars rowing. He is thus living in a state of exile, usually self-imposed, and as depicted in these texts he becomes the ultimate subversion of the original Southern hero, his literary precursor who could represent certain traditions with little of the self-consciousness that atrophies the communal sensibility of the wanderer. Yet the seductiveness of the idea that signifies his kinship with that hero clearly emerges from these texts. The past, which for the frontiersman, the statesman, the cavalier, the belle, and the matriarch represents a tradition and a way of life to defend, becomes for the wanderer an animated and dangerous reality that for his consciousness is as unpredictable as the future. The past is the psychological rattlesnake the wanderer must keep at arm's length, but his arm is shorter than his treacherous memory.

No Southern writer has been more intensely concerned with the significance of Southern exile than Robert Penn Warren, and his final novel, A Place to Come To, might well be looked at now as yet another variation on the narrative pattern I have been considering and as a touchstone for Warren's other treatments of the exile figure. I return to the novel for more extensive examination in chapters 5 and 6; here I want to concentrate on those elements that link it structurally to the pattern under discussion.

The protagonist/narrator of A Place to Come To is a renowned scholar who moves often, studies Dante, writes, teaches, fights in World War II, searches for love and friendship, marries, suffers the loss of his wife to cancer, has an adulterous affair, remarries, fathers a son, divorces, and gets stabbed by a mugger—all before coming to some sort of peace with the world he has been at odds with since the beginning. Jediah Tewksbury is not lacking in worldly experience, but in back of everything is his start in Dugton, Alabama, where he had the dubious distinction of being the son of Buck Tewksbury, an alcoholic subsistence farmer. Buck passes part of his time while drunk by reenacting Civil War battles he had never known firsthand, brandishing a sword that had reputedly belonged to an ancestor who used it honorably in the service of the Confederacy. On one such occasion Buck knocked himself out by falling against the hearth, an accident that represents the constant disturbance in the Tewksbury home. Then, finally, Buck Tewksbury "got killed in the middle of the night standing up in the front of his wagon to piss on the hindquarters of one of a span of mules and, being drunk, pitching forward on his head, still hanging on to his dong, and hitting the pike in such a position and condition that both the left front and rear wheels of the wagon rolled, with perfect precision, over his unconscious neck, his having passed out being, no doubt, the reason he took the fatal plunge in the first place. Throughout, he was still holding on to his dong" (9).

The shame and anxiety caused by this paternity cut Jed off from the community of Dugton as he grows up. Eventually, however, he assumes the distant and bemused perspective on his past illustrated by the tone of the passage quoted above. After he leaves home and wins recognition as a scholar, he even entertains first his fellow graduate students in Chicago and later his circle of acquaintances in Nashville with a comic reenactment of his father's death, complete with grotesque gestures for illustration. The story strikes most of his audience as wildly funny and, of course, too absurd to be true — even among the Nashville group, most of whom play very hard at being cosmopolitan.

Yet it is the Cudworths of the Nashville circle who offer a painful representation of the agrarian past for Jed. The Cudworths are farmers (horse breeders), and Sally Cudworth is pregnant, a fact the couple relishes. Their stability and fertility contrast with the chaotic and essentially sterile lives, including Jed's, revolving around them. Jed sees them as a dangerous force as Cud Cudworth tries to pull him into close friendship, but Jed is also quite capable of self-scrutiny. "At their place," he says of the Cudworths, "I had felt, now and then, a sense of unreality in their world, but now . . . the awareness struck me that I had clung to that notion of the unreality of their world simply because I could not face the painful reality of their joy. The joy sprang from their willed and full embracement of the process of their life in time, and I, God help me, was in flight from Time. I could not stand the reproach of the sight they provided" (254). The "flight from Time" is equated with what readers already know to be Jed's flight from Dugton, a flight from place. Warren suggests here what he had written in his 1932 review essay "Not Local Color": for the regionalist, "time and place are one thing" (154). Confronting the Cudworths means confronting the reality of all time, a breakdown of the illusory anesthetic of living solely in the present tense.

Seemingly to emphasize this theme, the novel uses two other examples of fulfillment in marriage and lives embracing time. One is the second marriage of Jed's mother, to Perk Simms back in Dugton. The other is that between Rozelle Hardcastle Carrington (also originally of Dugton and Jed's adulterous lover in Nashville) to a black Mississippian, another wanderer, who had for a time impressed the Nashville circle in the guise of an Indian mystic poet. As Rozelle describes it to Jed late in the novel, this marriage, like that of the Cudworths, is a reclamation of something lost: "We've been married a long time. . . . Not old exactly, but definitely slowed down. So, instead of ripping something off, sometimes we just get to talking about some special time in the past. Or we talk 'Ole-Timey down home' talk, about Dugton High and what happened. . . . And the longer we live with Wops and Dagos and Wogs and Greasers and Frogs — and even Limeys — the more we have a real Ole-Timey Confederate marriage, with the Stars and Bars tacked on the wall above our bed" (367).

With this striking image Warren seems to suggest deliberately the insideness of the outsider, the unusual union based on a felt sense of minority. There is even a suggestion that Warren is working with some sense of the ethnic analogy himself, an analogy that gets fuller play throughout the novel (and to which I return in chapter 6). Jed is more successful than Bowman, Shiftlet, or Christmas in reconciling himself to the past he has rejected, but the pattern Warren uses to dramatize his problem is nevertheless very similar to that used by Welty, O'Connor, and Faulkner.

What distinguishes Warren from these other Southern writers is the frequency with which he returns to the wanderer figure. For him, exile becomes an idée fixe. Jed Tewksbury is, in one sense, the same wanderer/son/poet who appears in much of Warren's poetry, early and late. And Warren himself adopts the voice of the exile in such studies as *Segregation, Who Speaks for the Negro?* and *Jefferson Davis Gets His Citizenship Back.* Though the impulse may be grounded in personal experience, he certainly saw the exile experience as representative of something larger. Particularly telling on this point is the specific "germ" for *A Place to Come To,* which the author contemplated for years before writing the novel: the life of a friend from Vanderbilt who had left the university after the first year for bigger things in the North. Meeting the friend years later, Warren spent an evening listening to him speak of his success, which he amply documented with photographs, until at last the friend looked at him and said, "I'm lonelier than God." For Warren the man captured the essential irony of the Southern exile, and in the same interview in which he acknowledged this incident as the germ of the novel, he provided a broader context for his thematic concerns: "I know many Southerners who, from babyhood on, hated the South, or felt inferior because of it, and so wanted out. Some are my contemporaries. I know some who have made great successes — heads of corporations, bankers, and so on. And at the same time, they never found a world to live in; they're people without place. They're cut off from one world and never really entered another one" (Watkins, Hiers, and Weaks 328).

Such statements should give us pause before we attribute the power in Warren's late work to his throwing off altogether what were all along the loosely fashioned chains of Agrarianism or of a regional identity. Among the more insightful critics, Hugh Ruppersburg sees Warren's career as a movement away from the position of a Southern Agrarian to that of an Agrarian of the Western world (36). Something like this is very much the case; indeed, in the interview cited above, Warren declared that he did not see any "mystic significance" in any particular place. But he also said that he did attach a great deal of importance to how anyone dealt with the place he was put down in, "his reasons for going or staying. And his piety or impiety" (Watkins, Hiers, and Weaks, 329). The question of Southernness generally and his own identity as a Southerner particularly was a burning one for

Warren, early and late—if anything, more intense in the later work as it grows out of a more personal quest for at-homeness in the world.

By looking closely at the career of his wanderer, one can learn much, I believe, about the significance of Warren's work, for the figure bears directly on most of the major issues that concerned him: the meaning of American history, race relations, and humankind's place in nature. Through the same figure he also establishes the consciousness that continually picks the scab (one of his favorite metaphors) of ontological being in relation to these major issues. It is also at least in part through experimenting with the wanderer theme and figure that Warren creates the new forms in fiction, nonfiction, and poetry which make him one of the most significant writers of our century.

So much has been written already about the nature of Warren's philosophy and literary theory that only a brief summary of his most basic ideas seems necessary here to establish a context for fuller analysis of how the wanderer relates to that body of thought. Warren pursues the foremost of his themes—the nature of man's knowledge of his identity—with two primary philosophical tenets: a conception of the world as an enormous spiderweb, and a conception of the past as a continuing influence in the present—another way of thinking of *time* and *space* as synonymous terms. The relationship between self-identity and spatial and temporal interconnection is the most important factor in Warren's thinking and art. He himself provided a statement of the basic elements of his philosophy in the important essay "Knowledge and the Image of Man." *Knowledge* for Warren is not simply the formal and scientific training of the mind that quells superstition and demythifies life; in fact, such axiomatic or technical knowledge is often the escape route for Warren's self-exile. It seems instead a state of constant revision of belief in a necessary conflict between intuition and reason. Warren's is the condition of the Romantic who doubts the verification offered by the world. He himself may be, as he said of Melville, a "mystic who hated mysticism" (*Selected Poems of Herman Melville* 31). Knowledge approached as a central human problem as well as a solution gives man his identity, he wrote, "because it gives him an image of himself. And the image of himself necessarily has a foreground and a background, for man is in the world not as a billiard ball placed on a table, not even as a ship on the ocean with location determinable by latitude and longitude. He is, rather, in the world with continual and intimate interpenetration, an inevitable osmosis of being, which in the end does not deny, but affirms, his identity" ("Knowledge" 241).

Such a statement and a great deal of his writing in the main seem to make Warren an unacknowledged father of the branch of contemporary regionalist theory known as bioregionalism, which holds that "individuals and communities . . . come into consciousness *through*, not apart from, the natural environment they inhabit" (Kowalewski 30). But the Agrarians, particularly Davidson, were emphasizing that point some sixty years ago; for that matter, Emily Dickinson was driven to the self-conscious statement that she saw "New Englandly" well over a century ago.

Warren, however, goes on to say that man's identity depends on how he distinguishes himself from nature: man "disintegrates his primal instinctive sense of unity" ("Knowledge" 241). The terms Warren often uses for this disintegration are separateness or original sin, terms that describe man's condition of separateness from God, from nature, and from other men. Warren's sense of original sin, defined by John Crowe Ransom as "the betrayal of our original nature that we commit in the interest of our rational evolution and progress" ("Inklings" 211), recalls the temperament of a Nathaniel Hawthorne or of Melville, who wrote of Hawthorne's "power of blackness" that it "derives its force from its appeal to that Calvinistic sense of Innate Depravity." Warren would agree with Melville that "no man can weigh this world without throwing in something, somehow like Original Sin, to strike the uneven balance" ("Hawthorne" 243). For Warren, this "uneven balance" leads a perceptive man to his agony, but the pain may itself move him toward redemption: "In the pain of isolation he may achieve the courage and clarity of mind to envisage the tragic pathos of life, and once he realizes that the tragic experience is universal and a corollary of man's place in nature, he may return to a communion with man and nature." He can "return to his lost unity" through "the discovery of love, and law. But love through separateness, and law through rebellion" ("Knowledge" 241–42).

His formal statement of philosophy in "Knowledge and the Image of Man" suggests the qualities that drew Warren to such writers as Hawthorne, Melville, Mark Twain, Theodore Dreiser, Faulkner, and Joseph Conrad. His essays on these authors, and on the poetry of John Greenleaf Whittier as well, are in fact all of a piece and define a tradition to which Warren's own name must be added. His definition of the wisdom he sees at work in the fiction of Joseph Conrad, for example, can, to his mind, be applied practically to any one of those writers:

Wisdom . . . is the recognition of man's condition, the condition of the creature made without gills or fins but dropped into the sea, the necessity of living with the ever renewing dilemma of idea as opposed to nature, morality to action, "utopianism" to "secular logic," . . . justice to material interests. Man must make his life somehow in the dialectical process of these terms, and in so far as he is to achieve redemption he must do so through an awareness of his condition that identifies him with the general human communion, not in abstraction, not in mere doctrine, but immediately. The victory is never won, the redemption must be continually re-earned. And as for history, there is no Fiddler's Green, at least not near and soon. History is a process fraught with risks, and the moral regeneration of society depends not upon shifts in mechanism but upon the moral regeneration of men. (*New and Selected Essays* 156–57)

Such a vision corresponds to Warren's definition of the self in *Democracy and Poetry* as "the felt principle of significant unity" (xi).

The term *felt* here identifies Warren with a body of Romantic thinking that refuses to privilege reason in the search for self-knowledge.
The intellect, in and of itself, implies a certain distance from the
object under consideration, as when Jed Tewksbury looks back on his
past in *A Place to Come To* or Jack Burden contemplates himself as
a subject in *All the King's Men*, each speaking of himself in the third
person, each attempting to become a disembodied mind. Emotional
response to experience, rather than "theoretical analysis," determines
the individual's identity, and a conflict between rationality and emotion is central in the struggle for knowledge which the wanderer goes
through as he attempts to distance himself from the painful past by
asserting the truth of an objective world. Warren was not, however, a
writer who suffered from a dissociation of his own sensibilities. What
he believed, put quite simply, was that individuals live necessarily by
ideas, which may give them an image of themselves, but that every
idea by which they live must be tested and borne out by experience,
which constantly influences the shape of the ideas. This may sound
like ordinary common sense, but it is of course not *common* sense,
for communities and individuals often operate with a mob mentality
that thrives on the purity of an idea. Acceptance of a perpetual conflict at the root of human existence is anything but *common* sense.
And Warren's drama, his *story*, unfolds from this essential human
failure.

Warren's tendency in his criticism of American authors is to find a
version of that story in their works. The studies of American authors
in his 1989 *New and Selected Essays*, his *Homage to Theodore Dreiser*,
and his editions of Whittier's and Melville's poetry combine to define
a central tension and a significant tradition in American literature. At
the same time, these are highly subjective and even personal works
that provide valuable resources for reading and understanding Warren's own poetry, fiction, and literary essays. To judge from the critical
principles he applies in each case—the relation between the author's
life and milieu, the test of what Warren calls inwardness, and the
identification of the poles of each writer's dialectical movement to-

ward knowledge—Warren was defining a tradition to which he felt he belonged. But he identifies with no other writer, not even Faulkner, as closely as he does with Melville, whom he saw as a kindred spirit, a "modern" one. He had, as he said, always been "crazy about" Melville (Watkins, Hiers, and Weaks 245), but his admiration was unusual: it was for Melville as a poet, a poet who, as Warren said, "needs some special interpretation" (*New and Selected Essays* 220).

In fact, his *Selected Poems of Herman Melville* may be the volume that reveals more than any other in his canon the relation between Warren's scholarship and his poetry, and it is useful, too, for the light it sheds on his inheritance from American Romanticism. Warren subtitles the volume *A Reader's Edition*, by which he does not mean, as one at first suspects, that he has put together a collection for the general public instead of for scholars. Rather, he means that *he* as reader has put together his own edition, revealing his own preferences and prejudices. At one level the statement that this edition of Melville's poetry is *Warren's* book seems literally true. Of its 455 pages, almost half (208) are taken up by Warren's introduction and his notes on Melville's texts. The approach to the poems suggested by the subtitle further reveals Warren's consciousness of the subjective base of criticism or, more precisely, of *reading*. A statement in the short foreword reveals even more: "I have dared to hope that, in the end, a true account of my experience with the poetry might be as useful as an edition designed for some idealized norm of 'the reader'" (vii).

Warren writes here not as a New Critic but as an adventurer/explorer, one who has traveled and "experienced" Melville and hopes now to render "a true account." His language is actually the language of an exploration narrative, and the region he explores in this case is the psychic duality of the "mystic who hated mysticism." Warren's daring is in offering this account of his experience as a model for reading modeled on and metaphorized in the broadest sense as a process of exploration and discovery—a model and metaphor so pervasive in Warren that especially during the latter half of his career they narrow the line between his critical and creative writing.

The impulse to *dare* is detectable also in the defensive tone of "Melville the Poet" and *Selected Poems of Herman Melville*, works undertaken warily with the knowledge that critics as distinct in their ideological and critical assumptions as Edmund Wilson and Allen Tate had concluded that Melville's poetry was of historical interest only. Warren answers the charge that Melville never learned the craft of verse by arguing that the wrenchings in Melville's poetry are attempts to establish his individual, "masculine," "nervous," "dramatic" style rather than signs of ineptitude (*New and Selected Essays* 221–22). The poetic form, in other words, is emblematic of the emerging philosophy. The complaint against Melville that Warren counters here is, of course, similar to complaints made against Warren's own poetry, and one may speculate that some of his defensiveness is attributable to his sensitivity to this fact. Still, his apology is instructive on the function of those "offenses" in Melville and, by reflection, in Warren.

There is a larger element of defensiveness in Warren's interpretation of Melville, however. There is no essay on Ralph Waldo Emerson in *New and Selected Essays*, nor any need for one, really. Emerson is the ever present hypercritic for Warren, whose critical and creative biases are for a very un-Emersonian, paradoxical, naturalistic spirituality and an equally un-Emersonian historical sense: a view of the past as simultaneously a text that has to be interpreted *and* a living body as "unpredictable," he writes in "I Am Dreaming of a White Christmas," "as the future" (*New and Selected Poems* 253).

What further distinguishes Warren from Emerson and makes him an interesting figure for modern and postmodern theory is his notion of the relationship between language and idea. Warren's thinking on the matter corresponds to his unusual brand of inclusiveness, an inclusiveness of the sort he saw in Melville. His argument against schematizing what he calls the polarity of *ideology* and *human values* in Melville's poetry makes this inclusiveness clearer: "One pair shades into another. One pole does not cancel out its opposite" in the "complex texture of life as lived." Yet "to live in any full sense demands the effort to comprehend this complexity of texture, this density and equivocalness of experiences, and yet not forfeit the ability to act" (*Selected Poems of Herman Melville* 22). To comprehend the "density and equivocalness of experience" and still to act is Warren's definition of heroic life, and he sees it as the heroic sensibility in Melville and in Hawthorne, Conrad, and Dreiser as well.

The reality of the coexistence of polar truths negates any theory of the purity of language for Warren; that coexistence makes language equivocal because language is a part of "life as lived." Instructive on this point is what he said about the difficult time he had completing the novel *At Heaven's Gate* because he was trying "to live the novel in the planning level." He discovered that he was "violating . . . a basic necessity," that the idea of the novel "must be in terms of the *language* of the novel" (Watkins, Hiers, and Weaks 118). Very interesting here is the phrase "trying to live the novel," for it implies that the inclusiveness necessary for living in any full sense is also necessary for composition. For Emerson, theoretically, the point of rest begins with the word, for the word, uncorrupted by society, is pure and does not resist itself. For Warren, language is a way toward a point of rest, but it is a maze that reflects the "complex texture of life as lived." This basic theoretical difference lies behind Emerson's championing of Whitman and Warren's championing of Melville.

To some extent, Warren's defense of Melville's poetry is based on his view of Melville as a corrective not only for Emerson but for American Romantic poetry generally. In fact, one of his most scathing critical remarks on a Melville poem — in this case, "America" — is that Henry Wadsworth Longfellow or James Russell Lowell might have written it (*Selected Poems of Herman Melville* 31). Warren understands the modernist view that Whitman, too, served as a corrective for some of the more blithe manipulation of nature in man's favor by the Romantics, yet Warren damns Whitman with faint praise to make his point that Melville's "analytical" poetry can be valued at an *aesthetic* level. Whitman, the democratic affirmer, misses something important that Melville, the democratic questioner, sees. Warren acknowledges that Whitman became something of a questioner himself with "some sobering second thoughts" in *Democratic Vistas*, but in the war poetry Whitman values the "will to possess"; Melville, the inner conflict (*Selected Poems of Herman Melville* 29, 26).

To put the matter another way, Warren finds in Melville's poetry the same tensions and tendencies to decenter vision that operated in his own aesthetic and regionalist sensibility. He distills the essence of Melville's difference from Whitman in his discussion of Whitman's "Come Up from the Fields, Father." In that poem "the family is safely Northern, . . . and the Northern reader Whitman was writing for could find his patriotism, his selfish interests, and all his human and humane feelings mobilized together and focused in the image — 'ritualized.'" All of which leads Warren to the conclusion that Whitman "was characteristically more concerned with intensity and purity of feeling than with any complexity or painful richness of feeling." Melville's tendency, on the other hand, was to take readers into unfamiliar and uncomfortable territory. Warren argues this point by implementing an imagined alternative scenario, a very common device in his prose: "If Melville had written [the poem], the farm might very well have been in Georgia, and the dead son one of those 'Slain Collegians' about whom he did write a poem; then the Northern reader, whose own son had been habitually shot at by the now dead Georgia lad, might have had some divisions of attitude to deal with. Like all decent poetry, that of Melville aims at the moment of poise, of synthesis, but for him the poise and the synthesis are hard-won, and often incomplete and provisional, and the awareness of that fact is the point, the 'truth,' of the poetry" (*Selected Poems of Herman Melville* 27).

The distinction drawn here is in essence a displacement of Warren's quarrel with Emerson and the party of hope generally. Whereas Whitman, for all his tendency to delineate experience, understood America poetically as a process of "aggregation or absorption" that aimed to wipe out distinctions, Melville understood it poetically as "an analysis to locate first principles," an "effort to achieve aware-

ness of the distinctions and paradoxes of life and to resolve them"
(*Selected Poems of Herman Melville* 30). Again, the distinction is between two kinds of inclusiveness, and Warren identifies in Melville
the kind central to his own vision. Warren values Melville as a poet
whose vision depends on knowledge as much as will—knowledge,
that is, as the product and process of a dialectic, as opposed to a pure
will that wipes out distinction in an Emersonian transcendence or
Whitmanesque "aggregation." For Melville, the Civil War "would
serve his need only if the centrifugal whirl toward violent action was
perfectly balanced by the centripetal pull toward an inwardness of
apparently irresolvable mystery, a tormenting ambiguity" (*Selected
Poems of Herman Melville* 11).

This inscrutable inwardness is the value that, in poetic form, creates both tension and a means of balance through resistance. One
example is the famous line from "Shiloh" (*Selected Poems of Herman
Melville* 22), "What like a bullet can undeceive!" —a line that undercuts not only youthful patriotism and expectations of glory earned in
action but the whole concept of enlightenment. Death makes friends
of foes in "Shiloh" while the swallows' flight over the battlefield in
the elegiac hush symbolizes the ambivalence of nature. It is a point
captured again by the personified elms in "Malvern Hill." Warren
finds a similar example in "The March into Virginia" in the paradox
of soldiers who go gaily into battle but either die "enlightened by the
vollied glare" or, surviving, are shaped for a truer, adamantine courage
in later battles (*Selected Poems of Herman Melville* 97).

Before considering how Warren's particular terms for valuing Melville shed light on his own relation to American Romanticism, I want
to consider some questions that those terms may raise for today's
readers. First, it seems too reductive to say, as some critics might, that
his terms for valuing Melville as poet merely reflect the fact that Warren was a New Critic for whom paradox, for whom irony, was the
primary poetic value—a critic who valued poems for the cleverness
with which they work up an ironic effect. Second, it seems equally
reductive to say, as some might, that by valuing a writer whose per-

sonal failure became absorbed into the great national conflict and, even more disturbingly, into a tragic and universal sense of human doom, Warren was participating in a conservative, conspiratorial privileging of genres that obscure the relation of writing to social problems at the expense of the literary reputations of such writers as Harriet Beecher Stowe, Frederick Douglass, and countless others less well known.

Either reading would obscure what Warren really values in Melville. Leaving aside the fact that, as anyone knows who has read a significant amount of Warren's criticism beyond *Understanding Poetry* and *Understanding Fiction*, Warren was not a New Critic as that creature is usually defined by its heavily armed hunters, I want to consider how his "special interpretation" of Melville may be special precisely because it affords him an opportunity to locate an American precedent for his own poetic irony. And it is an irony we misunderstand if we think of it as merely a way to undercut liberal positivism or a poet's technical plaything or simply a sign of Warren's "modernism."

The power in his later work lies not in the transcendence of the ambiguity/actuality dialectic that "troubled" Melville's poetry but in its superior development of the dialectical method. I do not wholeheartedly agree, therefore, with some otherwise instructive assessments of Warren's late achievement. Calvin Bedient, for example, argues that the power of Warren's late poetry stems from his exertion of will, over unbendable evidence to the contrary, to assert a positive interpretation of experience (4). Harold Bloom, rejecting Warren's philosophy, nevertheless finds power in the late Warren who shrugged off Eliot for a version of the American Sublime in which "the ontological self is identified with, and as, the flight of wild birds" (78).

Flight, most often the flight of hawks and other birds, does emerge from the late poetry as an important symbol for Warren's vision and does represent a moment of transcendence, often combining the terror and exhilaration associated with the Sublime. Yet the movement toward identification with the wild birds is accomplished only after an opposite experience has been, in a sense, ingested. The approach is decidedly Melvillean, a movement toward a mystic identification with the hawk which does not cancel the hawk's Otherness.

In Warren's 1975 poem "Evening Hawk," for example (*New and Selected Poems* 167), the sight of the hawk in flight leads to a state of acute attunement with the world. "If there were no wind we might, we think, hear / The earth grind on its axis, or history / Drip in darkness like a leaking pipe in the cellar." But it is important to note the qualifiers and negatives: "If there were no wind," "we might," "we think." Even the two activities, the grinding of the earth and the dripping of history, create a problem in exact interpretation because the first is placed solidly in the realm of nature and the second has been defined by Warren as the myth man lives (*Brother to Dragons*, 1979, Foreword xiii). Moreover, the image of history is troubling and quotidian rather than sublime. Though man may be moved by sights in nature to vision, pattern, or design, Warren keeps that vision grounded, so to speak, by emphasizing inherent human limitations.

Bloom is certainly correct in seeing Warren's hawk as a distinct achievement in the Romantic tradition. Warren's hawk is not William Cullen Bryant's waterfowl, or Whitman's untranslatable hawk, or even Wallace Stevens's ambiguous, undulating pigeons. It does, however, bear a strong resemblance to Melville's Man-of-War Hawk, whose flight is a "placid supreme" that neither thought nor arrow can attain—an image and a comment suggesting man's painful and destructive eschatological search. Warren's hawk is similarly beyond "Time and error" and is also "unforgiving." Yet the hawk alone does not stand for Warren's vision in the poem. The bat replaces the hawk at night and "cruises in his sharp hieroglyphics," a term that suggests both that man can "read" nature to learn something about himself and that this reading is difficult because it requires interpretation of what might be called the pictorial language of perfect adjustment. And in the reading, the hawk with its omniscient God's eye and the bat whose "wisdom / Is ancient, too, and immense" are apparently to be taken equally. The vision which is possible in this unresolved and irresolvable tension is suggested by the lines that follow the description of the bat: "The star / Is steady, like Plato, over the mountain." The comparison between the star and the philosopher closes the breach between man and nature; however, it is not Platonism which is "steady" here but Plato himself, perhaps because of the coherence of his illusion. Or perhaps the simile is an acknowledgment that the star is not really steady after all. It is steady only in the coherence the perceptive speaker makes with his knowledge that in an open universe the star is no more permanent than a man.

In one of his most acclaimed late poems Warren thus employs the principle of inner resistance which he valued so highly in Melville, but the principle may also be understood to work intertextually. For its relation to Warren's own body of poetry and to the tradition of American Romanticism which searches nature for moral instruction, "Caribou" is among Warren's most interesting late poems. In "Caribou" as in "Immortality over the Dakotas" (which immediately precedes it in the *Altitudes and Extensions* section of *New and Selected Poems*), Warren again uses flight but reverses the perspective by placing his persona in a plane. He often creates a rarified atmosphere in the cabins of airplanes to suggest either a cold idealism, in poems such as "Homage to Emerson," for example, or a relief from social or familial responsibility, as in scenes in *Segregation* and *The Cave*. In this case the poet flies in the company of scientists on an Arctic expedition; "Caribou" is a literal, if fictional, exploration narrative. The landscape is mystical:

Far, far southward, the forest is white, not merely
As snow of no blemish, but whiter than ice yet sharing
The mystic and blue-tinged, tangential moonlight,
Which in unshadowed vastness breathes northward. (*New and
    Selected Poems* 8)

Yet the animals that come lumbering from this otherworldly whiteness seem, like the bat, a complement to Warren's birds and perhaps

a commentary on all the poetic birds of Romantic poetry from Percy
Bysshe Shelley through Stevens in that they afford an opportunity to
consider natural phenomena in relation to human identity and destiny. Moreover, they bear more than a little resemblance to Melville's
phlegmatic, lethargic, and dull Maldive shark:

> The heads heave and sway. It must be with spittle
> That jaws are ice-bearded. The shoulders
> Lumber on forward, as though only the bones could, inwardly,
> Guess destination. The antlers,
> Blunted and awkward, are carved by some primitive craftsman. (8)

What beasts could make the meditation more awkward and pre-
posterous than these that don't seem natural at all, or suggest that
nature contains its own Gothic imagery carved by primitive crafts-
men? They break upon and mar the clean landscape:

> each shadow appears, each
> Slowly detached from the white anonymity
> Of forest, each hulk
> Lurching, each lifted leg leaving a blackness as though
> Of a broken snowshoe partly withdrawn. (8)

In their very individuation they break upon the poet's mystic dream
of a seamless nature without conflict. Warren's explication and appli-
cation of the "text" that the caribou write on the landscape affirms
the meaning of destiny revealed in the natural world and yet affirms
simultaneously that it is unavailable to man.

> We do not know on what errand they are bent, to
> What mission committed. It is a world that
> They live in, and it is their life.
> They move through the world and breathe destiny.
> Their destiny is as bright as crystal, as pure

As a dream of zero. Their destiny
Must resemble happiness even though
They do not know that name. (8)

It is *their* world, as the poet says, and in them we may find even
more than an image of that happiness we most long for — but not in
identification with them, for they exist outside language, even outside
image, while we are trapped in a world totally dependent on both.
The unavailability is further figured in the contrast between the in-
stinctual and mysterious path and destination of the caribou and the
mechanical and social dependencies of the passengers in the plane:

I lay the binoculars on the lap of the biologist. He
Studies distance. The co-pilot studies a map. He glances at
A compass. At mysterious dials. I drink coffee. Courteously,
The binoculars come back to me.

I have lost the spot. I find only blankness.

But.

They must have been going somewhere. (9)

The trappings with which the poet and his fellow travelers must
negotiate their way through the world — the plane, binoculars, map,
compass, "mysterious dials," even courtesy — seem intended to emphasize human distinction from creatures who "breathe destiny" as
easily as they find their way by instinct. Once these have obtruded on
the poet's own dream of zero — the unblemished snow at the beginning of the poem — he finds only blankness.

None of this is to say, of course, that Warren's vision does not concern itself with spiritual realities. His eschatological appetite is, in
fact, as large as the one that so fascinated him in Melville, and the
poems I have considered here are evidence of the depth of his spiritual quest. But what rationalization can there be for the final affirmation in "Caribou" that the animals "must have been going some-

where"? At least I read it as an affirmation, although literally the line states no more than what is naturally obvious.

We may return to Melville for an answer. The affirmation comes not despite the evidence of loss and blankness but with that evidence poised against other evidence already presented in the poem: the mystic landscape, the tracks of the caribou, the mechanical gadgetry, a hint of human communion, and even the narrative intrusion that asserts the resemblance between the caribou's destiny and human *happiness*, the word the poet *does* know. Going outside the terms Warren used in discussing Melville, a useful term for clarifying if not adopting Warren's irony is literary parataxis, as defined by Brooks Landon: "Rhetorical parataxis is the syntax of putting clauses together in a sentence without trying to relate them hierarchically. Literary parataxis extends this syntax to the larger structures and themes of the novel, juxtaposing seemingly incongruous sentences, narrative codes, and other forms or concepts within the text" (115–16). Warren's irony seems very like this, a parataxis extended to the larger elements of the poem. The result is an irony that is itself submitted to irony, that does not simply undercut the precedent vision but recuts it. It is the irony of the hero poet who sees through the illusion without necessarily devaluing the illusion. He continues to act, to affirm. It is Romantic irony. And Melville, if we believe the evidence of Warren's own criticism, was a precedent.

This specific irony, I would argue, describes the essential condition for the Southern exile. With this understood we may turn to Warren's second qualification of his definition of the self in his foreword to *Democracy and Poetry*: the term *significant*. He writes of two implications for this quality of the self: "continuity—the self as a development in time, with a past and a future; and responsibility—the self as a moral identity, recognizing itself as capable of action worthy of praise or blame" (xiii). Perhaps the worst thing that can happen to a character in Warren's poetry or fiction is that he or she loses sight of the past or the future as a shaping force in the present. The "osmosis of being," which Victor Strandberg has characterized as Warren's signal contribution to twentieth-century theological thought (*Poetic Vision* 192), has temporal as well as spatial implications. The spatial or social implications are suggested by Warren's emphasis on responsibility. As he makes clear in the passage just quoted, the acceptance of responsibility is crucial. If man does not recognize his condition of separateness and clings instead to a dream of innocence or meaninglessness, the consequences are disastrous. The imagery employed to present the idea of interconnection in "Knowledge and the Image of Man" is not nearly as frightening as Warren's most famous image of interconnection: Jack Burden's description in *All the King's Men* of the world as an enormous spiderweb that, touched, produces dire and unforeseeable consequences: it "does not matter whether or not you meant to brush the web of things. Your happy foot or your gay wing may have brushed it ever so lightly, but what happens always happens" (200).

Here lies the philosophical sticking point that has troubled many of Warren's readers; the language of his metaphysics recalls Jonathan Edwards more than John Donne. The argument that man is responsible despite his helplessness is too fatalistic for those who with Harold Bloom, for instance, "voted for Emerson a long time ago" (71). When Warren treated the theme in his 1968 *Incarnations*, the volume that Bloom sees as marking the turning point for the better in Warren's poetry, the perspective seems more pantheistic than Calvinistic, yet the world manages to seem somehow just as frightening.

One may come nearer understanding Warren by thinking of both the Calvinism and the pantheism as borrowed systems of thought, methods of accommodation to explain the way the self and the world mirror each other. For Warren, one who has achieved an adequate vision has a perception of his inner being which reflects the unity he perceives in the spiderweb world. Selfhood is an integration of elements—an acceptance of the past, a sense of the future, a sense of responsibility—and the individual is part of the larger integration of the one world. He is connected to all others who live and who have lived and who, in at least one respect, have a common experience with him: the tragic experience of man's separation from the innocence of nature. The important question is how man can achieve a vision that synthesizes his inner being and gives him a place in the world. All of Warren's writing has been addressed in one way or another to this question.

To summarize, Warren's remarks in "Knowledge and the Image of Man" reveal a three-stage paradigm of experience by which man may arrive at vision: (1) a disunion of the self with nature and society—original sin; (2) a struggle through a crisis of identity; (3) a return to unity based on the knowledge of the universal fall of man and an acceptance of experience and responsibility. The resemblance to a Christian paradigm is unmistakable, but Christianity for Warren was a metaphor for experience ("Conversation with Cleanth Brooks" 72), yet another borrowed system to explore the nature of true vision, which for Warren can come to an individual only out of the pain of isolation. If man does not recognize his separateness, his "fall" from the perfect unity of nature, any peace of mind he has is a false peace based on an illusory innocence. To discover a way to live in a community requires that man struggle through a process of coming to terms with the disparity between the "idea" of what he thinks life should be, his innocence (sometimes called by Warren the "original dream" in juxtaposition with "original sin"), and the "factuality" of his experience. Warren's definition of *reality* — "whatever any person might think validated his existence" (qtd. in Kehl 117)—reveals that in his lexicon it is a term synonymous with the "selfhood" that may follow knowledge. For the perceptive mind the disparity between the ideal and the factual is what Jack Burden calls the terrible division of the modern age (*All the King's Men* 462), but the body of Warren's work makes clear that the "terrible division" has always been a human problem.

The figure of the wanderer, the figure that Warren turned to again and again out of his impulse to test these issues, must finally be understood as a trope functioning at several levels. First, the wanderer partakes of Warren's personal experience, a broader regional and national experience, and finally a universal experience; the personal and the regional are set against a more abstract interpretation of experience which the exile internalizes as a form of escape from the pain of self. Second, as Warren's career began to take new turns after the 1940s, that strange decade of high accomplishment in prose and failure in poetry, he began to experiment—often with powerful results—with new ways to emphasize these multiple layers of significance. In doing so he did not outgrow but focused more and more on the central problem of the Southerner as the central problem of the American—the problem of *home*.

CHAPTER TWO

Warren's Wandering Son

A Study in Development

All the poems of the poet who has entered into his poethood
are poems of homecoming.

MARTIN HEIDEGGER, "Remembrance of the Poet"

◆ In many of his best-known early poems Warren uses an Ameri-
canized prodigal to tell a traditional story of flight and return.
Sometimes addressed explicitly as "wanderer," he appears in several
pre-1943 poems as a transient consciousness if not a full-blown character, one simultaneously repulsed and seduced by his home. "Revelation," "Original Sin: A Short Story," and "The Ballad of Billie
Potts" are all examples. Each is a narrative poem whose plot is a variation on a basic pattern: a parent is insulted; some ugliness or poverty
associated with home is rejected; some act opens a breach between
son and family. In "Original Sin" the wanderer is a Nebraskan who
seeks to escape the stain of his rural past. He goes to Harvard, becomes a fondler of axioms, and moves often without leaving a for-
warding address (New and Selected Poems 302). The story is varied in
"The Ballad of Billie Potts," in which the central wandering figure is
the outlaw son of a potbellied Kentucky innkeeper/bandit.

"The Ballad of Billie Potts" itself represented a shift in Warren's
poetry as his penchant for storytelling began to exert itself more in
his poetry. It anticipates the tales in verse that would follow: Brother
to Dragons, Audubon, Chief Joseph, "New Dawn." In fact, James Jus-

tus has noted that even earlier poems such as "Bearded Oaks" were derived "from the felt urgencies of narrative situations," for "the purely meditative lyric is too static to admit the exercise of a temperament such as Warren's given as it is to the interplay of excess, the dramatic clash of opposites conceived and drawn in large outline" (53).

"Billie Potts" tells the tale of a frontier Kentucky innkeeper and his family who supplement their income by informing highwaymen about "likely looking" travelers in return for a share of what can be stolen from them. On one occasion Big Billie, the innkeeper, sends his son, Little Billie, to inform one of their collaborators that a wealthy traveler is preparing to depart. Little Billie decides to surprise his parents by doing the job himself, but in his unprofessional attempt he gets shot. After first suffering the humiliation of being instructed by his intended victim how to do the job better next time and then facing his enraged father, he flees westward. He returns ten years later, having made something of a fortune. Planning to have some fun, Little Billie does not reveal his identity to his parents immediately (body fat and a long beard have made him unrecognizable to them). Big Billie and his wife, seeing only a wealthy stranger, plot to murder him for his money. They learn only after it is too late who he really was through a symbolic and tell-all birthmark on the corpse.

The story is itself apparently an old Kentucky legend and a good example of Warren's achievement with folk materials. It is the kind of story that would appeal to Warren, given Justus's analysis of the poet's temperament. Its basic irony allows for the development of some of the issues of most concern to Warren. Little Billie returns home feeling the tug of the past and expecting to find things as they were. Even after he is informed by Joe Drew, an old acquaintance whom he meets on the way to his parents' house, that his father has been running short of luck, he jingles the money in his own pockets to signify that he is bringing luck back to his parents. This is the second time Little Billie has tried to surprise his family by doing something good for them; ironically, of course, this time he succeeds.

The confusion over Little Billie's identity suggests the problem

Warren is trying to approach in the poem. For Little Billie not to be wary of returning to *his* parents' house in the guise of a wealthy stranger reveals the fatal flaw in his character. He is, in a sense, the same bumbler who botched the robbery because of a lack of experience; in this second instance his failure to see the significance of past events leads to his problems. He returns home with a nostalgic illusion of what home is and runs headlong into reality in the form of a hatchet set into his head.

Knowledge is not simply something that comes easily, however, even to people more intelligent than Little Billie, and perhaps his distrust of such homiletic conclusions led Warren to interrupt the vernacular folk ballad with commentaries in a style more suitable to philosophical meditation and clearly separated from the body of the tale by parentheses. In these passages Warren addresses a wanderer, a generic Little Billie, and analyzes his motivations. The parenthetical passages serve as a way of interpreting the action of the tale and raising that action to a universal or mythological level. The dual styles also suggest an imaginative doubleness, a criticism of both the low-style tale and the philosophical discourse of twentieth-century man analyzing its implications. If the split style is intrusive, that may well be the point. In much the way that Eliot achieves a functional incongruity in the mixed styles of *The Waste Land*, the incongruity of the styles here reflects the tension of the divided self that drives Little Billie, as well as his mother and father, toward the poem's tragic end.

What the tale suggests is that there is a continuity of life, an interrelatedness of the events of history. Neither Little Billie in his nostalgia nor Big Billie and his wife in their greed are able to recognize this fact until it is too late. Because recognition of the significance of the past is necessary to self-identity, returning home has a special significance as a motif in Warren's work. In one of the commentary passages in the poem, Warren provides a reason for the return:

Though your luck held and the market was always satisfactory,
Though the letter always came and your lovers were always true,

Though you always received the respect due to your position,
Though your hand never failed of its cunning and your glands always
 thoroughly knew their business,
Though your conscience was easy and you were assured of your
 innocence,
You became gradually aware that something was missing from the
 picture,

And upon closer inspection exclaimed: "Why I'm not in it at all!"
Which was perfectly true.
Therefore you tried to remember when you had last had
Whatever it was you had lost,
And you decided to retrace your steps from that point,
But it was a long way back.
It was, nevertheless, absolutely essential to make the effort,
And since you have never been a man to be deterred by difficult
 circumstances,

You came back.
For there is no place like home. (*New and Selected Poems* 295)

Here, as he often does, Warren adopts the vocabulary of popular
psychology and the marketplace to write about his wanderer and then
ends in the cliché which, as readers at the time could hardly have
missed, had been used as the closing line of dialogue in the film of
The Wizard of Oz. The tone is ironic, but like much of Warren's irony
it really affirms rather than undermines the popular understanding
or, rather, ironically *deepens* the popular understanding of the common utterances. There *is* no place like home. The urge that drives
Little Billie back is a universal memory of prelapsarian innocence.
His actions, though, have made that innocence irrecoverable, as it is
for all men. Little Billie is not thoughtful enough to understand why
he needs to return; he only feels the desire and wants, still, to impress
his parents with his adeptness. The wanderer in the commentary,
however, must return

back to the homeland of no-Time,
To ask forgiveness and the patrimony of your crime;

And kneel in the untutored night as to demand
What gift — oh, father, father — from that dissevering hand?" (297).

The nature of the Potts family makes the gift a shocking one, but Little Billie's motivation to return seems the same as the wanderer's: some impulse toward an identity with the past. The absence of the story Warren chooses *not* to tell in the poem is also significant for an understanding of his concerns. Billie's West is the Oz universal, which apparently needs no record. Here, at least, the return is all.

Given the significance of the impulse toward an identity with the past, one might be tempted to read the poem as an allegory of the lost cause, a version — albeit an ironic one — of what Richard King calls the Southern family romance (26). But even in that impulse Warren finds occasion to emphasize man's separateness not only from the past but from nature in an often cited passage near the end of the poem:

The bee knows, and the eel's cold ganglia burn.
And the sad head lifting to the long return,
Through brumal deeps, in the great unsolsticed coil,
Carries its knowledge, navigator without star,
And under the stars, pure in its clamorous toil,
The goose hoots north where the starlit marshes are.
The salmon heaves at the fall, and, wanderer, you
Heave at the great fall of Time, and gorgeous, gleam
In the powerful arc, and anger and outrage like dew,
In your plunge, fling, and plunge to the thunderous stream:
Back to the silence, back to the pool, back
To the high pool, motionless and unmurmuring dream.
And you, wanderer, back,
Brother to pinion and the pious fin that cleave
The innocence of air and the disinfectant flood

And wing and welter and weave
The long compulsion and the circuit hope
Back,

And bear through that limitless and devouring fluidity
The itch and humble promise which is home.
. . . .
And you, wanderer, back,
After the striving and the wind's word,
To kneel
Here in the evening empty of wind or bird,
To kneel in the sacramental silence of evening
At the feet of the old man
Who is evil and ignorant and old,
To kneel
With the little black mark under your heart,
Which is your name. . . . (300)

This passage is important not only in the Warren canon but in the
history of American nature poetry. Traditionally, in American Romantic poetry the solitary figure is aligned with elements of nature
in an attempt to learn something of nature's language, what it has to
teach. The progress toward a more modern poetry is marked by ever
more ambiguous treatments of the situation, as in Dickinson's "Apparently with no surprise" or Robert Frost's "Design" or, in fiction,
the conclusion of Stephen Crane's story "The Open Boat." Whether
the message is one of benevolence or indifference, in each case the
"language" of nature is treated as though it were final. But in Warren's
poem it is after the "wind's word" that the wanderer is forced to return, for the language of nature alone is not sufficient. The naturalism in the description of the creatures who carry their knowledge
with them is finally contrasted with the wanderer who, though he
salmonlike heaves at his own kind of pool, is clearly separated from
the naturalistic state of the eel and the bee, the goose and the salmon,
and the great serpent. He is, paradoxically, their brother, but a de-

fective one. Whereas they have the perfect knowledge and the peace of unity, the wanderer has "the itch and humble promise which is home," a dream and a desire. This separateness of the wanderer from nature is precisely what makes him human, but so is the desire to return to a unity with nature. And some sort of return, Warren suggests, is possible. The successful return, unlike Little Billie's, takes into account man's capacity for evil and his limitations of knowledge.

Even if the variety of experiences in these early poems seems to particularize rather than universalize experience, the technique emphasizes the fact that in back of all lies the figure of *the* wanderer, a literary figure derived from such sources as biblical narratives, Homer's *Odyssey*, Old English poetry, and the medieval legends of the Wandering Jew and the Pied Piper. Kenneth Tucker has demonstrated parallels between the Pied Piper legend and Warren's story "Blackberry Winter": a natural catastrophe strikes a community, a stranger is hired to repair the damage, the hirers refuse to pay, the stranger seeks revenge, and children follow the stranger away from home. Tucker argues that Warren's tramp and the Pied Piper are common figures of the Jungian archetype of the Trickster. Another prototype is Oedipus, in the Sophoclean sense that he wants to separate himself from his parents because he fears the role they will play in his fate. As John Burt has noted, even though Little Billie Potts suffers the reverse of the Oedipal crime, his rejection of the West is "like Oedipus' rejection of what he thought was his personal history" (*American Idealism* 91). That Warren in these early poems is depending on such archetypal conceptions of the wanderer is underscored by a number of poetic and rhetorical techniques, including biblical allusions and the parenthetical gloss in "The Ballad of Billie Potts." He achieves a similar effect by his use of the misleadingly impersonal pronoun *you* in "Original Sin" and "The Ballad of Billie Potts," a device that becomes even more prominent in later poems.

Floyd C. Watkins, analyzing the importance of the personal past in Warren's poetry, has written that Warren uses the pronoun *you* "with more frequency and accomplishment than any other writer [he] know[s]" (100). One can be more specific than this, however. Certainly Warren's *you* tends to suggest a universality of experience, and its frequent use may well suggest his keen awareness of the fact that poetry is an attempt to communicate with readers. At one level Warren's peculiar use of *you* reflects what Robert S. Koppelman describes as his dual commitments to teaching and to readers: "His commitment to literary language and to readers strikes a refreshing chord with a new generation of students of literary studies who find post-modernist rejections of all traditional belief systems and post-structuralist rejections of all faith in language ultimately unsatisfying" (149–50).

Another significant dimension of Warren's use of *you* must be understood as well. The ostensibly ambiguous second person, if it was not already functioning as such in these early poems, came to be a specific signification of the self, representing a core of individuality that was simultaneously inescapable and mysterious. Although akin to the *id*, which lies beneath the *ego* in its relation to *I*, it does not seem to be an exact synonym. The following lines from "The Interim," a poem from the mid-1960s in which the son describes the impending death of a surrogate mother—an old black woman who had worked for the family and whom he and his father have come to visit—lend credence to this interpretation:

Her hand rises in the air.
It rises like revelation.
It moves but has no motion, and
Around it the world flows like a dream of drowning.
The hand touches my cheek.
The voice says: *you*.

I am myself.

The hand has brought me the gift of myself. (*New and Selected Poems*
247)

At this ritualistic and archetypal moment of touching and naming, the importance of which is emphasized by the preponderance of two- or three-beat, end-stopped lines, the coupling of the pronouns *you* and *myself* suggests that the emphasis is placed on *you* not simply to capture some surprise in the voice of the speaker but to evoke the ritualistic and dramatic sense more commonly associated with the familial or tribal bestowal of a cognomen—a kind of christening, as it were. Warren's *you*, finally, suggests a complex identity that is both private and communal and continuous and, thus, a nag to the consciousness of the wanderer, who seeks freedom from that complexity.

For the son, whose attitude toward his past is at best ambivalent, the naming seems as much a conviction as a gift. The spoken *you* calls the wanderer back to an identity from which he has been dissociated, much as fate calls Oedipus back, with awful finality, to the origin and significance of his name. But the use of *you* in this manner to indicate the end of dissociation at the same time emphasizes the dissociation. Thus it also suggests the qualities that Warren's wandering son borrows from the modern outsider as that historical and literary figure has been analyzed and defined by modern critics and philosophers from Martin Heidegger to Colin Wilson. He is an individual alienated because he sees deeper into the human plight, or seems to, than does his community. His is the plight of the existentialist, who understands that man is dropped into a world in which he is not prepared to survive, in which meaning is not preexistent. The wanderer must make his meaning or perish. Often desperate for vision, Warren's wanderer is also Oedipal in the Freudian sense that he is seduced by the permanence that images from his past seem to offer. He longs for the changelessness that predates the Oedipal state, the condition of "No-Time," the primal identity, as Victor Strandberg puts it, that might be achieved through poetry ("Poet of Youth" 92).

One may say by way of summary, then, that Warren's early handling of the wanderer in his poetry as a figure akin simultaneously to an archetypal ancient wanderer and to a generic modern exile overtly universalizes his most urgent theme: a difficult quest for selfhood dependent on the sense of community and continuity Warren wrote of in *Democracy and Poetry*. Survival on these terms, as he shows again and again, requires a poetic integration of experience that the wandering son not only finds difficult to achieve but often actively evades. That poetic struggle for integration is often reflected in the form of Warren's works, even early on. The dual structure of "The Ballad of Billie Potts" stems from an attempt to gloss the experience of the unimaginative Potts family with the more imaginative voice of the poet, who interprets the experience by apostrophizing the archetypal wanderer in the parenthetical sections of the poem.

On the surface it appears that the impulse to explore his major theme through this archetypal figure in poetry—and all other poetic impulses as well—died just as Warren gave it its fullest treatment in "The Ballad of Billie Potts" (1943), for he completed no more short poems for ten years. He turned his attention to what he called more objective projects: *All the King's Men* and "A Poem of Pure Imagination," his essay on Samuel Taylor Coleridge's *The Rime of the Ancient Mariner*. With his own Jack Burden and Coleridge's Mariner, his mind was obviously still very much on the wandering figure, but his treatment of it through relatively formal and fixed genres, according to Warren's own testimony in "'Blackberry Winter': A Recollection," kept some distance between the figure and the author (639). It was immediately after producing those two works, however, that Warren took up the theme again in a more personal way.

The 1946 short story "Blackberry Winter" is a watershed in Warren's career as well as a link between the early and late poetry. His account of how the story came to be written reveals that its composition was a "poetic," personal effort: "I was going back into a primal world of recollection. I was fleeing, if you wish. Hunting old bearing and bench-marks, if you wish. Trying to make a fresh start, if you wish. Whatever people do in the *doubleness of living in a present and a past*" ("'Blackberry Winter': A Recollection" 640; emphasis added). Although Warren explains his own process of composition here as a return to a world, the process he describes in the story itself is a fleeing *from* that world.

The narrator of the story recalls his boyhood fascination with a tramp who, after unsuccessfully applying for permanent work on the family farm, provokes a near-physical confrontation with the father. As the vagabond leaves, the boy follows him until the man turns on him and says, "Stop following me. You don't stop following me and I cut yore throat, you little son-of-a-bitch" (86). After summarizing what has happened during the thirty-five years since this watershed incident, the narrator concludes the story by saying, "But I did follow him, all the years" (87). This final sentence, considered in a context that includes both the incidents told in the story and the process of the telling, creates a perspective that is strangely both prospective and retrospective. Within it the narrator seems to meet the boy he had been in an image that captures the "doubleness of living in a present and a past," much as O'Connor, say, in "The Life You Save May Be Your Own," has Shiftlet meet an image of his former self in the hitch-hiker. The "wanderer" looks back at himself in his innocence and finds himself even then staring at an image of what he was to become, or at least at an image of a kind of life he feels an affinity with now that he is an adult.

This dual process, going back to reexperience the moment that began the process of separation from home, is dramatized in a number of poems written after 1953. It becomes, in fact, a significant mark of Warren's later work in all genres. The process is not entirely new in the post-1953 poems, but whereas in "Billie Potts," for example, the wanderer experiencing the process and the poet interpreting it are distinct, in these more personal later poems they are two sides of one persona. The result of this fusion is that the wanderer becomes less a combination of the archetypal wanderer and the modern literary alien — less literary stock, in other words — and more a personal poetic persona. An attendant result is a powerful dramatization of inner tensions. Warren's statement that he was conscious of doing something new in "Blackberry Winter" deepens our perception of just how reflexive the story actually is. It is a watershed text in Warren's career that captures the wanderer pondering the significance of a watershed event in *his* life.

Poets' careers do not divide as neatly as the analyzers of their work might like, however. Poems from the mid-1930s through the early 1940s, such as "Picnic Remembered" and "The Return: An Elegy," adapt the wanderer theme to voices that anticipate the voice in the later poems. What distinguishes them is their form. The diction and rhythm of "Picnic Remembered" seem almost overt imitations of John Donne or Andrew Marvell; "The Return" reveals the strong influence of T. S. Eliot. Warren never lost his penchant for universalizing the experience of his wanderer by using biblical and classical allusions, nor did he reject completely the metaphysical diction and metaphors that marked his early poetry. Yet the forms of his later poetry seem to be wrested out of a personal struggle to find a form for *his* wanderer-poet in a process very different from adapting one's personal past to derivative poetic forms. In the poems written after 1953 the wanderer speaks directly in a highly personal voice as he recreates images of a past from which he is estranged yet toward which he is drawn because he needs to understand it. The collections from *Promises: Poems 1954–1956* through *Altitudes and Extensions, 1980–1984* (a collection published first as part of *New and Selected Poems*) contain a substantial number of these personal poems about the dilemma of the wandering son. They are distinguishable from the earlier ones by the way they collectively chronicle the struggle of a single protagonist trying to reconcile his worldly success with an inscrutable and plaguing past.

The later poems reflect this tension in a style and in structures uniquely Warren's. Several critics, most recently and perhaps most brilliantly Randolph Runyon in *The Braided Dream*, have noted that one of the chief features of Warren's sense of structure is the way his poetry creates its own context for interpreting individual poems. The later poems involve a sequencing that suggests, as a variation on narrative, a new path toward a redemptive knowledge. The recurrence of particular images and situations in "Natural History" and "I Am Dreaming of a White Christmas: The Natural History of a Vision" — both about the relationship between the poet-son and his parents — reveals the son's imaginative connection (or his aborted attempt to connect) with his experiences in a process to which Warren seemed determined to call attention. The poems are exemplary in the way they dramatize that process, and as companion poems they clarify the way in which the centrality of the wanderer's inner conflict shapes that dramatization.

The dilemma of the son in "Natural History" (*New and Selected Poems* 178) offers a good example of the root conflict. In the first twelve lines the son describes otherworldly visions of his dead parents — the father dancing naked in the rain, singing the song of understanding, and the naked mother counting "her golden memories of love" as if she were counting pieces of money. In its grotesque imagery the scene is similar to scenes in other poems. But the visions are seductive as well as repulsive, and the speaker's fear of this ambiguity is clarified in the closing lines:

> As much as I hate to, I must summon the police.
> For their own good, as well as that of society, they must be put under
>   surveillance.
>
> They must learn to stay in their graves. That is what graves are for.

The tension in this poem is between the past (or perhaps the eternal that the past can signify) and the present. The past is represented by the wild vision of the parents and the present by the stable, clock-conscious society to which the son happily gives his new allegiance. The incongruity of the two becomes clear when the ghosts create havoc, as dramatic ghosts are wont to do. They have the hyperbolic effects of stopping clocks all over the continent and causing the cancellation of flights out of Kennedy Airport. In addition to this hyperbole, the vision of the parents is marked by images of their frantic action: the naked father tries to dodge drops of rain, and the mother counts an "astronomical" sum with "maniacally busy fingers." The son's defense against their encroachment is detectable in the abrupt shift in tone, from hyperbole and maniacal action to the sedate and technical tone of the passage quoted above, which reveals the essentially professional nature of the son's relation to this society — and, by the way, marks his kinship with the protagonist of *A Place to Come To.*

The change in tone reveals a deadening transformation within the son from a stage in which he resembles Oedipus, the seeker, into one in which he resembles Creon, the restorer of order. The grave is essentially the prison to which disturbers of the psychic peace are consigned, but gravebreaks are a common problem for the wanderer. The significance or the reality of the past is resisted; as suggested by the term "surveillance" the mother and the father are something he must be on the lookout for. The legerdemain here is not really in the apparition of the dead but, with the irony characteristic of Warren, in the hocus-pocus of an infinite present in which the "good of society" corresponds to the psychological comfort of the individual, a present in which the son puts his faith to make the encroachers disappear again. The police are not merely "called" but "summon[ed]," the latter term seeming more nearly to suggest the son's final imperviousness to the past.

The poem is a powerful example of Warren's interest in the subconscious of the wanderer. The surreal images suggest a knowledge that the wanderer is not yet prepared to acknowledge, which is essentially his predicament: he knows more than he wishes to, and the knowledge disturbs the poise he seeks in his contemporaniety. The closest thing to this in modern American literature is the dream at the end of chapter 1 of Ralph Ellison's *Invisible Man.* There the young narrator sees himself at a circus with his dead grandfather, the man who had shocked the family with his deathbed talk of battle and struggle against whites and had disturbed the narrator in ways the young man did not understand. In the dream the grandfather will not laugh no matter what antics the clowns perform, for the clowns, we surmise, wear a mask of paint similar to the mask the grandfather had said the black man must wear in the war he fights with the white man. Yet he does, ironically, laugh when the narrator opens his brief-case (a prize for a speech he had given to an audience of influential white men) and, after working his way through a series of envelopes, discovers what should be his scholarship (another prize) but instead is only a sheet of paper on which is written, "To Whom It May Concern: Keep this Nigger-boy running." The young narrator awakens to the sound of his grandfather's laughter and concludes, "It was a dream I was to remember and dream again for many years after. But at that time I had no insight into its meaning" (26).

Of course, such use of dream and surreal imagery is common in modern literature, but Ellison's and Warren's purposes seem particularly close here. Each uses a dream of vague, hyperbolic, and disturbing content to suggest a troubled relation to the past in the mind of a central consciousness trying to evade the implications of that past for a newer, cleaner identity. There is an essentially Freudian element at the heart of each instance, but each asserts the continuing claim of the beaten "father" after the son's victory. The young man's grandfather, like the parents in Warren's poem, will not stay in his grave where he belongs. There is a further parallel between the "waking" dreams the two writers use: Ellison's narrator dreams of acceptance in the powerful white community, and Warren's persona dreams of temporal isolation. Both writers essentially juxtapose one dream with another to suggest the failure of a protagonist to reconcile himself to the "doubleness of living in the past and the present." Both Ellison and Warren were writers concerned with the way American society seemed to demand total devotion to the present and to the *burial* of difference. While we must not obscure the fact that because of his race Ellison's narrator has a very different stock in the dream from Warren's persona, we should note that both writers have something to say about the inwardness of the outsider who attempts to pass. It is not only a racial barrier that Ellison's book explores. It is the American tendency to efface the reality of the past for an emerging public identity.

However far "Natural History" and similar poems go toward an integration of the past/present and family/society dichotomies, the conflict that gives rise to the voice of the wandering son is almost always, though rarely simply, between seductive permanence and belonging on the one hand and psychologically defensive transience and isolation on the other. When the struggle goes further than the son allows it to in "Natural History," he undergoes a wrenching process of poetic imagination, weaving the two states together as best he can in an attempt to integrate the images of his life. This weaving of images is a key theme in Warren's most overt statements of his philosophy of knowledge: "Knowledge and the Image of Man" and *Democracy and Poetry*. From these it is clear that Warren's sense of the self is similar (but not restricted) to the Lockean sense that the scope of the self is defined by the extent of the consciousness into the past. What Warren attempts to do in more daring moments is to apply a Coleridgean secondary imagination to the individual's sense of the past, to stretch consciousness and, hence, the self. The wanderer resists the stretching; the poet shows its necessity.

In "I Am Dreaming of a White Christmas," a more complex and demanding poem, this treatment of the tension is accomplished by a juxtaposition of three sequential scenes that trace further the imaginative process begun and then aborted in "Natural History." In "Natural History" the imagination calls up the ghosts of the parents, and then fear shuts down the imagination to restore psychic order (associated with and emblematized as social order). In "I Am Dreaming" Warren pushes for an answer to the unarticulated but underlying question in "Natural History": why are the parents conjured in the first place?

The familiar fear of the past is aroused at the opening of "I Am Dreaming": "No, not that door — never!" (*New and Selected Poems* 180). The door is the door to the past in the poet-son's mind, and since he immediately enters despite this opening prohibition, one may assume that the conjuring act in both poems is an inevitability. But here the son is in a more daring mood because his agony is greater. In this second poem, in fact, the son's imagination runs a visionary obstacle course.

The first and most sustained scene, covering the first eight of the poem's twelve sections, is of a family Christmas remembered (or again *conjured*) from his childhood. Warren's approach illustrates the problems the son faces with knowing the past. The scene is not portrayed quasi-photographically, as if all elements were simultaneously present. It *becomes*, kinematically; over the course of the eight sections new objects appear in the vision, as if new props were being added to the stage of the son's memory. The sequential appearance of these objects might seem to underscore the entire poem's structure around a sequence of distinct scenes, to serve as the welded crossbars of the overall scaffolding, as it were. This is not precisely the case, however. Although the larger sequential structure reflects the son's attempt to divide his experience, this internal series of sequences, along with images and gestures that recur throughout the poem's major divisions, suggests the underlying and pervasive connectedness of that experience despite the wanderer's best efforts to divide it. All in all, the sequential structure circumscribes each separate experience recorded in the poem, but that structure is undermined by a counterstructure that suggests the "doubleness of living in a present and a past."

The larger sequence is marked by abrupt changes in atmosphere. A sense of decay pervades the opening sections. Words and phrases such as "brown" and "dust yellow" are repeated often, and once again there are grotesque depictions of the father and mother, both eyeless and motionless here. The mother is actually skeletal; the dry fabric of her dress "shroud[s] femurs" (182). The parents sit among pieces of faded furniture, and a dying Christmas tree is central in the imagined tableau: "[T]he floor / Is there carpeted thick with the brown detritus of cedar" (183). The atmosphere of disintegration and the macabre transports the son into a world beyond the here and now, a movement that he had more easily resisted at the end of "Natural History."

But here it is the imagination of the son that "moves," not the ghosts, as if Warren would clarify even more the psychological nature of the vision. On the mother's hand there are rings that shone on some evenings when in life she had sat with the father and that "[s]hine now" in the poet-son's imagination (182). Other details conspire with this one. A fresh green sprig of holly among the images of decay; the urgency of the son to know which of three brightly wrapped gifts under the tree is for him (*"Oh, which?"*); and even the father's voice, a past voice, audible in the present (*"No presents, son, till the little ones come"*) — these intensify the son's need to know, and to know more than what literal gift awaited him beneath the Christmas tree (184; original emphasis). The holly, the rings, the present, and the voice, in the way they lend a sense of presence to the scene, may be symbolic of the awakening imagination with which the son gives meaning to the image by a nascent and restoring kineticism. The "gift," at any rate, achieves a symbolic level of meaning in the poem, for what the son really needs to know is what meaning there is in his relationship with his parents *now*, what the *present* — both in the sense of a bestowed legacy and in the sense of time present — really is. One is reminded of the hand that brings the son the "gift" of himself in "The Interim" and of the important question asked in "The Ballad of Billie Potts," a question that is in fact important in all of Warren: "What *gift* — oh, father, father — from that dissevering hand?" (297; emphasis added). And the question is all the more relevant to consider here when one remembers that in "Billie Potts" it is asked by the archetypal wandering son who has returned to kneel before the father, essentially as the son in "I Am Dreaming" does through his imagination.

After the first eight sections of "I Am Dreaming," the son closes the door to the room of the past and turns for the poem's second scene to the present. The images here — from his surroundings in

New York City—emphasize madness and dereliction, and the language establishes a bond between the son and the indigent and insane who populate his present and who reflect his own longing for some fulfillment or escape from the contemporary mass mania that section 9 documents. An instance of a fearful madness controlled by the state echoes the control the son exercises over his nightmarish vision at the end of "Natural History": a female inmate at Bellevue, shackled to an iron cot, screams continuously as night is falling (185). In section 10 the poem continues the theme of contemporary mania as the son describes a street scene taking place in the "hysteria of neon" (186).

But section 10 offers particular complexities that turn out to be thematically relevant. It begins in hope:

> Clerks now go home, night watchmen wake up, and the heart
> Of the taxi-driver, just coming on shift,
> Leaps with hope.
>
> All is not in vain.

The details that follow suggest only vanity and failure, however:

> Old men come out from the hard-core movies.
> They wish they had waited till later.
> . . . .
> Meanwhile, down the big sluice of Broadway,
> The steel logs jerk and plunge
> Until caught in the rip, snarl, and eddy here before my face. (186)

That the son identifies with the old men coming out of hard-core movies is suggested by their staring up at a sky that "dies wide," a gesture the son will imitate in section 11. The recognition of the indigence of the self is similar to that of the narrator's identification of himself with the tramp in "Blackberry Winter." He deals with the disorder of the traffic jam in a familiar way. The description ends with the son's finding a kind of beauty in the figure of a mounted policeman, the same symbol of order that had to be summoned in "Natural History." As opposed to the eyeless dead in the earlier scene of this poem, the policeman's "eyes are bright with seeing," and he is "as beautiful as a law of chemistry" (186). Thus, section 10 moves from declarations of hope to images of futility and entanglement which can be mediated only by an imposed social order that is made comparable to a natural order.

But the idea of order will not hold here as it seemed to hold in "Natural History." The enormity of the psychic disorder and the son's difficulty in controlling it are suggested in several ways: by the clumsy movement of the traffic; by the conceit in which both the tenor (the traffic jam on Fifth Avenue) and the vehicle (the log jam) suggest the individual's discordant relationship with both society and nature; by the incongruous mix of slang expression and a higher diction in the section's final images—the horse's "rump / . . . gleams expensively," and the policeman "is some sort of dago . . . / as beautiful as a law of chemistry"; and finally by the ironic evocation in this image of the "law[s] of chemistry" which will inevitably lead us away from the kind of beauty emphasized here and back to decay (186).

But the resilience of the son is extraordinary, bordering on the comic. Since the images of social order and the beauty of an illusory perpetual contemporaneity will not calm the more active imagination at work in this poem, the son takes a bolder step to impose order. In section 11 he imagines himself into a Frostian situation, into (and here again diction is a key) "Otherwhere" (186). Specifically he imagines himself in the Nez Perce Pass where he knows that even "this early," snow will be falling (186). The phrase "this early" seems to associate his desperation with the desperation of the indigent old men who have gone to the porno movies too early. The son is working again to transport himself, this time from the here and now, and once again the diction reveals that his success is only partial. The meaning to be taken from this third scene is suggested in part by the description of the snowfall: "The first flakes, / Large, soft, sparse, come straight down / And with enormous deliberation, white / Out of unbreathing blackness" (187). But although the description is in part realistic, phrases such as "enormous deliberation" and "unbreathing blackness" work against that realism. Again a deliberate incongruity in diction proves highly functional, helping us to interpret the particular resonance of the adverb "Otherwhere" at the beginning of the vision.

Warren's friend and poetic mentor John Crowe Ransom had used the same word in a similar context in his poem "Somewhere Is Such a Kingdom." The lines are relevant enough to quote here:

> But when [birds] croak and fleer and swear,
> My dull heart I must take elsewhere;
> For I will see if God has made
> Otherwhere another shade
> Where the men or beasts or birds
> Exchange few words and pleasant words.
> And dare I think it is absurd
> If no such beast were, no such bird? (*Selected Poems* 49)

Warren's awareness of Ransom's use of "Otherwhere" may or may not have influenced him in "I Am Dreaming." In his essay "Notes on the Poetry of John Crowe Ransom at His Eightieth Birthday," Warren writes of the significance of this poem's placement in Ransom's volume directly after "Two in August," about a husband who, stepping into the night after a quarrel with his wife, hears ambiguous bird calls. I should add here that I am particularly indebted to Randolph P. Runyon (*Braided Dream* 84–85) for first drawing my attention to Warren's emphasis on the poem in his essay. Warren writes, "If the quarrel even of lovers is in the world (grounded in nature, even among 'birds'), then our role as men in our manliness is to create the vision of a loving peace" (*New and Selected Essays* 323). Warren sees in Ransom, then, a theme in common with Hawthorne, Melville, Conrad, and Dreiser. The son's imagined place in "I Am Dreaming," however, is quite different from that imagined by Ransom's speaker, and understanding this helps us to see that the contortions of mind Warren puts the son through are quite extraordinary.

The point may be particularly confusing because Warren does write of imagined places similar to Ransom's in other poems. In "Bearded Oaks," for example, lovers supine beneath the oaks learn how they "may spare this hour's term / To practice for eternity" (*New and Selected Poems* 307). Another instance occurs at the end of *Chief Joseph of the Nez Perce* (and here the danger of misreading is made even greater by the reference to the Nez Perce Pass in "I Am Dreaming"), where the poet imagines a stranger who might withdraw from the hysteria of traffic and, "standing paralyzed in his momentary eternity, [look] into / His own heart . . . while he asks / From what undefinable distance, years, and direction, / Eyes of fathers are suddenly fixed on him" (64). It is not at all the epiphany of a "momentary eternity" that engages the son in section 11 of "I Am Dreaming." He has neither the lovers' "we" in "Bearded Oaks" nor the stranger's sense of the presence of ancient fathers in *Chief Joseph*. The relationship between Ransom's otherwhere and Warren's is an ironic one. Ransom's speaker imagines a place of men, beasts, and birds exchanging few and pleasant words—a conceivably less maniacal society. The son in "I Am Dreaming" imagines a total negation of life marked by an "unbreathing blackness," essentially a nowhere, a void into which the son plunges, the ultimate Other.

The plunge, however, may be necessary. The void here is described in terms that link it to Jed Tewksbury's assertion in *A Place to Come To* that orgasm was "like the 'black hole' of the physicists— a devouring negativity." But Jed continues by calling orgasm "the death in life-beyond-Time without which life-in-Time might not be endurable, or even possible" (220–21). A similar void or "Otherwhere" may well be the *public* that Warren defined in *Democracy and Poetry* by the same metaphor that Jed uses to define orgasm: a black hole, a "devouring negativity" (62). In the novel, however, Jed comes to this conclusion through hindsight. The son in Warren's poem plunges into the visionary landscape otherwhere to escape his immediate pain much as Jed plunges into orgasm, or Issac Goldfarb into his cleansing *public* identity at the end of *The Cave*. The reason this evasion fails is clarified by the sudden eruption of the question first posed in the poem's opening scene as the poet virtually screams for what has been left out of this third scene change and third psychological turn: "But tell me, tell me, / Will I never know / What present there was in that package for me, / Under the Christmas tree?" (187).

Just as in section 9 the woman chained to her asylum bed screams to escape the falling night, here in section 11 the son screams to escape the void to which his escapism has ironically led him. These lines rupture the "dreaming" of the kind of white Christmas that negates time. Furthermore, the passage shows that as in "Natural History" the mother and father will not stay in their graves; but whereas in that poem the son seems to quell the nightmarish vision by exercising a tone of control, in "I Am Dreaming" the sedate tone of section 11 is broken by the sudden reemergence of urgency in the son's voice. He must face the fact that the mother and father will not learn to stay in their graves where they belong because there is a part of them that is not dead. What that part is has something to do with the past as a determining factor in identity; the problem is how to know just what significance the past has as such. The entirety of "I Am Dreaming" seems an exercise in using memory and imagination to settle this important issue. That the son has an understanding of the value of this process is demonstrated in the lines that constitute the whole of section 12:

All items listed above belong in the world
In which all things are continuous,

And are parts of the original dream which
I am now trying to discover the logic of. This
Is the process whereby pain of the past in its pastness
May be converted into the future tense

Of joy. (187)

These final lines of "I Am Dreaming" constitute an explicit, even prosaic statement of the wandering son's dilemma and the way he attempts to solve it. The poem probes the complex relationship between experience and vision and records the process whereby the son obtains his vision through the working of his imagination on the stark images haunting his memory. All of this perhaps relates one version of what Warren has called "the movie in our heads" (*Homage to Theodore Dreiser* 118). Together, "Natural History" and "I Am Dreaming" establish a pattern of movement from a static image to a dynamic one. In the first poem the horrifying image from the past is denied by the mind's need for a simple order. In the second the anguish is greater, driving the son by way of various stages toward an awareness that the mind achieves meaning through the integration of past and present. The result may be a conversion of religious significance (the word *converted* almost slips by the reader in the final lines of "I Am Dreaming" because of the reversion to the clinical tone). Moreover, the process is as much Warren's method here as it is his meaning. By their structures as well as their content, "Natural History" and "I Am Dreaming" evoke the drama of the doubleness of living in the present and the past.

For what they say about the process that leads through anguish toward knowledge, the final lines of "I Am Dreaming" are comparable to a similar epiphany when the son in "The Interim" declares that the only way to learn how to live is to eat the dead, which echoes Warren's eating metaphor for reading poetry in "Pure and Impure Poetry." Since I will have other occasions to refer to Warren's eating metaphors, I quote them both here:

There is only one way to conquer the monster [the poem]: you must eat it, bones, blood, skin, pelt, and gristle. And even then the monster is not dead, for it lives in you, is assimilated into you and you are different, and somewhat monstrous yourself, for having eaten it. ("Pure and Impure Poetry," *New and Selected Essays*, 4)

You must eat [the dead] completely, bone, blood, flesh, gristle, even
Such hair as can be forced. You
Must undertake this in the dark of the moon, but
At your plenilune of anguish. ("The Interim," *New and Selected*
    Poems, 249)

Again, the significance of the striking similarities between these two passages lies in Warren's use of identical metaphors for the process of reading and understanding poetry and for the process of "reading" and understanding history — in the case of the poems I have considered here, personal history. As Burt has written, the similarities "point out how close the cauterizing grief elegy evokes and assuages is to the experience of poetic meaning generally, that poetry itself is a crucial but dangerous thing one must approach as once approaches grief" (*American Idealism* 81). The necessity of poetry in general which Burt emphasizes and its definite link to grief are certainly revealed in the two poems I have analyzed here. The emphasis on the ironic process of transforming grief into joy and the personalizing of his wanderer are twin developments that give Warren's post-1953 poems their sometimes convoluted yet methodical form — and, to my mind, much of their power. Poetry is knowledge, Warren wrote in "Knowledge and the Image of Man," a knowledge of form (244).

But poetry is also, in a sense, a place, if *place* is understood to mean a matrix of relationships rather than simply a geographic spot on the globe. That the metaphor for reading the past is identical to that for reading poetry suggests the poet's necessity of injecting *you* into the picture of his own life or, to adopt another way of critical speaking, of establishing his relations to a "text." I use that term with its several

layers of meaning not so much because it is in vogue as because here
Warren's own eating/reading metaphors seem to require it, especially
if we extend to its logical extreme the communion analogy they in-
vite — that in eating the body of the dead one eats the Word.

Warren's concern with the high psychological costs of placelessness
in contemporary American society intensified, if anything, during
the last two decades of his career. In *Democracy and Poetry* he wrote
that "the ordinary, decent, intelligent citizen, functioning in the
morally neutral world of technologies, easily begins to assume that
the only self worth having is one to be defined primarily by its capacity to deny its 'self.' Fluidity of selves replaces integrity of self as a
source of effectiveness, and identity is conceived of in terms of mere
action, with action determined completely by the fluctuating contingencies of environment" (58–59). In such a paradoxically deterministic world, he continues, "the fundamental role of the citizen is no
longer that of producer but of consumer" (60). That statement, while
echoing the Agrarian manifesto, also finds a corresponding thought
in a historian such as Daniel Boorstin, who argues that as America
entered its technological age, the idea of community was significantly altered and the ancient idea of a "fellowship of skill was displaced by the democracy of cash" (89). As society drifts toward the
abolition of self, Warren adds, people take time off to find themselves,
not realizing that "the self is never to be found, but must be created"
(89). What people have lost, then, in this shifting of value and process, is essentially a dominant metaphor or myth for the value and
process of making the inward self.

The fluidity of selves describes not only the condition of "the ordinary, decent, intelligent citizen" but also the dilemma of the Southern exile. In that figure, however, the condition is intensified; it is
a condition the exile seeks rather than one he "easily begins to assume," for any exposure to a less fluid way of life haunts him — be the
revelatory images of either stasis or stability. A belief in moral neu-

trality and determinism, or rather a need to believe in them, leads Jack Burden to his theory of the Great Twitch and Jed Tewksbury to his "identity with Fate." Yet both are, like Issac Sumpter in *The Cave* and Brad Tolliver in *Flood*, oxymorons — professionally successful drifters.

A poem of the late 1970s, "Blessèd Accident," reveals that Warren was also continuing to explore the paradoxical question of contingency — the ratio between accident and logic in the determination of fate — through his wandering-son persona. The one sure thing for "you" in this poem is that "Success, / Particularly of a vulgar order, tends / To breed complacency in the logic of / Your conduct of life" (*Rumor Verified* 12). Here as elsewhere, however, the "mysterious anger" or mysterious grief, as the nameless and haunting feeling toward the past sometimes manifests itself, draws the alien from his complacency. The dissatisfaction is a completely illogical feeling, for it comes to those who have made successes of themselves: "Though your luck held and the market was always satisfactory," says "The Ballad of Billie Potts." In "Original Sin" and several later poems the feeling, figured often as an animal, comes in the night as the persona lies awake. "What Was the Thought?" provides a typical example wherein the persona, shocked by the suddenness of a nameless disturbance, tries to fend off the feeling with logic.

> You feel
> Your heart settle to the old guaranteed rhythm.
> You know that constellations also are
> Steady about their allotted business. Your children
> Are healthy. They do well at school. Your
> Wife is faithful. (*Rumor Verified* 57)

Diction here emphasizes the contrived nature of the consoling order, an order in which biological functions and heavenly bodies are ostensibly controlled by market terminology: "guaranteed," "allotted," "business." Yet "[s]uddenly, / You feel like weeping" because the thought, like a mouse, has crept "along the baseboard of the dark mind" (57). Figuring the mind as a house or a room, as he had done in "I Am Dreaming of a White Christmas," gives Warren an accurate metaphor for the security the wanderer should feel as well as the opportunity to metaphorize encroachment on that security by the "Nightmare" of the past. It is something physical to be cornered, captured, and destroyed. The family cat, associated with the daylight self of the persona, effectively kills the mouse that disturbed his night peace in "What Was the Thought?" But in "Nameless Thing" the persona must do the hunting himself:

I hold my breath. I am ready. I think of blood.
I fling the door open. Only a square
Of moonlight lies on the floor inside. All is in order.
I go back to bed. I hear the blessèd heart beat there.

But once, on a very dark night, it was almost different.
That night I was certain. Trapped in a bathroom!
I snatched the door open, weapon up, and yes, by God! —
But there I stood staring into a mirror. Recognition

Came almost too late. But how could I
Have been expected to recognize what I am?
In any case, that was what happened. I now lie
Rigid abed and hear namelessness stalk the dark house.

I wonder why it cannot rest. (*Rumor Verified* 27–28)

Several characteristics here are very common in what one may think of as Warren's insomnia poems, which appear rather frequently in *Rumor Verified, Being Here,* and *Now and Then*: the night panic, the "thing" in the house, the reassurance of everything's being in order, the heartbeat (or breathing) of the loved one beside the speaker in the bed, the image in the mirror or the photograph. And the mirror or photograph represents the primal self, the other identity that the logical self would figuratively beat with a poker to keep it out of the orderly house. Among American authors one thinks only of Edgar Allan Poe and Dickinson, perhaps Henry James, using architectural metaphors for the mind with such similar effects and effectiveness.

To be taken alongside these poems because of the similarity in their situations are the four poems in section 5 of Warren's final volume of verse, *Altitudes and Extensions*, a collection that in some ways, especially with its emphasis on *last* things, reflects a consciousness of its "finalness." One poem especially seems to carry on the important images and themes associated with the wanderer/son, but in fact all four of the poems in section 5 are linked by the memory of boyhood in Kentucky. They also have in common the impulse that Strandberg has seen: the impulse to find through poetry the lost "innermost identity of the octogenarian poet," the identity that is "lost somewhere among those vanished voices and faces" called back in these poems ("Poet of Youth," 92).

The first of the four poems, "Old-Time Childhood in Kentucky," invokes the familiar image of Warren's maternal grandfather, Gabriel Penn, and ends with the speaker as a child in a prospective moment wondering about his future, most of which, in the poem's typical doubleness of perspective, has of course already occurred. In the third poem of the four, "Last Meeting," the persona, on a return visit back home, meets an old black woman who in the frailty of age seems an emblem of the goneness of the past and who during a bittersweet conversation calls out "Ro-Penn, Ro-Penn." (It is interesting how often Warren refers to himself in muted or abbreviated forms in his poems—e.g., R.P.W. in *Brother to Dragons*—as if to suggest that in investigating a part of the past he is unwilling to invest the self too quickly or assuredly with a full identity.)

The second and fourth poems in the group need more attention here. In the second, "Covered Bridge," Warren again shows his wanderer facing the problematical link between present and past.

Another land, another age, another self
Before all had happened that has happened since
And is now arranged on the shelf
Of memory in a sequence that I call Myself.

How can you think back and know
Who was the boy, sleepless, who lay
In a moonless night of summer, but with star-glow
Gemming the dewy miles, and acres, you used to go? (*New and Se-
lected Poems* 47)

Structurally the poem seems much more conventional than "I Am
Dreaming" with its shifting verse forms and tones. Yet in these first
two stanzas the poet uses first- and second-person pronouns and the
third-person "boy" all to refer to himself, suggesting the complexity
of the problem by simultaneously splitting the subjective self and
universalizing the central question evoked by the poet's experience.
Line four, furthermore, seems highly reflexive, referring perhaps to
the use of sequencing rather than straight narrative in the wanderer
poems as a way to explore the doubleness of living. The "covered
bridge" of the title becomes a symbol of the separation:

Till you wondered what night, long off, you would set hoof
On those loose boards and then proceed
To trot through the caverning dark beneath that roof.
Going where? Just going. That would be enough. (47)

Reading casually here, one assumes the presence of a horse in the
prospective journey, but the trope in "you would set hoof" suggests
the transformative power of traversing the cavernous bridge. Identity
is complicated even more as the poet becomes satyr or minotaur in
an image recalling the bestial imagery so significant in the definition
of man in *Brother to Dragons* — particularly the myth of Pasiphaë,
which the bitter Jefferson ponders early in that poem. The only crime

here may be the aimlessness suggested by the final line of the stanza.

Yet in the penultimate stanza the prospective separation that obviously did, in time, occur is followed by an uneasy return:

> Then silence would wrap that starlit land,
> And you would sleep—who now do not sleep
> As you wonder why you cannot understand
> What pike, highway, or path has led you from land to land. . . .

A connection between then and now is suggested by a dash in midline (a reconnecting bridge?) and also by syntax: a relative clause identifies the man with the boy he was, rejoining what the multiple points of view had seemed to separate in the first two stanzas. Even as this connection is made, however, the poet goes on to ask the same question about his fate that he had asked in earlier poems:

> From year to year, to lie in what strange room,
> Where to prove identity you now lift up
> Your own hand—scarcely visible in that gloom. (47–48)

The characteristic sleeplessness connects this poem with those such as "Blessèd Accident" and "What Was the Thought?" as the older poet's insomnia becomes the occasion for poetry. But the image of the lifted hand, which seems to emphasize anatomically a reversal of the original transformation—from hoof to hand—also echoes images from another group of related poems, especially "Mortmain" and "Tale of Time," Warren's poems about the deaths of his father and mother.

In "Mortmain" the father's lifted hand from his deathbed proves enigmatic. In "Tale of Time" the mother's lifted hand, or her surrogate's, names the poet. But both actions tend toward a paradoxical effect of separation. The poet is left "naked in the black blast" of his dying father's love (*New and Selected Poems* 264), and the mother figure's touch is the disservering touch of his own identity, the gift of

"Myself." The fact that the hand he now watches is his own emphasizes the poet's aloneness, and "Covered Bridge" does not go further. There is no self-contained epiphany here, but in the gesture itself there is the connection with the other figures from the other poems.

The language needs close attention as well. Though the hand is "scarcely visible in that gloom," the gesture is not a feeble attempt to prove identity; it does prove identity. At one level, in isolation, the affirmation of identity seems a knowledge based only on physical evidence. Read in connection with the earlier poems, however, the gesture becomes an affirming reenactment. The father's falling hand in "Mortmain" absorbed all boyhood experience from the poet; here his own hand seems to contain the past symbolically. It does not, of course, solve the mystery of how the speaker came to be in the strange room, but it does connect the present self with the former self almost ritualistically. The gesture is what the persona would do after he had "eat[en] the dead." The poem absorbs the previous ones in a sense, in part through Warren's development of a private system of symbols associated with his wanderer.

The final poem of the four, "Re-interment: Recollection of a Grandfather," is another study in the incongruous but real connections of experience between childhood and adulthood. This time, however, the metaphors for the mind multiply as if the poet cannot settle on an appropriate one to contain the image. The title suggests the mind as grave, breaking the earlier pattern of the mind as a cityscape or a house terrorized by the gravebreakers, but in the first stanza the grandfather's image ("it") is figured as a fetus, carried in the poet's head as a century and a half earlier it had been carried in a woman's womb. The psychic discord, metaphorized as civil unrest, which results from the grandfather's having to inhabit space with all the others in the poet's mind (all of whom certainly came from a different world) requires more room—"the great dome my shoulders bear"; however, the head then becomes the "jail" the grandfather claws to get out of. Formally illogical, the shifting metaphors suggest the wrangling that the grandfather's memory represents in the diverse experience of the wanderer's life. Although civil unrest is the dominant metaphor, there is here no need to "summon the police." Instead, the aging poet comes paradoxically to feel more like the old man himself, even as he emphasizes the lastness of a world the grandfather represents:

> Some night, not far off, I'll sleep with no such recollection —
> Not even his old-fashioned lingo and at dinner the ritual grace,
> Or the scratched-in-dust map of Shiloh, and Bloody Pond,
> Or the notion a man's word should equal his bond,
> And the use of a word like *honor* as no comic disgrace.
> And in our last communal trance, when the past has left no trace,
> He'll not feel the world's contempt, or condescending smile,
> For there'll be nobody left, in that after-while,
> To love him — or recognize his kind. Certainly not his face. (*New and*
> *Selected Poems* 50)

A poem that begins as one more night tussle of the insomniac poet turns into one more homage to Gabriel Penn and what he stood for both in the poet's life and in the body of poetry that was the attempt to make sense of that life. There is a sense of guilt here for prolonging the suffering of the old man who cannot die until the last person who knew him dies. It is a strange guilt, like Bowman's strange guilt in the tenant house in Welty's story, but through it the poet manages to make death less solitary; it becomes a "communal trance." One must also recognize that in the poet's final identification with the grandfather there is a quiet, a disturbingly quiet, condemnation of a world that would not recognize his kind, just as in the personal family legacy there will be none to recognize the face. A world that values a fluidity of selves cannot value Gabriel Penn. The wanderer is that figure who has had to live in two times, in two worlds, and the conflict is the harangue and the strange guilt suggested by the mind as a jail for the old man, as if he has kept him prisoner by living.

The fusion of the poet and the wanderer into a single figure is a major stroke in Warren's development, yet the pervasive presence of the wandering son is a sign that the very real and significant changes in the kind of poetry Warren wrote after 1953 were not just the result of a sudden affirmation of meaning, as Calvin Bedient, for one, believes (4). They were instead the result of a lifelong and traceable struggle for form, which was for Warren the struggle for knowledge, which was in turn a struggle for *place*. If Warren's later poetry is his highest accomplishment, it is so in part because he grappled his way into it, not simply by returning to the personal past as a source but by returning to it with the dual sense of estrangement from it and the need to create it. It offered him a redefining inner conflict between permanence and transience — redefining because each poetic foray into the past brings new knowledge into the self and makes the self "somewhat monstrous."

The examples considered here can represent something about the wholeness of Warren's vision and how it relates to his conception of the link between knowledge and the form that reveals the knowledge. In each case it is the structuring of the material — the ordering that is a literary effort analogous to "eating the dead," the process that gives life and ultimately meaning to the nagging icon or ghost — that drives Warren's treatment of the theme. Paraphrasing the passage from Heidegger (233) that serves as the epigraph for this chapter, one might say of Warren that the poems are not poems about homecoming but are themselves a homecoming. And even though I have focused on one strain of his poetry, that which can be said to have this wanderer theme, a very similar conflict seems to drive his treatment of those "representative" men from American history — James Audubon, Thomas Jefferson, Chief Joseph — whose lives as represented in Warren's poetry are a struggle between pure ideas and recalcitrant facts as they strive for that achievement of being at home in the world.

Warren defined *home* as "not a place" but "a state of spirit, . . . of feeling, . . . of mind, a proper relation to the world" (Watkins and Hiers 102). Whereas Audubon, Jefferson, and Joseph represent to some extent Warren's historical treatment of the theme, the wandering son is perhaps his more personal response to the dilemma of home in the modern world: estrangement from a familial and regional identity when the only alternative to such an identity appears to be immersion in a society that seeks the abolition of the self and disturbs the "proper relation." Such a troubled relationship with *home* in this sense has, of course, been a rich theme for modern writers, particularly modern Southern writers, but few have pursued the theme as relentlessly and through such remarkable evolutions of form as Warren. Examining his use of the wandering son is one way to enter into his work and begin to understand with greater clarity his enormous contribution to our literature and to our time.

CHAPTER THREE

Brothers and Rebukers

The Race Question(s)

It is easy to say to the Southerner that he should give up his Southernness and just be a good American. It is easy to say to the Negro that
he should give up his Negro-ness and just be a good American — who
is got up in blackface. Negroes and white Southerners do, in fact,
want to be Americans, but by and large they want to be themselves
too; and the fact that both belong to minorities means that both may
cling defensively to what they are, or what they take themselves to
be. They may refuse to be totally devalued, gutted, and scraped before being flung into the melting pot. But that is one solution, and
some Negroes and white Southerners, in self-hatred — sometimes
self-hatred disguised as liberalism — or in self-seeking, accept it;
they "pass."

ROBERT PENN WARREN, *Who Speaks for the Negro?*

◈ John Burt has written that "the difference between the drifter
and the fanatic" in Warren "is only a difference in time; it is
not a difference in kind" (*American Idealism* 185). Although this may
be putting the matter too absolutely, there are certainly elements of
kinship between the two. In some ways we may say that the difference lies in what Warren identified in writings such as *The Legacy of
the Civil War* as the difference between a traditional man and a new
man who developed out of the war and its attendant logic. As a "vital
image" of identity, the Civil War is the Homeric period that marks

America's true beginning for Warren. Its heroes are "figures," "images," as well as humans, often differing from men of the present, Warren argues, in their individualism. They achieved identity by attempting to come to a moral awareness in a process that contrasts with the practices of the present age of conformity and uniformity. Without irony or, more accurately, with an insistence on the necessity of irony, Warren also recognizes that a corollary to this individuality is a sense of community. He points, for example, to George Pickett's admonition to his men at Gettysburg before charging: "Don't forget today that you are from Old Virginia!" Warren comments that "the notion of place has a natural relation to the notion of identity in community, in the shared place" (*Legacy* 91). In short, the heroic figures of the war exemplify the dialectic of moral awareness outlined in *Democracy and Poetry*: a sense of oneself as a development over time and a sense of oneself as a responsible member of a community. Warren realizes that the appeal of such images of the men of the war is nostalgic, at times even absurd. This does not to his mind, however, make the images less "true," for it is finally the "inwardness," or doubleness, of the Civil War illustrated by such images that he seizes to demonstrate an American form of a human dilemma.

What one may come to realize after some scrutiny and synthesis is that Warren's history of the Civil War encodes the conflicts and the psychological defenses of the wanderer on a regional, thence a national scale. Looking at that history reveals something valuable about Warren as a Southern and an American poet. It also establishes an important background for understanding more fully the significance in his canon of a work such as *Segregation*. And, finally, it makes clear that the wanderer's kinship with the fanatic of an earlier time reveals only a part of his story.

Strong Union sentiment in the South is one example of the doubleness Warren sees in the war. More dramatic examples include the relationship of Generals Simon Bolivar Buckner and Ulysses S. Grant. Though they were enemies in war—Buckner, who had once lent money to the destitute Grant, surrendered to him at Fort Donelson—Warren emphasizes the irony of the visit Buckner paid later to the dying Grant: "When Buckner had come out from the dying man and the reporters demanded what had passed between them, he said, with tears in his eyes, that it was 'too sacred.'" And Warren adds, "We may remember the Confederate generals, in their gray sashes, walking as pallbearers at the funeral of Grant" (*Legacy* 85–86). Such images, even in the piety they evoke, give the war its inwardness, its double-sidedness, the significance of which Warren clarifies to some extent by contrasting it with the Revolutionary War, which was in some ways too easy for Americans; at least as it exists in the national imagination, it offers no inner conflict. The fascinating theory is that only through inner conflict was America born, and the same principle applies to the individual.

In contrast to the Civil War's inwardness, Warren sees that systematic thinking about the North-South conflict tended to be more polarized and self-absolving than double-sided and self-incriminating. The worst excesses of Northern "higher-law" thinking led to John Brown and his backers. Perhaps Warren's most frightening example of zealous higher-lawism is a rhetorical one: James Redpath's assertion that if only one black slave survived the general slaughter of his race as the price of freedom, the price would be cheap for the return of that freedom (*Legacy* 20–21).

The South, on the other hand, became a closed society, a defense for itself as real in Warren's eyes as the guns pointed north. By refusing any criticism of itself from the inside, the South stopped growing and rigidified. Warren's analysis superbly maps the psychological development of that rigid South which William Faulkner and other Southern writers, including the Agrarians, dramatized in its clash with a new order of pragmatism and technology. Yet although a "new man" emerged in the war whom Warren sees represented in various degrees by Grant, W. T. Sherman, Abraham Lincoln, Justice Oliver Wendell Holmes and William James, the failure of the Southerner in the end is the same as the failure of the abolitionist and transcendentalist branches (sometimes overlapping) of Northern reformism:

the lack of willingness to be self-criticizing. In *The Legacy of the Civil War* Warren regards self-criticism not only as a path to an essential knowledge but also as a means of practical solutions to social problems. The pragmatism practiced by such men as Lincoln, Holmes, and William James was a reaction to the disaster of the polar alternatives of higher-law thinking and "legalism," the treatment of the Constitution as sacred and inviolable text. For Warren, "the philosophy of pragmatism represented an attempt to establish the right relation between intellect and society—the relation which had been violated by the Transcendentalist repudiation of society and Southern repudiation of criticism" (41).

Warren's frequent comparison of Davis's thinking to Lincoln's in *Jefferson Davis Gets His Citizenship Back* adds to his discussion of the "new-manism" begun in *Legacy*. It is also a good indication of the evenness of his treatment. To say that the president of the Confederacy saw no magic in emancipation would draw a wry grin from many readers, but to point out in the same paragraph that the Great Emancipator held similar notions (*Jefferson Davis* 42) undermines one of the most cherished images of Northern self-righteousness and presents a different kind of irony: the irony of the Melville-Warren tradition that I want to call the irony of inwardness.

Warren also compares the two men in terms of their ambition: Neither of them had a simple ambition at either extreme, not "the trivial vanity of strut and preen, with no relation to accomplishment," or "the fuelling, depersonalizing devotion to an objective endeavor, the locale of which may be a poet's desk or a soldier's battlefield" (*Jefferson Davis* 52). The ambition of both is complex and ultimately unknowable in relation to the one's success and the other's failure, but in the complexity of their motivations Warren locates their difference from modern men. The difference involves and is involved in their struggle for moral awareness in action, which Warren often contrasts with what he sees as the moral complacency of modern America.

Analyzing the differences between Davis and Lincoln in the context of polarized interpretations of the Constitution, Warren contrasts the pragmatism that developed in the North—at first as a wartime attitude—to the attitude of Southerners to show that the differences between Lincoln and Davis to a large extent reflected differences between their societies. Lincoln's willingness to suspend habeas corpus during the war is indicative of the evolutionary attitude the North generally took toward the Constitution, whereas many Southerners, including Davis, "saw the Constitution as equivalent to the tablets that Moses delivered from Sinai" (62). Yet there is no simple irony in Warren's subsequently writing that Davis did not regard slavery as an institution sanctioned by holy writ, for Warren sees in Davis a pathos not unlike that which he finally discovers in John Brown: his beliefs rigidified along with those of his region.

The basic difference in regional attitudes is further reflected in the pragmatic tactics of the North and the codified behavior of the South. Southern commanders were shot practicing the outmoded chivalric gesture of charging the enemy on horseback at the front of their troops. In fact, Warren argues, it was the Civil War that brought the change from chivalric battle to modern warfare, as exemplified by Sherman's policy of total war. This change was the result of the "logic of experience": "There is a straight line of logic leading from Sherman's theory to Coventry, buzz bombs on London, the Dresden fire raid, the Tokyo fire raid, and Hiroshima." Grant's "swap system" is another example of the practical new-manism. Grant "had an incalculable amount of blood to swap," and to strengthen his position he refused either a truce for tending to dead and wounded or prisoner exchanges (*Jefferson Davis* 66–67).

Warren's theory of new-manism is comparable in some ways to R. W. B. Lewis's theory of the American Adam as applied to post–Civil War culture. The new men of pragmatism were cut off from traditional society and its notions of values and conduct. Their emergence during the war, set against the rigidifying process of the Southerners, polarized the conflict between men of antique values and men of developing new values. The implications of that conflict are crucial to Warren's epistemological themes: in many contexts he looks to the war and the late nineteenth century as the time when social upheaval led to shifting values for individuals and communities. Most notably, the new man was a man of educable consciousness; the traditional man had been a man of conscience. The chivalric gesture and strong sense of state loyalty that strike us now as absurd were signs of the strong hold of that conscience. But conscience was also signified, Warren argues, in the reservations about waging war on civilians of such (pre-Sherman) Union officers as George McClellan, George Meade, and Robert Shaw (*Jefferson Davis* 65).

The conflict between a rigid society and the emerging consciousness in the works of Mark Twain, Henry James, Kate Chopin, Edith Wharton, Stephen Crane, and Theodore Dreiser reflects the conflict Warren is identifying here, and like his predecessors he is interested in the effect of the conflict on self-knowledge or, to use the more Jamesian phrase, the growth of consciousness. Warren's comparison between Lincoln and Davis and the broader comparison between Northern and Southern societies are ultimately comparisons between two ways of knowing.

From these polar reactions of North and South to the war, Warren formulates in *The Legacy of the Civil War* his dual theory of regional absolution: the Treasury of Virtue and the Great Alibi. These he labels interestingly as "psychological" costs of the war because each represents a way of repressing individual and regional connection to and responsibility for its horrors. Clearly, Warren was labeling the automatic and axiomatic tendencies in regional history that characterize the intellectual narcotics taken by the wandering son to soothe his guilt and order his psychic world.

With his theory of the Great Alibi, the Southerner's sense that he is trapped into certain patterns of thought and behavior by history, Warren launches his most scathing attack on his home region and his most perceptive explanation for its failure to deal humanely and responsibly with the poverty and racial strife that have plagued it. But whereas the Southerner feels conveniently trapped in history, the Northerner feels automatically redeemed by history, thanks to his heritage of the Treasury of Virtue. Here the image of the self may be based on a rewriting of history that suits the deepest needs of the Northerner with his "ikon of a boy in blue striking off, with one hand, iron shackles from a grizzle-headed Uncle Tom weeping in gratitude, and [with] the other passing out McGuffey's First Reader to a rolypoly pickaninny laughing in hope" (*Legacy* 60). Together, the Treasury of Virtue and the Great Alibi represent a complete failure to achieve the dual consciousness requisite for selfhood: the sense of continuity and the sense of responsibility. Inheritors of the Treasury of Virtue fail to recognize the relevance of history to the present, and those of the Great Alibi fail to realize their responsibility in an interconnected world. In the end Warren relates the disparate regional responses to the war to the importance of the study of history for the individual in the present. Selfhood is simultaneously an achievement of imaginative interpretation of historical fact and a perspective from which to study the past.

It is with something of this perspective that Jack Burden comes to understand and to explain in a rather scholastic fashion the split represented by his two friends Adam Stanton and Willie Stark in *All the King's Men:* "Each had been the doom of the other. As a student of history, Jack Burden could see that Adam Stanton, whom he came to call the man of idea, and Willie Stark, whom he came to call the man of fact, were doomed to destroy each other, just as each was doomed to try to use the other and to yearn toward and try to become the other, because each was incomplete with the terrible division of their age" (462). Even though the "terrible division" Jack refers to has more or less always been a human problem, in Warren's interpretation of history it was intensified by the advent of certain strains of pragmatism, progressivism, and scientific positivism after the American Civil War. For Warren, that war rather than the First World War marked the rise of modernity. His fascination was personal as well as intellectual, however; both his grandfathers had fought for the Confederacy, and the maternal grandfather, Gabriel Penn, on whose farm

Warren spent his boyhood summers, becomes an image or even an icon of the era in much of Warren's prose and poetry. But through this personal doorway Warren returns to the war again and again because he sees it as a central conflict that intensified the "terrible division" and paradoxically *created* the nation. For both North and South the war represented a loss of innocence. It was an inner conflict not only in the sense that it was a *civil* war but also in the sense of division within each region and within individuals who fought. The war, our only "felt" history, represented at multiple levels the inner conflict between innocence and experience, the fact and the idea, knowing and not-knowing, love and separateness — all of which are terms Warren uses in various contexts to label the conflict he is most concerned with. For him the process toward knowledge is dramatic and narrativistic as it follows the basic paradigm I outlined in chapter 1, but it is simultaneously dialectical as the individual swings between the poles of the central conflict. And the combination of these two movements has an enormous influence on Warren's structures.

The individual quest for selfhood overrides all other subjects in Warren's oeuvre. History, race relations, family, politics, composition, art, religion, nature are all treated with an eye for what they mean to the individual. All are linked to the theme of the self developing through the process toward a knowledge suggested by the basic paradigm of experience. Yet the secondary subjects are nothing less, in some cases, than obsessions for Warren. No other writer has been more consciously influenced by American history. American history and American literature were important, interrelated subjects — testing grounds really — for his developing theories of knowledge. His historical subjects — Thomas Jefferson, John Brown, the Civil War, Jefferson Davis, segregation, the civil rights movement — all have in common the disparity between how they have been viewed by official history, how they viewed themselves, and how Warren interprets them as something between the idealistic notions associated with them and the factuality of the sociohistorical context that shaped men or movements into what they were.

The large historical event or figure, however, is not ultimately Warren's chief concern as a historian. Rather, he presses to uncover the link between personal history and national history. These are interrelated in his writing, even in the formal histories and social criticism. It can be reasonably argued that the integration of the individual personality is the major theme of works whose seemingly broad scope is reflected in such titles as *Segregation, Who Speaks for the Negro?* and *The Legacy of the Civil War.* Behind them all lies Warren's key belief that the individual must accept and respect the facts of history, personal or national — insofar as it is possible for human beings to know them — in order to develop selfhood through knowledge. As L. Hugh Moore, Jr., has demonstrated, Warren believes that man must respect historical fact for very specific purposes: first, to confront his own flawed nature; second, to temper idealism. Finally, confronting the facts of history — as inheritors of the Treasury of Virtue and the Great Alibi fail to do — "will free one from a dependence on history, on the notion that things will work out well, that life is not a tragedy; this realization throws one back on his own human resources" (Moore 14). The exile inhabits that space between the Treasury of Virtue and the Great Alibi, is stranded there as he attempts to move between the two modes of thought. The real "blessed accident" is that he becomes, paradoxically, a model for developing a more real, crucial, and usable knowledge.

Thus, although Warren insists in the end on a stoic self-reliance, it is a far cry from the Emersonian brand, which finally alienates man from man and man from history with its majority-of-one philosophy and its disdain of the past. Closer philosophically to Melville and Hawthorne, Warren implicates man in a brotherhood of complicity and defines the self as the awareness that may grow out of acknowledging that brotherhood.

We have already begun to see that one way to read Warren's life's work is as an effort of constant revision, even a rewriting, of a central "text." Or we may say that at the core of his massive canon is a single story. I do not mean to be reductive here or to slight Warren's achievement. On the contrary, he managed to make his readers conscious of the "central significance" of his work, an accomplishment that he himself said was one mark of a writer's greatness ("Irony" 107–08). Productivity, of course, is not to be equated with greatness, but neither is sparsity, and it is not unreasonable to see Warren's prolificacy in several genres as at least one measurement of his special genius.

At one level his productivity is simply a sign of his enormous mental (and physical) energy, an energy his close friend and associate Cleanth Brooks witnessed and described ("Robert Penn Warren" 591). But the abundance of his work is also a sign of the urgent need for knowledge: knowledge of humanity's place and of the individual's place and the extent to which these two entail conflict, knowledge of the limits of human responsibility, knowledge of the terms on which individuals can be moral beings even as they are forced more and more to rely on their own consciousness in searching for those terms. Abundance is one sign of Warren's willingness to risk much in the pursuit of a sustaining knowledge. There is another kind of abundance in the very multifariousness of forms: of the novels, of the poems, and even of the biographies and social histories. That diversity testifies to Warren's need to test the characteristic vision of the spiderweb world in as many situations as possible. Perhaps the ultimate "relevance" of Warren's work is that he keeps pressing the issue: how can one live separately from a society and also in identification with it? The abundance finally testifies to the belief that human beings live by the constant process of knowing themselves, not by formula or by an isolating antinomianism but by a willed and full embrace of life in time which demands a recognition at once of context and of individualism.

Warren is therefore neither a moral relativist nor a skeptic who turns to tradition because knowledge extraneous to tradition is ultimately unobtainable. This may be what Burt is saying when he writes that Warren's characteristic movement is toward an absolute understanding from which he draws back just on the brink, that Warren "negotiates between romance and the necessity of restraint" (*American Idealism* 125). I would add that the negotiation is the work of a predominantly Coleridgean imagination strained through Hawthorne, Melville, Conrad, and Thomas Hardy. Warren's is an imagination grounded in experience (the Southern past, the American past, the personal past), and it works to know what no one can ever fully know. The struggle is Sisyphean, of course, but not meaningless. The meaning is the meaning of all tragedy, whether the story of Oedipus, Macbeth, Clyde Griffith, Willie Loman, or Willie Stark: man's potential greatness and his inevitable failure are ineluctably and inextricably joined in one life.

Warren's body of work arises from a special genius thriving on his particular experience and vision. But it can also be reasonably viewed as a response to two great dictums: the Greek "Know thyself" and the American/Emersonian "Trust thyself." Only by self-knowledge, the body of Warren's work says, does man become a truly moral agent. In self-reflection, however, he may learn that his values are illusions. The danger of such knowledge is that even the "new man" — perhaps especially he — may become alienated, withdrawn from society while paradoxically *busy*, maniacally so at times; almost always in Warren this condition is a sign of flight from the self. He believed what he saw as the central issue in Conrad, Melville, and Dreiser: the heroic thing is to "continue to walk in the world." The unillusioned individual must finally come to trust himself and the values he makes for himself, and he must realize that life, like history, means the continuous revision of values. The unillusioned knows what the fanatic and the drifter cannot accept and what the "hero" never had to face, that he is a constant "failure," and his greatest value may be pity for the illusions of others. Warren's *pity*, the term he uses again and again in his essays on American authors to define their insight, seems for him a term synonymous with *empathy*, for it depends on a recognition of like conditions. Relevant too are the words describing the agony of Audubon, the Warren protagonist who seems to come closest to fulfilling both the commands of "Know thyself" and "Trust thyself":

> He thinks: "What has been denied me?"
> Thinks: "There is never an answer."
>
> Thinks: "The question is the only answer."
>
> He yearns to be able to frame a definition of joy. (*New and Selected Poems* 221)

This yearning, this urgency to know and utter in a world where "the question is the only answer," is the poet's dilemma as well as the naturalist's and lies at the bottom of Warren's intense revisions. The textual history of *Brother to Dragons* provides clues for us here: it nagged Warren from the time of its first publication in 1953 until the new version was published in 1979 — really a new poem in significant ways. Furthermore, it is not too much to say that *Segregation* and *Who Speaks for the Negro?* — to whatever extent they owe their existence to Warren's engagement with the racial tensions of the 1950s and 1960s — are in some ways rewritings of the earlier, nagging text "The Briar Patch." Yet another text on race, the remarkable poem "Old Nigger on One-Mule Cart Encountered Late at Night When Driving Home from Party in the Back Country," actually seems to be about the process of such revision. It stands as a central text in the Warren canon because of its place as a statement on race and its place as an index to what its author was doing in the later work and how he was going about doing it. I return to this poem for a fuller discussion later in this chapter. First, an examination of the evolution in Warren's thinking on the problems of race in America and an analysis of the form of his fascinating and powerful book *Segregation* will establish a context for that discussion and demonstrate the relation between the personal and regional experiences in the development of his protean wanderer figure.

Links between the wanderer trope and Warren's historical sense become clearer after one realizes that one of the most important subjects of Warren's nonfiction prose after 1953 is the web of social conditions that gave rise to the psychological traits of the Southern exile. An adequate reading of these texts reveals the predominance of a voice rising out of a matrix of which the central defining factor is the conflict between an inscrutable and plaguing past and the need for a well-ordered present. It is the same conflict that gave rise to the wanderer figure lost between the two worlds of past and present in Warren's poetry and fiction. And it should be noted that the first of Warren's later studies of race relations appeared in 1954, spurred by *Brown v. Board of Education* but also closely following his reemergence as a poet in 1953 after ten years of publishing only prose criticism and fiction.

It is no mere coincidence that Warren's more personal essays on social issues accompanied his acclaimed reemergence as a poet. Many of his poems and short stories as well as his final novel, *A Place to Come To*, are deeply personal works; the later prose studies in race relations and history are explorations of his own regional identity. Except for his late memoir *Portrait of a Father* (1988) and certain parts of *Jefferson Davis Gets His Citizenship Back* (1980), *Segregation* (1956) and *Who Speaks for the Negro?* (1965) represent Warren's most overtly autobiographical prose. Both are replete with personal anecdotes that reveal their author's connection with (and in some cases his rejection of) the people he is interviewing or observing. Other passages reveal just as strongly that Warren's is the predicament of a double isolate, at home neither in the Southern culture he is writing about nor among the "Pharisees" who judge it from the outside. In both works Warren's perspective is that of one who should be an insider yet is the outsider—the Southern expatriate who, as he put it in *Segregation*, feels relief as he leaves the South and knows that he does not have to live in the turmoil of racial strife that his book so poignantly records. "Out of Memphis," he writes, "I lean back in my seat on the plane, and watch the darkness glide by. I know what the Southerner feels going out of the South, the relief, the expanding vistas" (3).

Those "expanding vistas" are detailed in the later "flight" from the south of Warren's fictional exile Issac Sumpter, who, after exploiting the death of the spelunker Jasper Harrick, flees north "where *he, Issac Sumpter, Ikey, Little Ikey, who wanted to be good, and had paid the price, could at last be totally himself*" (*The Cave* 372). Warren's narrative irony in ending this novel is similar to the irony with which Katherine Anne Porter's "Old Mortality" concludes. Porter's frustrated Southerner, Miranda, having given up ever understanding the massive complexity of the experiences and feelings of her father's generation, thinks, "At least I can know the truth about what happens to me." But Porter's narrator comments that the thought comes to her "in her hopefulness, her ignorance" (221). These similar moments bring relief to both fictional exiles, but the poet *as* exile, as we saw in the preceding chapter and see again in the narrative stance of these examples, must go on to analyze the relief—revealing that it is only temporary. Similarly, in *Segregation*, Warren reckons the cost of living the alternative life—that is, a psychological as well as literal relocation in the North:

I feel the surge of relief. But I know what the relief really is. It is the relief from responsibility.

Now you may eat the bread of the Pharisee and read in the morning paper, with only a trace of irony, how out of an ultimate misery of rejection some Puerto Rican school boys—or is it Jews or Negroes or Italians?—who call themselves something grand, The Red Eagles or the Silver Avengers, have stabbed another boy to death, or raped a girl, or trampled an old man into a bloody mire. If you can afford it, you will, according the local mores, send your child to a private school,

where there will be, of course, a couple of Negro children on exhibit.
And that delightful little Chinese girl who is so good at dramatics. Or
is it finger painting?

Yes, you know what the relief is. It is the flight from the reality you
were born to. (51–52)

Here the word *you* obviously inscribes the collective experience of
the Southern exile, but the pronoun is still hardly "impersonal." It
refers to Warren himself as well as to a type, and the experience is
generally an experience he participates in, down to the self-conscious
"trace of irony." But the irony is doubled as the self-scrutinizing exile
ironically catches himself in his less reflective irony.

Such passages of self-indictment are central to an understanding
of Warren's political thinking and its relation to his poetic vision, a
vision he did not set aside when he sat down to write social criticism.
Most often in *Segregation* and *Who Speaks for the Negro?* he simply
allows racism to reveal itself, reserving greater rhetorical treatment
for party-line, "officialized" thinking (what Warren sometimes called
"right" thinking or, here, eating "the bread of the Pharisee"). In such
passages Warren often reveals his deep regionalist sense and his belief
that the white Southerner, as an outsider with respect to the main
forces and values of modern American life, has something in common with the black American, Southern or otherwise. The most dangerous thing they have in common is the tendency to "accept the
values of the dominant group and internalize them," and "the most
destructive value that can be internalized is the certainty which the
dominant group holds of its own total superiority" (*Who Speaks?* 55).

In the epigraph for this chapter—a passage that does much to raise
the book above whatever datedness in terminology it suffers as a so-
ciological study (Ruppersburg 131)—Warren reveals yet another interconnection of these seemingly polarized groups. At the same time he
essentially explains one motivation of the Southern exile. Warren saw
Southernness, or perhaps any regional identity, as at least to some
degree analogous to racial identity. His ideas, in fact, seem quite con-

temporary in the light of recent regionalist theory. He was interested in the high psychological costs of "passing," whether he was exploring them through a poet-son's relation to a lost home, as he often did in his verse and fiction, or through his own relation to an inter- and intraregional conflict. The fact that the theme crosses the lines of genre reveals that the distinction between the personal and the regional level is by no means absolute. If the scope, or perhaps simply the canvas, of the prose works seems broader than that of the personal poems I considered earlier, they are nevertheless driven by similar impulses — even poetic impulses perhaps — and have in common with the poems the imaginative depiction of the process of "going back." The common driving impulse is suggested by the "poetic" organizations of the prose works: that is, much like such poems as "I Am Dreaming of a White Christmas" and "Old Nigger on One-Mule Cart" or short stories such as "Blackberry Winter," they are visionary explorations. A summary of Warren's thinking on the matter of race relations should help prepare us, then, for a deeper consideration of the relation between the process of discovery and literary form in a work such as *Segregation*.

It is a revealing fact of Warren's development that his two most important early writings dealing directly with race relations — *John Brown: The Making of a Martyr* (1929) and "The Briar Patch," his contribution to the Agrarian manifesto *I'll Take My Stand* (1930) — are the two works with which he later expressed his greatest dissatisfaction (except perhaps his dramatic exploration of racially motivated violence, the 1953 version of *Brother to Dragons*, which he rewrote and published in a new version in 1979). Despite the fact that Warren's ideas in "The Briar Patch," compared with those of some other Agrarians, were actually *progressive*, as Donald Davidson thought (Fain and Young 251), these early works include some of what have been taken to be his most politically damnable and archaic comments — for example, the argument that the Southern black was best suited to life on the farm. Readers would be too complacent to see "The Briar Patch" simply as a reflection of Warren as a man of his place and time. That conclusion ignores too many issues: that David-son thought the essay radical; that the thinking of Warren's place and time was not totally represented by his Agrarian associates (as evidenced by the controversies they sparked within the South); and, most telling of all, that Warren himself was dissatisfied with the piece from the time he wrote it. The essay is not so much a reflection of his time and place as evidence of the incompleteness of his own thinking, as William Bedford Clark has emphasized (*American Vision* 28). Warren's arguments in "The Briar Patch" and his association with the Agrarians generally have made some critics so uncomfortable with him that they reject him out of hand. In this age, when the sometimes simplistic notions of a writer's supposed politics determine his or her reputation, that response testifies to another kind of complacency and comfort.

To reject Warren's significance as a social critic because of his early thinking on race, or, perhaps worse, to misread the later work in the light of the early, or to dismiss the early works too readily as reflections of a state of mind at last transcended, would be to miss one of the most extraordinary developments of an American writer in the twentieth century. Warren's emotional, intellectual, and artistic growth becomes collectively a dramatic image of a man's inward wrestling for knowledge. He moved from the position of a humane segregationist in the 1930s, when he wrote the two early works, to that of a forceful critic of segregation in the 1950s and 1960s. In the meantime he had taken a hard look not only at himself but at American society in general and Southern society in particular.

Yet one important aspect of his vision did not change. He remained a social critic who insisted on seeing segregation (as he insisted on seeing slavery) in the context of the culture in which it existed and on connecting that culture somehow to the internalized notions of the individuals who made it up. In a self-revealing passage in *Who Speaks for the Negro?* Warren remembered the Romantic view he had held of the country dweller who retained his individuality by his close ties to the land and his isolation (or insulation) from modern industrial America. That view had informed his composition of "The Briar Patch" when he was a Rhodes Scholar at Oxford, far removed geographically from the South (287). An earlier passage in the same book described the circumstances under which the essay was written: "I was a student in England, and had been out of the South for almost five years; and the image of the South I carried in my head was one of massive immobility in all ways, in both its virtues and vices—it was an image of the unchangeable human condition, beautiful, sad, tragic" (12).

It could be charged that this passage merely represents Warren's apologetics for his earlier defense of segregation. But a thorough reader of Warren will understand that the immobility the passage describes is an image employed often in his poetry and novels to suggest an inadequate or inflexible vision, even a haunting vision. In "I Am Dreaming," for example, there are the early macabre visions of the parents in their profound motionlessness, and in "Old Nigger on One-Mule Cart" the image of a black man's face frozen in a moment of abject terror. In both cases the movement of the poem is the movement of the speaker's imagination animating the frozen figures and discovering their highly subjective reality in the present, even years after the recalled event or condition that sparked the meditation. In Warren's longer works, too, such images often figure prominently. In *All the King's Men*, for instance, Jack Burden clings to an image of Anne Stanton forever floating on her back in water beneath a changeless sky (126), and Jack's problem is that he cannot reconcile that image with the living Anne Stanton who goes on with her life, including her love affair with the anything but static Willie Stark.

One reason for some of the structural as well as thematic and even political differences between his early and later work begins to be clearer as Warren goes on in *Who Speaks for the Negro?* to describe how the "unchangeable human condition" had changed and how the Depression had made him aware there was no way to escape the notion of change. The need to "claw out" of the desperation of the Depression made change necessary. Warren puts what he has learned about the inadequacy of his vision of the South in terms of another image by alluding to a primary myth of Western knowledge — the myth of the Fall: "You had to take a bite of the apple from the mysterious tree that had sprung up in the Confederate — no, the old American — garden. The apple might, incidentally, have given some knowledge of good and evil; but it certainly gave a knowledge of more profound consequence, the knowledge of the inevitability of change" (12). This may seem a rather blasé knowledge upon first consideration, but one should keep in mind that Warren was describing a personal, *felt* knowledge, not a strictly rational knowledge. What he says he learned about the South is, of course, important, but just as intriguing is his fascination with how he learned it and his impulse to metaphorize and universalize that process.

Basic to Warren's epistemology is the idea that man's image of himself is constantly modified (if he is intellectually honest, anyway); and if he is to be taken at his word, the South's experience during the Depression was the instigation of that way of thinking for him — at least of his way of thinking about his homeland. One can detect the influence of this discovery in the somewhat circular process toward knowledge that his very personal persona undergoes in a number of poems. After repressing the past by putting it in its grave where it belongs in "Natural History," for example, he attempts to "claw out" of the psychic depression that repression causes in "I Am Dreaming of a White Christmas." The process worked out in these companion poems parallels Warren's description of the South's attempt to claw out of an economic depression, at least to the extent that both require a grappling with the need to change the image by which an individual or a region defines his or her or its subjective reality. In the logic of Warren's pervasive eating tropes, the bread of the Pharisee must be forgone for the bitter apple or for the corpse that, ingested, brings knowledge.

For both its method and its theme of self-division, *Segregation* is especially important in Warren's development of the Southern exile figure. The book's subtitle, *The Inner Conflict in the South*, refers not just to a regional division but to a common division both *among* and *within* Southerners. Though most of the book is a meditative replay of Warren's conversations with Southerners during the spring of 1956 on the boiling issue of desegregation, it can actually be regarded as a book of three parts, a structure reflecting the familiar theme of discovery: its pattern reveals Warren's own separation from the experience he is exploring; his recollection of his recent engagement with Southerners speaking their minds on the issue; and, finally, his inward assessment of the meaning of what he has heard and experienced.

Warren's way into his subject is personal:

> "I'm glad it's you going," my friend, a Southerner, long resident in New York, said, "and not me." But I went back, for going back this time, like all the other times, was a necessary part of my life. I was going back to look at the landscapes and streets I had known—Kentucky, Tennessee, Arkansas, Mississippi, Louisiana—to look at the faces, to hear the voices, to hear in fact, the voices in my own blood. A girl from Mississippi had said to me: "I feel it's all happening inside of me, every bit of it. It's all there."
>
> I know what she meant. (3)

This opening passage announces a tension that, as we have already seen, is common in Warren's work: the primal necessity of "going back" despite the protest of the rational voice, represented in this case by the words of the friend. It also clarifies that the "going back" is necessary because it is a defining, internal action.

But Warren leaps immediately from this beginning to the end of the experience, entangling and blurring the two, a structural manipulation that comes as no surprise from a poet who in his "Identity and Argument for Prayer" described a year as a serpent swallowing its own tail (*Now and Then* 67). Specifically, he shifts the scene to his departure from Memphis; the plane's-eye view of the South encourages the feeling of separateness in the native son who had come back not for comfort, like a prodigal, but for an understanding of what it was that he felt separated from. From the plane the South seems very distant as Warren hyperbolizes time: last week seems a hundred years ago (4). As he makes clear in the larger context of the theme of inner division played out in the book, this distancing of himself from the *then* is, for one thing, the psychic defense of the wandering son soaking himself in a timeless *now.* Airplanes are a favorite setting for Warren's moments of idealistic distance, as in "Homage to Emerson": "At 38,000 feet Emerson / Is dead right," and the persona's heart is (shades of Warhol) "as abstract as an empty / Coca-Cola bottle" (*Selected Poems* 153). And again in the late poem "Immortality over the Dakotas": flying through darkness, "You feel as though you had just had a quick dip / In the Lamb's mystic blood" (*New and Selected Poems* 7).

In *Segregation* Warren thus associates his leaving the South with the clean, abstraction-bound consciousness his poetic persona and fictional exiles seek beyond the contingency of earthly matters. A further purpose of the sudden reversal in his introduction, however, seems to be to make the body of the book appear as the content of his memory: the experiences of the preceding few weeks are framed as "past" experiences over which his mind now pauses. Thus they are presented not as straightforward, journalistic reports but as memories the writer is putting on the pages. This process suggests that he must *go back* yet again, this time into the experience of the interviews to gain some meaning from them, just as he had to go back to the South to conduct the interviews in the first place. At the level of the book's framing structure, Warren thus captures an essential dualism by emphasizing with one device two nearly opposite meanings: a geographic and emotional distance that separates and an aesthetic distance that prepares the way for imaginative understanding and paradoxically brings the experience closer.

Turning to the conversations that make up the bulk or body of *Segregation,* the reader is almost immediately struck by the rich oral mode of discourse. The vignettes become in effect a collection of

voices with which Warren creatively suggests the multiplicity of perspectives on the problems of racial segregation in the South. He himself acts as interlocutor, iterating the questions that spark the talking:
"What are the white man's reasons for segregation?" "What does the
Negro want?" "What's coming?" And the related questions: "Is it only
power [the white man] wants to retain?" "Do the feelings of the black
man toward the exclusions of segregation differ from the feelings of
any man confronting the necessary exclusions of life?"

This last question may well tip Warren's philosophical hand. It
might be argued that the very question indicates a conservative insen-
sitivity to the "difference" that race gives rise to. But balance is largely
restored by the multiplicity of answers, whether the questions apply
to both or only one of the races. Within the space of a few pages, for
example, the reader hears one black man admit that the white man
is a complete mystery to him. Another says with certainty that the
white man is motivated by fear of mongrelization. Then a "hill-man"
organizer for the white Citizens' Council says, "The Court . . . hit
caint take no stick and mix folks up like you swivel and swull eggs
broke in a bowl. Naw . . . you got to raise 'em up, the niggers, not
bring the white folks down to nigger level." And when Warren asks
how, the organizer answers that by education—segregated, of
course—the blacks will be raised. Then follows a black grade school
teacher: "You ought to see the school house I teach in . . . set in the
mud and hogs can come under it, and the privies set back in the
mud. And see some of the children that come there, out of homes
with nothing, worse than the school house, no sanitation or clean-
ness, with disease and dirt and no manners. You wouldn't blame a
white person for not wanting the white child set down beside them."
Then speaks another white segregationist, a spouter of ethnology, saying, "Take India. They are a pure white people like you and me, and
they had a pretty good civilization, too. Till they got to shipping on a
little Negro blood. It don't take much to do the damage. Look at 'em
now." A Baptist minister with an intellectual air, invoking Acts 17:26,
speaks last in this section: "This is the passage the integrationists are

always quoting to prove that integration is Christian. But they won't quote it all. It's the end that counts." And Warren plays his part by supplying the passage, without commentary: "And [God] hath made of one blood all nations of men for to dwell on all the face of the earth, and hath determined the times before appointed, and the bounds of their habitation" (18–26).

The method—multithemed, pluralistic, perhaps even cacophonous—seems at first to be simply to let people talk, to listen to the human voice trying to express human feeling. One realizes within a few pages that Warren was revealing his technique when he opened the book by saying he was after "the *voices* in [his] own blood" (emphasis added). Moreover, the method of presenting the material as memory intensifies the sense that the words and events are indeed happening inside Warren himself. One effect of this particular treatment of the theme of "inner conflict" in *Segregation* is Warren's emphasis on his belief that the fate of the individual is tied ultimately to the fate of a society, to a brotherhood. But by framing the experiences as memory he is also able to impose his arrangement of the voices: the juxtaposition of the Citizens' Council organizer's call for raising the Negro by education with the black schoolteacher's description of the horrid conditions in which she is expected to teach; the juxtaposition of the black man's certainty of the white man's fear of mongrelization with the white ethnologist's polemical example of India, which seems to some extent to confirm the black man's theory. The particular structuring of the material suggests that the individual's fate is tied to the society, but the vision is neither fatalistic nor deterministic. The structuring also suggests that through imagination both order and meaning can be discovered.

The closing frame of the book, however—accomplished by Warren's returning again to the narrative of his flight out of Memphis and the relief from responsibility he felt as the Southerner leaving the South—implies the same relief from responsibility his friend had expressed in the book's opening line: "I'm glad it's you going [back to the South] . . . and not me." Warren recognizes the feeling as the relief of flight from reality, a major theme in all his work, for it is often by flight that he illustrates the failure of man to live up to himself. Given Warren's very open definition of reality as that which "any person might think validates his existence," flight from reality is a flight from self. In this case he realizes that the flight from the reality one is born to is a flight from "the fact of self-division." He sees the fact of self-division as a modern universal, but as a Southerner he is drawn to treat it in the particular terms, such as segregation, that alienated the Southerner from himself. Warren insists simultaneously on the peculiarity of the condition *and* its representativeness.

The structural ploy he uses in the conclusion of the book carries his major theme even further. Conducted as an interview with himself, it suggests simultaneously the problem of self-division and the inward approach the problem requires. The voice of the interviewer is rendered in the tone of a somewhat distanced journalist who seems to have eaten "the bread of the Pharisee" and taken on certain assumptions about the racial turmoil in the South; the voice of the interviewee, in the tone of a Southerner who, although he speaks defensively, reveals his awareness of the responsibility of self in relation to a region. The technique is not without a certain trite posturing, yet it reveals a doubleness in Warren himself which gives yet another meaning to the "voices in [his] own blood." A brief passage will illustrate the tone and pattern:

Q. You're a Southerner, aren't you?

A. Yes.

Q. Are you afraid of the power state?

A. Yes.

Q. Do you think the Northern press sometimes distorts Southern news?

A. Yes.

Q. Assuming that they do, why do they do it?

A. They like to feel good.

Q. What do you think the South ought to do about that distortion?

A. Nothing.

Q. Nothing? What do you mean, nothing?

A. The distortion — that's the Yankee's problem, not ours.

Q. You mean they ought to let the South work out a way to live with the Negro?

A. I don't think the problem is to learn to live with the Negro.

Q. What is it then?

A. It is to learn to live with ourselves. (63)

A far cry from the old states' rights theme, the implied argument here seems nevertheless a risky political stance, a paradoxical Thoreauvian approach to regionalism or even an anachronistic eighteenth-century isolationism. Yet taken in the context of the rest of *Segregation* and, indeed, Warren's writing in the main, the consistency of these statements with a world view that depends on a metaphysical and social *integration* becomes clearer.

One might cite *Brother to Dragons* as another example from among Warren's other writings. Published a year before *Brown v. Board of Education*, the poem dramatizes and analyzes an act of racial violence so graphically and thoroughly that readers can hardly miss the root cause: the frustration and the failure to live with himself of the murderer Lilburne Lewis. It is an epidemic frustration, really, infecting each of the characters (including the embittered Jefferson), a frustration arising from a failed dream, a *loneliness*, to return to the words of Brad Tolliver, profound and mysterious, which makes the black a rebuke to the white. Though *Brother to Dragons* is set in "no place" and at "anytime," R.P.W., the Southern exile in this poem, twice refers to what "anybody raised down home" knows — the rivalry between Mammy and mother (58), and the slave as the "spy" goading white conscience (69–70). References to what folks know "down home" give "no place" a geographic relation to the consciousness similar to the North of the Pharisee in *Segregation*. "No place," which in these references seems the antipode of the South, is what that land is for the exile in his peculiar relation to it, *no place*. Similar situations in the Cass Mastern episode of *All the King's Men* and in

Band of Angels help clarify the consistency with which Warren made the argument that the problem was not a matter of one race learning to live with another but a matter of the white Southerner's learning to live with himself. In *Segregation* he is not evading the question; he is reiterating the theme of the profound ambiguity of the white Southerner.

As William Bedford Clark has remarked, Warren held to the "Platonic notion that the polis is the individual writ large" (*American Vision* 8). Nothing testifies to the accuracy of this observation better than the multiple levels of meaning of "inner conflict" in *Segregation*. The region's conflict is the individual's conflict, and the internalization of the public issues gives the book its unique form as both meditation and social criticism. Understanding the inclusive nature of Warren's vision as Clark articulates it may help us see that *Segregation* is, in some ways, a "poetic" attempt to point out just how the Southerner can learn to live with himself without "passing" into the Treasury of Virtue and the false security of a redemption from history, and without adopting a segregationist's position or evoking the Great Alibi — the two apparent psychological dangers of thinking that the race issue in particular and history in general are somehow external to the individual. And the extrinsic valuation system extends to the "Yankees" as well, with their distortion of Southern news to make themselves feel good. Set against such external and "superior" approaches, Warren's book is an attempt to lead readers to a deeper and more real way of seeing, or reading, the region's conflict, not through the harangue of rational political analysis but through the same kind of aesthetic *experience* they expect from fiction or poetry.

In addition to Clark's observation, however, one would do well to remember what Warren thought of the "public," as distinguished from the polis. Writing on the subject in *Democracy and Poetry*, echoing American predecessors such as James Fenimore Cooper in *The American Democrat* and Melville in *White Jacket* and taking his cue on this particular occasion from Søren Kierkegaard, Warren compares the public to the physicist's "black hole," a "devouring negativity" (61). It is the same metaphor, as I noted before, that Jed Tewksbury would use to describe the psychological effects of orgasm in *A Place to Come To*. To assume responsibility for the self in relation to a group is to become a member of the polis. To "pass" is to disappear into the "black hole" of the public (or, in Jed's case, the mechanistic universe represented for him by orgasm). The dilemma of the Southern exile is too often that he sees no option but the latter.

Warren calls instead for a politics of inwardness "to break out of the national rhythm, the rhythm between complacency and panic" (*Segregation* 66). In one sense *Segregation* is a highly unusual defense of the South, for Warren argues that the South might lead the nation in this attempt, not because of its old ideals and traditions but because in its history it has had to deal concretely with the troublesome issues. The book is a warning against a widespread faith in abstractions, pointing out the inherent dangers of abstract thinking about such social issues as the loss of self and "the national rhythm . . . between complacency and panic." Oddly, its highly personal nature does not undermine its value as a social document. In some ways it retains political relevance much better than *Who Speaks for the Negro?* which was the work of a decade later and in which more than any other Warren took off his poet's laurels to play the role of social scientist (though even there the shift to a more objective approach was far from complete). What he said of James Baldwin might well be said of Warren himself in *Segregation*: the fact that he speaks for himself is "the source of [his] power. Whatever is vague, blurred, or self-contradictory in his utterances somehow testifies to the magisterial authenticity of the utterance—it is the dramatic image of a man struggling to make sense of the relation of personal tensions to the tensions of the race issue" (*Who Speaks?* 296).

Segregation, with its competing voices, could never be regarded as a reflection of unity in diversity, of course, but it is nevertheless something of a prose song of the self roughly woven from the recalcitrant material of inwardly haunting voices. Whatever vision is achieved is achieved through the inward knowledge of doubleness. The self-interview that closes the book reiterates the relation between form and knowledge which the collage of voices throughout the book has been pointing to. The Southern exile is an exile because of an inner conflict he is trying not to face up to. He is caught between the nagging pull of home — that seductiveness which complicates feeling and, with Faulkner's Quentin Compson, makes him tell the truth even while he appears to be protesting too much by saying he does not hate the South — and the cleaner vision of the outsider by which he attempts to erase the last traces of irony that might intrude upon his assumed virtue. The South, inasmuch as it inevitably becomes a part of the Southerner's being, is far too complex either to love or to hate cleanly. But those who "pass" try to hate it cleanly by reducing it to its purest ugliness. "I'm glad it's you going back" is an expression that affirms a certain knowledge of the South's northern border and implies total rejection of the myth of the Old Unchanging South. Set against the total rejection is the knowledge that "it's all happening inside of me, every bit of it." And the two conflicting attitudes are indicative of the destructive national rhythm Warren describes: the rhythm between complacency and panic can be played out in the individual as well as in the nation. Warren's little book exposes that momentous rhythm with a powerful one of its own.

"Old Nigger on One-Mule Cart Encountered Late at Night When Driving Home from Party in the Back Country" has in common with "I Am Dreaming of a White Christmas" and *Segregation* the theme of the exile's estrangement from and imaginative recovery of the past. Collected with the poems of *Can I See Arcturus from Where I Stand?* — a group of largely personal or meditative poems on emerging self-knowledge — it is (along with "Red-Tail Hawk and Pyre of Youth") among the most ambitious of Warren's shorter poems on the complex relationship between experience and vision. It follows the pattern we saw earlier in the wandering-son poems, the movement from a dream state through terror toward a psychic readjustment to the past. The persona, now overtly a poet, again accomplishes this movement by meditating on a past experience called up as a static image from memory.

The long, headline-like title explains the central event from the past that provokes the meditation. The party the speaker is returning from is described in the opening lines in terms that place it in a world outside time, the effect of the music, motion, and "booze" that are the accoutrements of sexual Otherwhere:

> Flesh, of a sudden, gone nameless in music, flesh
> Of the dancer, under your hand, flowing to music, girl-
> Flesh sliding, flesh flowing, sweeter than
> Honey, slicker than Essolube, over
> The music-swayed, delicate trellis of bone
> That is white in secret flesh-darkness. What
> The music, it says: *no name, no name!* — only
> That movement under your hand, what
> It is, and no name, and you shut your eyes. . . . (*New and Selected Poems* 170)

The collapse of ordinary reality at this backcountry party is underscored by the fact that the speaker cannot recall the name of his dance partner from that night. Human volition is minimized as flesh is "music-swayed" and human identity absorbed in that movement. Alliteration and consonance lend a feeling of euphonic nothingness. "Flesh flowing" sounds like a kind of unity itself; "sliding," "sweeter," "slicker," and "Essolube" combine to create a sense of the easy movement of a dream — though trouble is foreshadowed by the incongruous union of honey and Essolube, with the latter term also foreshadowing the automobile that will figure prominently and soon in breaking the spell. The hyphenated "girl- / flesh" reduces the girl to all flesh even as it breaks her apart and paradoxically suggests the unbroken rhythm of dance by its place in the run-on line. In short, the dance here is rendered as a ritual of self-forgetting, and central to the process is the touch that leads to indistinguishability. Unlike the dissevering touch of the parent, sexual touch is often evoked by Warren for its effect of self-negation.

The encounter on the way home, by contrast, stands out as *something*; it must be analyzed and interpreted in the poem. Yet Warren achieves a connection between the passages that describe the two central events—the dance and the near collision with the junk collector—by the consistency with which he uses images of contrasting darkness and light (as he had done effectively in "I Am Dreaming" and as early as "Bearded Oaks"). At the party, white bone is hidden in "secret flesh-darkness." In the Louisiana night, stars that are "whitely outrageous" because they are in a "blackness of velvet" and dust that is "whiter than star-dust" mark an even stronger clash between light and dark (170). When the speaker's car nearly collides with the cart of junk on which the black man sits, the headlights reveal out of the night darkness the image that strikes so harshly that it stays in the speaker's memory.

> the mule-head
> Thrusts at us, and ablaze in our headlights,
> Outstaring from primal bone-blankness and the arrogant
> Stupidity of skull snatched there
> From darkness and the saurian stew of pre-history
> For an instant—the eyes. The eyes
> They blaze from the incandescent magma
> Of mule-brain. (171)

Behind the mule's eyes appears another light/dark contrast: the "Man-eyes, not blazing, white-bulging / In black face" (171).

After skidding, barely missing the mule and cart, the speaker passes on, leaving the junk collector alone and "unmoving," and the

> dust of the car's passage settles
> White on the sweat-sticky skin, black, of the forehead, and on
> The already gray head. This,
> Of course, under the high stars. (171)

The white stars and the white dust fringe a blackness that during the encounter is suddenly illuminated by the car's headlights. Formed in the speaker's mind in that instant is an image with the permanence, though certainly not the effect, of Keats's leaf-fringed Grecian urn.

The subsequent elaborate meditation on this image demonstrates the poet's need to wrest some meaning from the object and the difficulty involved in achieving such meaning. But part of the process is, once again, an imaginative movement far away from the central image in the poem. In a passage reminiscent in its subject of Frost's "Stopping by Woods on a Snowy Evening" or even Stevens's "The Snowman," yet distinct from both in its urgent tone, images of whiteness again play an important part, offering an escape from the problems of existence. The lines, in fact, recall the snowy-night Otherwhere in "I Am Dreaming of a White Christmas":

> Have you ever,
> At night, stared into the snow-filled forest and felt
> The impulse to flee there? Enter there? Be
> There and plunge naked
> Through snow, through drifts floundering, white
> Into whiteness, among
> Spectral great beech-boles, birch-whiteness, black jag
> Of shadow, black spruce-bulks snow-shouldered, floundering
> Upward and toward the glacial assertion that
> The mountain is? (172)

As in "I Am Dreaming" the speaker has changed venue, apparently to New England, and the passage adds to the continuing light/dark dichotomy a pattern of heat and cold. In this new, colder air "purer / Than absolute zero" he fantasizes that *you* could "stretch forth your hand over / The bulge of forest and seize trees like the hair / Of a head you would master" (172).

One function of the light/dark dichotomy would seem to be to suggest this speaker's tendency to frame his experience in black and white, finding in those polarities images of being and of the nothingness that is at once frightening and seductive. But the racial significance can hardly be missed. Anthony Szczesiul has noted that early in the poem the speaker, through his very language, participates in communal racial assumptions: the "fool-nigger" with his cart was on the wrong side of the road *naturally*. The assumption is seemingly that such behavior is all you can expect from a "nigger." The poem's imagery also suggests the self-consciousness of this participation in a cultural myth. The coating of *white* dust stirred up by the car and settling on the *black* man shows symbolically how the "old nigger" is interpreted, initially, through a layering of white suppositions. There may even be something of double entendre, aiming the poem toward its theme of unmasking, in the phrase "black face." Diction and images whitewash, as it were, the black man, and readers who understand the ironies involved in Warren's approach at this point can better see why later in the poem the distinctions between white and black are less absolute.

Certainly Warren is doing something quite deliberate with racial epithets and bigotry at the poem's beginning. And it may well be that the effect is to document the poet's earlier assumptions of an "unchanging" South, the romanticized vision of the "backcountry" dweller. The moment of the near-collision bears a striking similarity to another incident in Southern literature: in Erskine Caldwell's *Tobacco Road*, Dude Lester smashes a car into a wagon driven by a black man, leaves him for dead alongside the road, and continues home in the now dented brand-new automobile he has acquired along with his brand new-wife. When told of the incident, Dude's father, Jeeter, says, "It looks like niggers will get killed. It looks like there's nothing to be done about it" (159).

Of course, both Warren's and Caldwell's passages call to mind the best-known literary instance of what has been taken to be the white South's collective mind. In *Huckleberry Finn*, Huck (pretending to be Tom Sawyer) tells Aunt Polly that no one was hurt in the (fictional) steamboat explosion that delayed his arrival at her farm. The accident only "killed a nigger." Aunt Polly is *naturally* relieved: "Well, it's lucky; because sometimes people do get hurt" (173). Readers may even recall a similar treatment of the subject in Faulkner's *Light in August* when the white community's assumptions about Joe Christmas alter completely with the revelation that Christmas is a "nigger" (although the novel never establishes his racial identity with certainty). The town is deeply confused, for Christmas acts "like he never even knew he was a murderer, let alone a nigger too" (306–07). Each of these literary instances is a fiction that treats a fiction (an assumed and general communal mind-set), and in Twain and Faulkner the dubious nature of the communal fiction seems to be emphasized even more by the compounding of fictions, or lies.

Warren's poem, like these other texts, may well have a referent in the white South's assumption of what was *natural*, but it also has a referent in another context—his own poetry. It is to that referent that one must turn to understand the bearing of these issues on his wanderer theme. "Old Nigger" raises and absorbs earlier poems—most clearly, "Pondy Woods" and "Ballad of Mr. Dutcher and the Last Lynching in Gupton," both of which were apparently based on the lynching of Primus Kirby in Warren's hometown of Guthrie, Kentucky, in the summer of 1926 (Watkins 71). There is in "Pondy Woods," which Warren was working on in 1927, a split between elevated and low diction, an attempt to marry forms without the parenthetical divisions he would employ in "The Ballad of Billie Potts." Floyd Watkins observes that the mixture may function to capture Jim Todd's ironic situation—hiding from a lynch mob in the marshy ground of Pondy Woods while wearing patent-leather shoes and his Sunday best (74).

But the greater incongruity in the poem is in the device Warren uses to create a second perspective on the fugitive: buzzards who speak a language infused with classical phrases and notions. "Nigger, your breed ain't metaphysical," they say to Todd, an objectionable line only if readers take it as a direct statement from Warren and reduce Warren to a twentieth-century Confederate writing a metaphysical poem; such a reading fails to understand the significance of the buzzards. As Watkins points out (74), Warren, like Ransom and Tate, was not a man impressed by the metaphysicians the buzzards symbolize, the "beaked tribe" who "eat the gods by day and prophesy by night" (*New and Selected Poems* 320). M. L. Rosenthal has said that Jim Todd epitomizes "the nameless guilt and unearned doom of all humanity" (501), and the fact that he is likened by allusion to the "Jew-boy" Christ suggests some such universalizing of his plight. But the general treatment damns the particular class that the buzzards represent as *they* take the poem's sentiments aloft to the nonracial world of abstractions and universals.

> "Nigger, regard the circumstance of breath:
> *Non omnis moriar*, the poet saith."
>
> Pedantic, the bird clacked its gray beak,
> With a Tennessee accent to the classic phrase;
> Jim understood, and was about to speak,
> But the buzzard dropped one wing and filmed the eyes. (320)

The black man is silenced in "Pondy Woods," as he is in "Old Nigger," but the implications of the silencing seem clear. Warren is not an innocent spokesperson for a monolithic society mouthing metaphysics to sidestep social realities. He is instead revealing the source of that silencing, and in this instance it is not the stereotypical redneck lynchers Jim Todd flees but the Brahmin buzzard:

We swing against the sky and wait;
You seize the hour, more passionate
Than strong, and strive with time to die —
With Time, the beaked tribe's astute ally. (320)

The "pedantic" buzzard counseling Jim Todd to strive less and accept his death with the knowledge of more than a physical existence may well be associated with the class Warren wrote of again in 1960. An essay that was not actually published until 1994, after it was discovered among Warren's papers by James Perkins, "Episode in the Dime Store" is angry in its tone. Its being unfinished of course limits what one may conclude about how it reflects Warren's thinking, but it may well assume an important place among his nonfiction for that very difference in tone from the other writings. The essay was written in response to three photographs in *U.S. News and World Report*, taken during a sit-in demonstration in Nashville. They picture a white youth being pulled from a lunch-counter stool to the floor and kicked by other whites. In one passage Warren draws a line of logic which again examines motives. The "hoodlumism" displayed in the dime store reflects a society "without the undergirding of right," a society of force. He goes on:

It may be objected that hoodlumism does not rule in Nashville — that the "better element" as well as the man behind the stool would forbid anybody's sitting there. That is precisely my point. By staying home in Bellemeade, or wherever it happens to be, the "better element" has left the administration of force to the hoodlum behind the stool. Those who approve the intent of the hoodlum's act would, in one sense, be more worthy of respect if they themselves came down to the dime store and jerked somebody off a stool and kicked him.

Suppose all citizens of Nashville and the South do condone the act of the hoodlum, then what kind of society do we have? In that monolithic society of force the thing the Southerner supposedly holds most dear — the right to his individual judgement — would be violated. . . .

> In that monolithic society of which the dime store was a microcosm
> all possibility of discussion and criticism would be cut off. No longer
> could anybody ask the crucial question about the motives and conse-
> quences of an act. ("Episode" 655–66)

The inhabitants of "Bellemeade, or wherever," prefer, in a sense,
the "blue tense altitudes" of the buzzards to direct involvement (*New
and Selected Poems* 319). If we read the buzzards as representing this
class and attitude, we see that Warren gave such high-caste groups
rhetorical hell—whether Southerners as in "Pondy Woods" or New
Englanders as in *John Brown: The Making of a Martyr*—well before
he wrote a balanced view of culpability, with the Treasury of Virtue
and the Great Alibi, in *The Legacy of the Civil War*.

Warren's text is a criticism of a monolithic society he fears equally
with the power state. The essay anticipates, in even harsher terms,
Martin Luther King's criticism of complacent whites in "Letter from
Birmingham Jail." But the essay's other thrust is personal, for Warren says the pictures in the magazine have robbed him of something:
his identity. "At home you wander around the house and sit where
you like. It is a shock to realize that in Nashville, Tennessee, I can
no longer sit where I like. . . . I am deprived of citizenship in that
place [of] which I had felt myself most fully a citizen" (655). Whereas
Segregation depicts the relief of the Southern exile, who dips himself perhaps into the metaphysical complacency of the buzzard and
avoids the front-line involvement of the youth beaten in the dime
store, in this essay Warren is attempting to cast himself in the position
of the black man: "Now any white person in Nashville knows what it
feels like to be deprived of the right to sit on that stool. He can, fleetingly, for a moment, know something of what it feels like to be a
Negro in that dime store" (655).

The attempt is rather awkward, if honest, with its multiple qualifiers (*fleetingly, for a moment, know something of*), and perhaps Warren felt the awkwardness of trying to say in prose argument what
he felt the connection was, the connection of exclusion that the

Southern exile felt with the Southern black. Perhaps this awkwardness contributed to his decision not to finish and publish the essay. In any event, he did go on to find the form to say what he had attempted here.

If the buzzards of "Pondy Woods" represent not Warren's own metaphysical distance from the action but the capstone of a society that assumes it knows the "nigger," Warren wrote of a tier of that society closer to the level of violent action in "Ballad of Mr. Dutcher and the Last Lynching in Gupton." Included as part of the single poem *Or Else-Poem/Poems 1968–1974*, "Ballad of Mr. Dutcher" is linked with "Natural History" and "I Am Dreaming" both textually and thematically; it is yet another poem on the subject of a childhood mystery whose meaning continues to be explored by the adult poet removed from the original locale.

The object under consideration in this instance is a small, inarticulate gray man (recall the "gray beak" of the buzzard in "Pondy Woods") who in hindsight seems to have carried with him all along a secret knowledge until one day he says to an assembling lynch mob in a hardware store; "Gimme / that rope." Then,

> Quick as a wink, six turns
> around the leader, the end snubbed,
> and there was that neat cylinder
> of rope the noose line could slide through
> easy as a greased piston or
> the dose of salts through the widow-
> woman, and that was what Mister
> Dutcher, all the days, weeks, and years,
> had known, and nobody'd known that he knew. (*Or Else* 27)

As a poem on the problem of complicity in an act of violence, "Ballad of Mr. Dutcher" raises two other passages from Warren texts that are not under immediate consideration here but further illustrate the intense revisionary nature of his work. In *All the King's Men,* in his dramatic speech before the capitol just after the impeachment proceedings against him have failed, Willie Stark uses a language of violence in asking the inspired crowd to help him defeat his Senate opposition: "Gimme that meat ax!" Jack Burden reports that "the crowd roared" its assent (277–78). The similarity between this scene and a later one in *Brother to Dragons* (both versions) should not be missed. About to kill the young slave John, Lilburne Lewis says to his brother Isham, "Hand me that meat-axe, Ishey." Isham complies as automatically as Willie's crowd had roared approval to the same words. Reporting his compliance, Isham says, "And me, I did" (*Brother to Dragons*, 1979, 82).

The specific words and even the similarity of syntax and rhythm in these passages indicate the centrality of the impulse toward violence or complicity in violence in both of Warren's masterpieces. The crowd and even the individual find it easy to hand the meat-ax over to the strong man when there is no integrated self or individual judgment, only the forfeiture of individual volition required in a monolithic society or tyranny. And perhaps the ultimate meaning to be taken from the comparison is that it is possible, even frighteningly easy, for a single individual to exhibit the mindlessness typical of a mob. In much the same way, Percy Munn is stirred to violence by important men and his own failure of selfhood in *Night Rider*, and "all the king's men" and women have similar feelings of completeness through their attachment to Willie Stark at some point in the later novel. Warren demonstrates again and again the danger of the senseless and selfless mentality that can make anything right by force or make anything meaningless in a dream of nothingness.

But what are we to make of Mr. Dutcher's apparent echo of the two strong men Willie Stark and Lilburne Lewis when he says to the lynch mob in the hardware store "Gimme / that rope." No strong man — in fact, a symbolic little man in the pervasive grayness of his life — he imitates two of the profoundest instigators of violence in Warren's canon, a canon so marked by violence in both action and language that it is sometimes criticized for being too Jacobean. The mystery of Mr. Dutcher is that he possesses a skill useful at least occasionally to the society he astonishes with it. He can come out of his grayness and slip back into it and "walk the same old round like a blind / mule hitched to a sorghum mill" (*Or Else* 27). The image may suggest the paradox of peace after the eruption of violence or may capture the monotony that fueled the violence to begin with, but the greater significance is that the little man has in common with the great one the desire to fulfill himself in action, even violent action. What Warren attempts to do with Mr. Dutcher is to write a version of the "root tragedy" he identified in Dreiser. All tragedy is concerned with destiny, but "the root tragedy . . . seeks the lowest common denominator of tragic effect, an effect grounded in the essential human situation" and "based on the notion that, on whatever scale, man's lot is always the same" (*Homage to Theodore Dreiser* 138).

Just as important as the "study" of Mr. Dutcher, however, is the relation of the persona to the object. The speaker in this case seems to draw his view in part from the common well of the Great Alibi. The lynching itself is, in fact, displaced as the subject by the particular *horror* of the event, and for that horror the communal voice can place blame on the victim.

> Well, what
> happened was not Mister Dutcher's
> fault, nor the rope's, it was only
> that that fool nigger just would not
> cooperate, for when the big
> bread truck they had him standing on
> drew out, he hung on with both feet
> as long as possible, then just
> keeled over, slow and head-down, in-
> to the rope, spilling his yell out
> like five gallons of fresh water

in one big, bright, out-busting slosh
in the sunshine, if you, of a
sudden, heave over the crock. So,
that fool nigger managed never
to get a good, clean drop, which was,
you might say, his last mistake. One
man started vomiting, but one
put six .44's in, and that
quieted down the main performer.
Well, that was how we came to know
what Mister Dutcher'd thought we'd never know. (*Or Else* 27–28)

The epithet "fool nigger" (used each of the first four times the speaker refers to the victim), the rhetorical displacement of subject and cause (the victim, not the lynchers, becomes the "main performer"), even the colloquial "Well" beginning each of the two sentences framing this section, point to the speaker's insider status with Mr. Dutcher's society. He continually emphasizes the communal assumptions of the black man's ignorance and irrationality, suggested by "fool nigger." After shooting a liquor store clerk in a failed robbery attempt (shades of Little Billie Potts), the victim had fled toward Gupton "in happy / ignorance that the telephone / had ever been invented" (26).

What Warren does not do in his depiction of the violent South is make things easy for his readers. In fact, he seems determined to do what he saw Melville doing in his poems, to create tension *within* his readers. He does not make the black man an innocent victim of mob violence — it is he, in fact, who commits the first two acts of violence — so those who need a simple portrayal of violence against the Southern black by the Southern white may well be dissatisfied with the "truth" of the poem. Moreover, if Southern readers are not discomforted by the displacement first of the subject and then of the blame, by the sheer baldness of the defense, they must notice the paradox that the sympathy with Mr. Dutcher, at this point at least, is

an anti-Christian sympathy. The speaker defends Mr. Dutcher for his
secret knowledge:

> But isn't a man entitled
> to something he can call truly
> his own — even to his pride in
> that one talent kept, against the
> advice of Jesus, wrapped in a
> napkin, and death to hide? (28)

Mr. Dutcher's knowledge of the hangman's noose, his *talent*, seems
for the speaker the chief mark of his identity, therefore his most pre-
cious possession, a thing not to be risked. In sympathizing with
Mr. Dutcher the speaker simultaneously makes him an object for our
sympathy, an emblem of the eternal sorrow that Rosenthal says Big
Jim Todd represents in "Pondy Woods." At the same time, that sympathy depends in part on the shared assumptions of a society which
tends rhetorically and emotionally to make its victims its offenders.
Warren portrays the black men in both poems as people who live
vitally, who live in fact with Dionysian force against the Apollonian
will of whites, who have the rope and the rhetoric to manage such
vitality.

But at the end of "Ballad of Mr. Dutcher" the speaker shows himself estranged from that society. He begins, in fact, to sound more like
the exile of other poems:

> I'm the one man left
> who has any reason at all
> to remember [Mr. Dutcher's] name, and if
> truth be told, I haven't got so
> damned much.

Time, then, has separated the persona from the event, but so has
distance: the speaker considers "going back" sometime to try to lo-

cate the grave of Mr. Dutcher. And then he concludes the poem with lines that show a shift of perspective marked by a different level of diction: "I might even try to locate / where that black man got buried, though / that would, of course, be somewhat difficult" (29).

The emphasis comes back in the end to what has been the true subject all along: the significance of all these events to the identity of the poet. Whether or not Warren literally ever tried to locate Mr. Dutcher's grave, the poem itself is an attempt to locate the little man in the consciousness of his personal persona. But the inclusion of the black man in the prospective search has a powerful suggestiveness, and the transformation of the victim from "fool nigger" to "that black man" in the final stanza links Dutcher and his victim in a whole new way. They become equal victims of a larger fate perhaps, but only after the psychological tricks of the communal will have been brought into the light and burned away by time until the speaker is left, alone, to reinterpret what happened. Both the "gray man" and the "black man" are vested with a fuller humanity and made worthy of remembrance by the poem's end, but Warren acknowledges the social realities of the South during its darkest era since the Civil War. The fact that the black man's grave would be difficult to find indicates the place he had held in that society. But even Mr. Dutcher's stone might be impossible to find if the grass and ragweed were too high — that is, if neglect obscured him in death much as his mumbling and his general grayness had once obscured him in life. Warren's interest in social realism, however, feeds the deeper psychological realities of the region's turmoil and of the individual whose relation to that region is a divided one. If "Ballad of Mr. Dutcher" is an attempt to locate in that consciousness of *self* or sense of *home* the secret behind the grayness represented by Mr. Dutcher, "Old Nigger on One-Mule Cart" may be the "somewhat difficult" attempt to locate the black man within that consciousness.

Returning now to a consideration of heat and cold as the second major image pattern in "Old Nigger," one can see fairly easily its significance in the Dionysian/Appollonian dichotomy found in other poems. Whereas the Louisiana setting is dominated by images of heat, dust, and sweat, the New England setting provides an air "purer than absolute zero." The heat corresponds to namelessness and meaningless motion; the cold, to the desire for and belief in definition or even mastery of experience: "Have you ever / Had the impulse to stretch forth your hand over / The bulge of forest and seize trees like the hair / Of a head you would master?" (*New and Selected Poems* 172). The last line with its obvious racial implications and its particular referent — perhaps the head that stands out as the nightmare to be settled in this particular poem — leads directly into a complacency like that which led to sympathy with Mr. Dutcher in the earlier poem: "Well, / We are entitled to our fantasies, for life / Is only the fantasy that has happened to us, and / In God's name" (172).

But this speaker cannot rest in that complacency. As in "I Am Dreaming," the illusion of innocence and command over nature and other men is snatched away suddenly by the agonizing need for meaning:

> In the lyrical logic and nightmare astuteness that
> Is God's name, by what magnet, I demand,
> Are the iron and out-flung filings of our lives, on
> A sheet of paper, blind-blank as Time, snapped
> Into a polarized pattern. . . . (172–73)

Several things are to be noted in these lines. First, the phrases "lyrical logic" and "nightmare astuteness" seem to draw together the two primary images established early in the poem — the lyricism of the dance and the starkness of the mule, cart, and man — and as God's name they perhaps represent poles of human experience. (Though I realize that, grammatically, they could be read as plural, the sense seems singular to me; that is, the relative "that" clause refers to both "lyrical logic" and "nightmare astuteness," not just the latter.) Then, too, the imagery used to describe the matrix of any individual's experience as a boy's experiment, organizing what is random, contains a pun, a cleverness. The trope signals that all is certainly not pure in this poem, for while it suggests the potential culmination of vision, it simultaneously suggests the particular method of arriving at it in this case — poetry, and the agon of the poet: "A sheet of paper, blind-blank as Time." Once again, albeit less overtly here, there is a suggestion of the link between the poet's boyhood and his manhood in terms of a repeated action, or an attempt to repeat an action that is difficult. There is the same agony here that is detectable in the voice of the son asking what "gift" there was from his parents. Both questions reveal a desire for a confirmation of a "felt" unity of self.

Here the demand is answered immediately by an act of the speaker's own imagination, which creates a new image based on his experience. He sees the old man arriving at his shack after the encounter and stopping to urinate, his face "lifted into starlight, calm as prayer."

> He enters
> The dark shack, and I see
> A match spurt, then burn down, die
>
> The last glow is reflected on the petal-pink
> And dark horn-crust of the thumbnail. (173)

Although it is not always easy to pin down exactly what is accomplished by the play between light and dark in this poem, in this last image — which exudes an overriding sense of calm in contrast to the terror associated with the earlier image — the light, through its connection with the old man especially, seems to represent the possibility of vision, a way to have meaning in the seeming darkness of fate or the fantasy that happens to us. It is important that the old man carries his light with him. It is equally important that action is continuous; the frozen image has been unlocked by the work of the imagination toward establishing kinetic meaning. Not only is this second image juxtaposed with the earlier static, stark image of terror, but also, in its insistence on awareness, on light, on sight (as opposed to touch, which reduces life to tactile sensation), it is functionally juxtaposed with the initial dream of nothingness that the dance represents. So a larger kinesis is in the familiar movement from image to vision through a "plot" of return and discovery.

The animation of the late image leads the poet to address the junk man as "Brother, Rebuker, my Philosopher past all / Casuistry" (173). The "Old Nigger," a socially constructed *object*, has been transformed into a "Brother," a signifying *subject*. Through a creative process the old man becomes yet another "speechless" symbol, but a symbol of whatever degree of vision the poet may attain. He is familiar as a "Rebuker" and may be likened to Warren's many fictional father figures in that he represents something that is hard to live up to. But he is also one of a type in the Warren canon often represented by a black, Jew, European exile, tramp, or military deserter—an Other who becomes paradoxically representative of the self's experience. The black man here, as a "Philosopher past all / Casuistry," reminds the poet that moral identity does not depend on a set of theories or "fondled axioms," as in "Original Sin," or on seizing the head you would master, as in this poem. From his final image of the old man the poet seems to learn at least the importance of striving for a communion that relieves the primal terror but that is not based upon an illusion of the flowing nothingness represented by the dance. It is instead a communion that depends first upon

> a name . . .
> A hard-won something that may, while Time
> Backward unblooms out of Time toward peace, utter
> Its small, sober, and inestimable
> Glow, trophy of truth. (173)

Such an identity is hard-won because it depends first on the pain of isolation.

Something else hard-won, however, is the recognition of the black man as a brother, and this recognition is associated with the self-knowledge achieved in the poem, for the black man has first to be transformed from the "old nigger" of the poet's past. It seems quite clear that he was at least associating the self he was then with the poet he was then, a poet struggling with form. In yet another episode of insomnia in Warren's poetry, the speaker attempted a poem on the experience on the very night of the encounter:

Get up, get paper and pencil, and whittle away at
The poem. Give up. Back to bed. And remember
Now only the couplet of what
Had aimed to be — Jesus Christ — a sonnet:
One of those who gather junk and wire to use
For purposes that we cannot peruse.

As I said, Jesus Christ. (172)

The language describing the attempted composition, especially the phrase "whittle away," suggests the inadequate vision of the poet, who thinks the experience must be something he can capture by whittling a block of experience into a standard form. Szczesuil has pointed out that the original couplet bespeaks a common Romantic view of the "old nigger." Perhaps so, in the context of the present poem; however, Warren's literary executor, John Burt, has discovered the original sonnet among Warren's papers. He reports that the early attempt gives no indication that the junk collector is black ("Reflections"). The inadequacy of the sonnet form can be looked back on in irony now. Through the imagination — which requires a form that reflects the process of that imagination, a form marked by juxtaposed images, meditative passages, and the interplay of lyricism with jagged syntax and brutal diction — and through night sweats and distance, the poet comes to a state of knowledge in which the "old nigger" is transformed into his "Brother." But this knowledge of external fact is self-knowledge as well, for the Brother is also a "Rebuker" and a "Philosopher past all / Casuistry." The *idea* of the sonnet and the *idea* of the "nigger" are inextricably linked in their association with the a priori assumptions of the poet's earlier self, a time and self represented in the poem by the dream of the dance and the stark terror of the frozen image caught in the car's headlights. And these perhaps are representative of the idealism/naturalism alternative to be worked through in the movement toward a new kind of knowledge.

It is significant that after shocking the sensibilities of late twentieth-century readers with his title, Warren uses the term "nigger" — "fool nigger," in fact — only once in the text of the poem, and that early on. Verisimilitude might in part explain the use of the term, but the word *nigger* had a very particular connotation for Warren which dovetails with the epistemological theme of the poem. Warren made the significance clear in his comment that "Faulkner . . . undercuts the official history and mythology of a whole society by indicating the 'nigger' is a creation of the white man" (*Faulkner* 259). In other words, the "nigger" exists only as a wish fulfillment, which is what the poet of "Old Nigger," I believe, has already learned as the result of his "encounter" — not then, but now, through this second attempted poem. It leads to a deeper knowledge, for the process involves the recognition not only of a society's creation of the "nigger" but of the poet's own participation in that communal racism by his creation of the figure on the junk cart. Hardly the exercise in casuistry Calvin Bedient believes it to be (185), the poem is an act of *re*creation, an act of *re*vision.

One object of the central image early in the poem, then, is transformed from "nigger" into "Brother." But another object within it needs consideration: the mule. Again the object is historically accurate, but Warren uses the mule for more than verisimilitude. To return again to the passage:

>   the mule-head
> Thrusts at us, and ablaze in our headlights,
> Outstaring from primal bone-blankness and the arrogant
> Stupidity of skull snatched there
> From darkness and the saurian stew of pre-history.

For an instant—the eyes. The eyes,
They blaze from the incandescent magma
Of mule-brain. (171)

With terms of naturalistic horror, this passage captures the nightmare of animal existence frozen in a moment of terror and thus presents a contrast to the dream of nothingness in the earlier description of the dance. The poet moves from that dream of nothingness to a fantasy of power and finally to a hard-won knowledge of kinship with the black man in a calmer vision of acceptance of meaning and the limitations of meaning. Does the poet likewise move from the naturalistic horror to a new peace with nature? We do not see the mule again until, near the poem's end, it is unhitched and staked—controlled, in other words. But we see the significant emblems of nature associated with the mule's primal significance at the moment of deepest reflection in the poem: the snow-in-woods section; they strike at the heart of the poet's agonizing need for meaning at the moment before the poetic vision of the junk collector arriving at his shack.

In the final line the speaker asks, "Can I see Arcturus from where I stand?" This is an obvious reference to the image of the old man gazing calmly at the night sky, and the great star Arcturus is intended here as a symbol of vision, a lofty vision, its inestimable value suggested by the name. The poet has, however, moved through experience and pain to an earned knowledge of at least the need for self-identity. The poet lives, so the question is unanswerable, but the question itself affirms his deep need for meaning. Like the wandering son, the poet has moved toward an identity in separateness; but he has also, again like the son, moved toward a healing of the pain that comes with that separateness by realizing his bond with others through the figure of the old man. Both the son and the poet (the son/poet?) have undergone the process of envisioning that leads them from a stark image to a knowledge of kinship and the implications of selfhood.

By its thematic structure, then, "Old Nigger on One-Mule Cart" can be linked with the wandering-son poems, but there may be other reasons to link them. James Perkins has argued convincingly that Warren's personal wrestling with the race question in the 1950s cannot be separated from the personal happiness that he and others cited as being responsible for his rejuvenation as a poet. Perkins points out that while Warren was spending blissful summers with his new family in a ruined fortress by the sea in Italy, he was also spending much of his time traveling the South and working toward what would become *Segregation*. As his experiences with his new family sent him researching the significance of the old one — his mother and father, his grandfather — "going back" in *Segregation* was a similarly freeing experience (Perkins 73).

The external evidence is intriguing, but if the poet *behind* "Old Nigger" was exploring family and regional pasts simultaneously, the poet *in* "Old Nigger" was definitely finding common ground between the two. Here is the passage leading into the compulsion to attempt the original sonnet:

And go on: to the one last drink, sweat-grapple in darkness, then
Sleep. But only until
The hour when small, though disturbing, gastric shifts
Are experienced, the hour when the downy
Throat of the swamp owl vibrates to the last
Predawn cry, the hour
When joy-sweat, or night-sweat, has dried to a microscopic
Crust on the skin, and some
Recollection of childhood brings tears
To dark-wide eyes, and the super-ego
Again throws the switch for the old recorded harangue.
Until waking, that is — and I wake to see
Floating in darkness above the bed the
Black face, eyes white-bulging, mouth shaped like an O. . . . (171–72)

He does not dream of the black face; he awakens to it. Both the childhood memory alluded to and the recurring vision of the black face are elements below the level of the ego, coming at the poet's weakest moments when his own physical nature is aligned with the night voice of nature. They are elements to be controlled by activities of the "super-ego"—writing sonnets, summoning the police, taking a metaphysical vacation in the Nez Perce Pass—because they are elements that disturb the order achieved by the Appollonian super-ego, especially when it has the tenuous nature of the consciousness of the Southern exile, who, eating the bread of the Pharisee, knows he is a usurper of someone else's peace to begin with. But the new poem is also an attempt to control, to form, experience. What the poet does here again is forge the *terms* of his own peace by struggling to discover the new form that does not so much contain the experience as revise it, necessarily and honestly revise it.

CHAPTER FOUR

Lying Words

The Adult Problem

[I]rony is always, and only, a trick of light
on the late landscape.

ROBERT PENN WARREN, *Brother to Dragons*

◆ In Warren's second historical biography, the 1980 hybrid biography/memoir *Jefferson Davis Gets His Citizenship Back*, there are significant structural parallels with the late poems as well as with *Segregation*. The chief similarity is that in *Jefferson Davis* Warren again casts himself in the mold of the returning wanderer. Again he confronts the massiveness of his regional past. And he considers even more deeply, in the wake of prose works such as *The Legacy of the Civil War* and *Democracy and Poetry* and poems such as "Old Nigger on One-Mule Cart," the problems of language that the wanderer must confront in order to know the past.

One prominent method by which Warren attempts to explore the significance of actual events is constructing alternative scenarios. His most sustained and successful use of this technique is with an if-clause motif in his novel *Wilderness*, about which I have written at length elsewhere ("Warren's Wilderness"). *Jefferson Davis Gets His Citizenship Back* uses one such scenario in a comparison of Lincoln and Davis:

Less than a year after little Jeff's birth — before he could have character or aspirations worth mentioning, of course — another man-child was born, some hundred miles away in Kentucky, in another log cabin, to even poorer parentage. The parents of Abraham Lincoln were somewhat ambitionlessly caught up in a drift northward, across the Ohio and into frontier country, where, in spite of poverty and hardship, the boy, driven by some remorseless will to excel, reached out for learning and for a place in the world of power which would be worthy of the self he felt he was. By early middle age, the boy born in the frontier cabin was a success, living in a spacious white house in town, practicing law for good fees, and dabbling in politics. . . . What would have happened if Thomas Lincoln had followed the drive to Mississippi as the land where energy and cunning in a new fluidity might make a man great — the same land that William Faulkner's great-grandfather came to as a penniless youth and that Faulkner himself was to write about? Or what would have happened if Samuel Davis had sought his luck northward across the Ohio? How much is a man the product of his society? (28–29)

Warren makes his point, not atypically, by interrogatives, a rhetorical device that suggests the tenuous nature of knowledge. Yet the main point of the rhetorical inquiry is not that all could have been different, though it does operate by raising that possibility; it is instead that human beings are known in context. This means not that they are doomed to think a certain way but that the way they do think is tested against the way of their society. Imagining the alternative scenario is, finally, an exploration of the possibility of meaning and definition in the actual scenario of history, or in as close an approximation of that scenario as human effort can bring us.

The theme of imaginative knowledge is also a corollary to Warren's personal or inward approach. *Who Speaks for the Negro?* offers a good example. James Justus has said that *Who Speaks for the Negro?* is personal in that Warren invokes the subjects and themes which he depends upon to unify his work on the whole (150). Hugh Ruppersburg writes that the value of *Who Speaks for the Negro?* lies in Warren's attempt "to investigate in the matrix of contemporary affairs the important themes of his poetry and fiction" and also that the book is "informed by Warren's characteristic vision of American history in process" (116). What both Justus and Ruppersburg help us to see is that even this book, which on the surface would appear Warren's most journalistic, sprang like his poetry and fiction from his own need to know what the issues meant in the complex of an interpenetration of self and society. The almost constant interplay between personal and social experiences makes the book's underlying theme of the interconnection of human experience all the more obvious. When Robert Moses, for instance, mentions a conversation he once had with his father and thereby triggers Warren's memory of his own father, Warren provides a brief résumé of his father, emphasizing (as he would again in *Portrait of a Father*) the personal sacrifices Robert Franklin Warren had made for his family. Then he returns to the subject at hand:

> I am remembering what the father of Robert Moses said to him "about whether he was satisfied or not—you know, his whole purpose in life," and how "he had decided to put his energies into his personal family," and I hear in my head, clear as can be, my own father's voice—an old man's voice—saying to me that he had had to choose, had had to realize that certain things were not for him, but he was happy.
>
> I think, then, that I understand something about Robert Moses. (*Who Speaks* 100)

The realization of the limits of individual freedom is a major theme in Warren, perhaps most significantly of all in the figure of Audubon, who appealed to Warren as a subject because he had learned how to accept his fate (Watkins, Hiers, and Weaks 244). The knowledge Warren writes of here, however, comes through the imaginative act that creates connections, this time through a double layering of memory: the memory of what Robert Moses has recently said and the memory of what his own father had said years before. The fact that the connection seems accidental, even immaterial in some sense to the race question, undermines the commentary as social science but reveals Warren's personal concerns with the race issue. He is still speaking for himself as he considers who speaks for the African American.

Warren's feelings about his own father were very important to his development and led him late in his life to write the memoir *Portrait of a Father*, in which he elaborated on the sacrifices that marked his father's life. Warren, in fact, suffered what Joseph Blotner calls a "strange sense of guilt, as a successful poet, for having somehow appropriated the vocation his father had vainly cherished, living out his small-town life as an unsuccessful banker and stoic storekeeper" (207). An awareness of those sacrifices might even have prompted the question Warren had put to Moses which led to the revelation of their parallel experiences to begin with: "Had your father had ambitions like your own?" (*Who Speaks* 90). Considering Warren's relationship with his father will help reiterate and clarify the point about Warren's personal and imaginative approach to history.

Like much of the late work, *Portrait of a Father* is a memory piece not only in name but in its very structure. Warren admits that there is much he does not know and that the book is a memoir, not the product of extensive research into his father's life. His real concerns are suggested by his preference for "a chronology of vividness and sequence, not of event, but of recollection" (30). What he attempts to set down is what the father is in the son's mind; this is the significant reality for Warren, as the book itself suggests. Corroborating this interpretation is a passage Warren wrote in a letter dated January 7, 1985, two years before "Portrait of a Father" first appeared in essay form in the *Southern Review*: "I never really knew my father, except as a kind of benign presence until after my mother died—when I had been away since the age of fifteen. Then I discovered him [and] for many years—until he died at the age of 85, we saw each other often. Often took trips together. And discovered each other. After his death he became more real to me than ever. If being an obsessive subject for poems means 'being real'" (letter to the author).

There is a parallel between the development of Warren's father from a "benign presence" to a dynamic part of his son's life and the awareness Warren expresses in *Who Speaks for the Negro?* of how his thinking about the South had changed. The parallel is in the kinetic process of a subject's transformation from a static image into a moving one. The imagination's importance in the transformation is strongly suggested by one sentence in the letter quoted above: "After his death he became more real to me than ever." The composition of *Portrait of a Father* may have been Warren's attempt to vitalize that reality just as the composition of *Who Speaks for the Negro?* was part of an attempt to vitalize and clarify another reality: that change, including changes in attitude toward a place, is essential.

In *Jefferson Davis Gets His Citizenship Back*, Warren approaches the familiar and intertwined processes of self-making and -remaking, which he explores in much of the poetry and nonfiction I have considered, essentially as problems of language. His way into history, as in *Segregation* and *Portrait*, is once again personal. The first twenty-six pages are autobiographical, in fact, and early in the book appears the common scene of the boy Warren listening as his maternal grandfather Gabriel Penn talks about the war. The image is an example of the second of the two kinds of memory Warren defines: "One is narrative, the unspooling in the head of what has happened, like a movie film with no voices. The other is symbolic—the image, say, of a dead friend of long ago, with a characteristic expression of face, which may be called up by name" (*Jefferson Davis* 1). Warren makes no distinction in value between the two kinds of memory, yet one of the important impulses behind the book is to account for a change from what seems to be symbolic memory into a more mature narrative memory achieved through the process of historical imagination. It may simply be, however, that meaning is given to the symbolic memory, which is static, through historical imagination, which is dynamic or narrative memory.

Certainly there are similarities between this process and the process dramatized in the poems and in *Segregation*, and the result is that as a subject of biography Jefferson Davis is treated by a method very different from the way John Brown was treated fifty years earlier. Of course, with fifty years separating the publication of the two books, it would be remarkable if there weren't significant differences between Warren's first historical biography and his last. But it is finally because both are really attempts to tell an American story that some of the differences are especially significant. They cannot be accounted for simply by the fact that the later work is less the product of a defensive sensibility than the earlier, though it is. Rather, the later is a more conscious effort on Warren's part to treat both the historical personage and the process of imaginative knowledge as subjects. One major thrust of *Jefferson Davis* is to show how Robert Penn Warren came to *know* Jefferson Davis. That is, how Jefferson Davis the figure changed from an image in the "old dark wordless flow" of the author's childhood to a figure clouded in adult-world fact and mythology. From this one learns something essential about Warren's sense of the writer's relation to his audience: his belief that his own subjective wrestling with the subject will be as valuable as any objective analysis, a critical approach he had spelled out explicitly in the volume of Melville's poems he edited.

In a large way Emerson, or at least Emersonian thinking, had been the subject of Warren's *John Brown: The Making of a Martyr*, for it is the Eastern abolitionism of a William Lloyd Garrison combined with the higher-law thinking of Emerson and, finally, the ego of John Brown himself which actually *make* the martyr in the earlier biography. The biases of that book have long been noted, and Warren himself later said it was "shot through with Southern defensiveness" (*Who Speaks?* 320). As several perceptive readers have noted, however, the book did introduce certain figures that Warren would go on to develop, and despite its bias it is not without certain powers that became typical of his later works. L. Hugh Moore, for one, has praised Warren's accomplishment in rendering the "texture" of the time and place (28). Yet Warren's achievement goes beyond verisimilitude in *John Brown*. Political matters such as the Compromise of 1850 and the debate over the future of Kansas are treated with the same evenhandedness and wholeness of vision exemplified in the much later *Legacy of the Civil War*.

The failures of this first book, however, ultimately reveal more to the Warren reader, for the "Southern defensiveness" is inextricably related to the not unworthy purpose of debunking American martyr-making. As an object for study, Brown appealed to Warren on several fronts. There were dramatic events to be rendered, which suited Warren's taste for the "big" scene in drama. There was the political conflict, played out in Warren's interpretation by the free-soil/slave-state polar contingencies. There was the corrupting influence of the West, the old Wilderness theme to which Warren would later give powerful treatment in *World Enough and Time* and *Brother to Dragons*. There was, of course, the maniacal figure of John Brown himself, who presented a fascinating study in the "image of man." And then there was the Sage of Concord, who did not act but commented in a way that drew Warren's verbal assaults, usually ironic but without the tensions of the counterirony that characterizes his mature work. There is even a greater demonstration of sympathy for Brown than for Emerson, since Emerson had a greater hand, finally, in "making" the martyr.

Foreshadowing the tack his career would take is the fact that the subject of Warren's first book had become a focus of debate between the Hawthornesque and Emersonian schools of American Romanticism. Within this context, Warren's treatment of Emerson, his early pronouncements on race, and his use of Brown as a study of the way man makes an image of himself are of primary importance to an understanding of the contribution this book makes to its author's developing epistemology. More specifically, considering some important elements of the book will prepare us to consider how Warren's second biography reveals even more the tendency of revision we have already seen in the poetry. *Jefferson Davis Gets His Citizenship Back* is not just an aside from or an addendum to the poetry but an integral part of a larger body of work cast in the wanderer mold. The development to be traced reveals, I believe, a strong link between Warren's development as a historian and the Warren who developed the wandering figure as a primary image of his poetic vision.

Warren saw Brown, then, as an Emersonian man, a man for whom the past was nothing: "John Brown never looked back; his past and history were simply an instrument for framing [an] astounding future" (*John Brown* 310). As such a man, Brown is a prototype, as Moore has said, for the Warren character who denies the significance of his own past (110). But Emerson too is targeted as another type who was to develop in Warren's later fiction—the complicitor. Warren wrote that Emerson (and Thoreau) praised John Brown out of a failure to see the facts. He attacked Emerson's comparison of Brown with Lincoln as a comparison that was true in matters of rhetoric but inconsequential in matters of fact (414). The statement might seem a sign of Warren's straining "Southern defensiveness" but also reveals the young Warren's keen sense of the disparity between language and "truth." The transcendentalists took Brown on Brown's own terms, accepting too easily his own valuation of himself. Emerson, Warren wrote, thought Brown was "something . . . which would correspond to the fine ideas and the big word" of Transcendentalism (*John Brown* 245). The Sage's chief failure, Warren contends, was that he lived in words, not facts. Brown, finally, was an Emersonian man only in part. For him vocabulary was only a valuable instrument, for the Brown whom Warren reveals is utilitarian rather than idealistic, and Emerson, who exemplifies one strand of American innocence, could not understand how Brown's rhetoric could differ so from his own (245). It is perhaps more accurate to put the case this way: through Brown, Warren reveals how close any utilitarian and idealistic philosophy come together when adherents assert their comprehensiveness. One can see in his interpretation of the relationship how early Warren was working out the split he would dramatize with Willie Stark and Adam Stanton in *All the King's Men*.

Warren also attempts to divorce Brown from the rhetoric and casuistry of Emerson, Garrison, Theodore Parker, and others whom he sometimes conveniently lumps together according to their responses to Brown. The relation of Brown to these men as Warren depicts it in the biography is interestingly like the relation of Willie Stark to his constituents in *All the King's Men* and the relation of Lilburne Lewis to most of his relatives in *Brother to Dragons*. All are dangerous relationships between the man of action, sometimes the fanatical man of action, and those who would have their ideas fulfilled vicariously through the man of action. John Brown acted murderously and was hailed, to Warren's great disgust, as an exemplar of the higher-law thinking of distant Boston. The relationship was reciprocal, for the man of action needed the complicitors' support: Brown "heard remotely, as an echo, the shouts from many people, thousands of people, who filled the paved streets of cities far to the East, the well-mannered applause of great men sitting in large, richly furnished rooms. That echo rose and multiplied in his mind, as the cheering rose between the poor, unpainted shacks and dwindled out into the wide silence of the prairie" (215).

To characterize Brown further, Warren uses the dialectic of higher law and self-interest. In relation to the theme of self-knowledge, Brown exemplifies yet another strand of American innocence. In several ways Warren's Brown seems to be borrowed from Fitzgerald's Gatsby and to look forward to Faulkner's Sutpen, a prototypic figure for such later fictional creations as Warren's own Jeremiah Beaumont, Arthur Miller's Willie Loman, and Thomas Berger's Custer: an "innocent" to the extent that he is single-minded and dependent on the public. Very conscious of the public figure he makes, Warren's Brown is a man who long before the culmination of events at Harpers Ferry learned the habit of dramatizing himself (20). And his willingness to act independently signifies not self-reliance so much as an ego that precludes joint action (106). The massacre at Pottawatomie is central, for it was there that Brown first developed a Machiavellian attitude toward means: that is, he learned that a higher-law man, as Warren most often uses the term, is not obligated to regard the morality of his means. This interpretation certainly looks forward to Jeremiah Beaumont's murder of Cassius Fort in *World Enough and Time* as well as to Willie Stark's meat-ax political methods. For Brown, such thinking was justified by his favorite biblical verse: "Without the shedding of blood, there is no remission of sin."

Warren is aware of the curious marriage of pragmatism and divine ordinance at work in such a way of thinking and believes that Emerson understood only half of Brown's motivation when he said that Brown had made the gallows as hallowed as the cross. By contrast, the heart of Warren's interpretation of John Brown's motivation is that Brown drove maniacally forward to achieve meaning for himself in the world. According to Warren, Brown refused to avail himself of an insanity plea at his trial because "it would have meant a repudiation of himself, and in comparison to such a thing the danger of the noose was inconsequential; it would have meant that he himself was nothing, and all his life, since the youthful period of doubt when he felt a 'steady, strong desire to die,' had been spent in a ruthless, passionate attempt to prove to the world that he, John Brown, was something" (401). Earlier I quoted a very similar passage from Faulkner's *Light in August* as Joe Christmas resists the seductive pull of a life of peace and ease married to Joanna Burden: "No. If I give in now, I will deny all the thirty years that I have lived to make me what I chose to be" (232). Both Faulkner and Warren were interested in the figure whose mania was made manifest as the need to preserve the created self. Warren's purpose is much more than the debunking of a martyr. He has an interest in the psychology of the maniacal drive to publicly *be*. It is an interest that also informs his studies of Twain and Dreiser, and to one degree or another similar motivations impel his fictional characters Willie Stark, Percy Munn, Jerry Calhoun, Jeremiah Beaumont, Murray Guilfort, and Jediah Tewksbury. In John Brown, Warren saw what he interpreted as one side of a two-sided American phenomenon: the desire for recognition as a means of achieving identity. Its antithesis is a desire for obscurity, an escape from self, which Warren dramatizes through several characters (Jack Burden,

Jeremiah Beaumont, Amantha Starr, Isham Lewis) as westward flight. These are the terms of conflict captured in the figure of the wanderer. But it is also through his wanderer figure that in his late work he seems to press hardest for solutions to the conflict.

Warren writes in *Jefferson Davis* of the vagueness of his feeling as a boy and his wondering about the significance of history, both stirred by his several visits—made alone in the family Chevrolet and not without an element of quest—to Fairview, Kentucky, to see the monument erected to Davis's memory.

> Was the blank shaft that was rising there trying to say something about that war of long ago when young men had ridden away from the same countryside to die for whatever they had died for? Was the tall shaft, now stubbed at the top, what history was? Certainly these words did not come into my fuddled head. Childhood and adolescence do not live much by words, by abstractions, for words freeze meaning in its living surge, or come only as bubbles that rise and burst from the dark, unpredictable flow of feeling. And, looking back years later, we know how hard it is to sink ourselves again into the old dark wordless flow. We have more and more words now, and being truly adult is largely the effort to make the lying words stand for the old living truth. (24)

Warren's point that the fall from the prelapsarian "flow" is a fall into language — "lying words" — suggests his full awareness of his dual subject: the object of the biography, and the verbal process of coming to know the object. The effort to understand the past in its relation to the present, which is the effort of this book and most that Warren wrote, is a painful process because of the limitation of words. But it is necessary, as *Segregation* and the poems make clear, though the limitations of language intensify the difficulty, even the anguish, involved in the attempt to "focus some meaning, however hard to define, on the relation of past and present, old pain and glory and new pain and glory" (*Jefferson Davis* 25).

We might even say that history—the activity of coming to know the significance of the past—is reducible to a struggle of language for Warren, but we must understand what this meant for him. Despite being known as one of the chief figures of New Criticism, he actually shares with poststructuralist theorists a sense of the inadequacy of symbol and metaphor and of the distance between language and the idea or object that language attempts to signify. Yet as Fred R. Thieman has adroitly demonstrated, Warren can be distinguished from Jacques Derrida, Michel Foucault, Paul DeMan, and any number of other postmodern theorists in that for him the fact that symbols are never pure "does not 'deconstruct' those symbols, what they symbolize, or (perhaps least of all) symbolization itself" (311). In some ways Warren's development immunized him against an intellectual fascination with poststructuralist conclusions about the false relation between language and reality much as, according to his own testimony, it immunized him against the allure of as diverse solutions to human problems as Christian orthodoxy and Marxism. He attributes that turn of his mind, in fact, to his having read Henry Thomas Buckle's *History of Civilization* when he was a boy: Buckle's linking of history and geography was the "one-answer system" that immunized him against other one-answer systems (Watkins, Hier, and Weaks 26–27). If we remember that in "Pure and Impure Poetry" Warren was not prepared to call the poetry of Shakespeare's lovers complete until it was spiked with the blasphemy of Mercutio, we may begin to see that his writing resists honest deconstructionist methods precisely because it goes so far in that direction to begin with. No poem in American literary history that I am aware of treats history as a problem of language more rigorously than Warren's own great *Brother to Dragons*. Consider one of its most remarkable features, but seemingly one little remarked on: its reflexive nature.

By the poem's reflexive nature I mean the consciousness of the characters that they are involved in a process of creating, even in a process of composition. They often speak with a keen awareness that their words, to borrow Warren's own phrase, rise to the surface like bubbles and then burst, failing to contain their meanings. Setting the tone for his debate with R.P.W. throughout the poem (a dialogue that has its literary cousin in Quentin Compson and Shreve McCannon's trying to flesh out the final third of Faulkner's *Absalom, Absalom!*), Jefferson announces the theme of the inadequacy of language in his opening speech in the 1979 version (to which my citations refer unless otherwise specified): "Language betrays. / There are no words to tell Truth" (7). The point is emphasized perhaps even more in the language of the 1953 version: "I had not meant to speak thus. Language betrays. / What I mean is, words are always the truth, and always the lie" (8).

Jefferson's qualification of his speech here foreshadows the general tendency in the poem for characters to speak, retract, and respeak, to press language to the very edge of its usefulness and then try again. Talking of the house where the murder took place, for example, R.P.W. presses a naturalistic interpretation of history and then resorts to a line of colloquial diction that seems a verbal shrugging-off of all he has said:

> I have seen [the house]. Or saw,
> Rather, all that remained when time and fire
> Had long since done their kindness, and the crime
> Could nestle, smug and snug, in any
> Comfortable conscience, such as mine — or the next man's —
> And over the black stones the rain
> Has fallen, falls, with the benign indifferency
> Of the historical imagination, while grass,
> In idiot innocence, has fingered all to peace.
> Anyway, I saw the house — (9)

The theme of the mind's collusion with nature in forgetfulness is treated with a tone somewhere between the irony of Carl Sandburg's "Grass" and the despair of Edna St. Vincent Millay's "Spring," and with echoes of both, perhaps. But R.P.W. lacks confidence in his tropes in the end and somewhat shiftlessly abandons them.

Another example of this pattern of assertion and retraction is captured when Lucy Jefferson Lewis speaks of her love:

I loved my children. Love them. But know, too,
The way my husband's face looked locked in sleep,
When leaning in the night, the lamp unlit,
I said, "He lives in some dark place where I
May come to take his hand, if I love well."
But never came where he inhabited.

Came only to Kentucky, by my love.
I did the best I could. No, that's a lie.
I did not do my best. I died. (17)

What we witness continually in the poem is more than voices countering other voices, thesis and antithesis played out between the voices and within the struggling consciousness of single voices. We see in several of the characters' speeches a continuing inward struggle to frame the truth accurately in language that continually fails. There is thus no synthesis in the usual sense, yet the recognition of the failure of their language is part of the success finally.

This self-conscious use of a language that fails to hold truth often marks other Warren poems, as in the opening of "Mortmain," on the death of the poet's father:

In Time's concatenation and
Carnal conventicle, I,
Arriving, being flung through dark and
The abstract flight-grid of sky,
Saw rising from the sweated sheet and
Ruck of bedclothes ritualistically
Reordered by the paid hand
Of mercy—saw rising the hand—

Christ, start again! What was it I,
Standing there, travel-shaken, saw
Rising? What could it be that I,
Caught sudden in gut- or conscience-gnaw,
Saw rising out of the past, which I
Saw now as twisted bedclothes? (*New and Selected Poems* 263)

Here is yet another instance of the later poet confronting his former self and discovering the inadequacy of old forms. The strained metaphysical style and stentorian utterance will not work, and he begins self-consciously striving for a more exploratory form. The moment has its parallel in "Old Nigger" when the poet remembers trying to write "what had aimed to be—Jesus Christ—a sonnet." But it also has its parallel, perhaps even its precursor, in *Brother to Dragons* when Jefferson and R.P.W. debate form. R.P.W. says he had once considered making a ballad about the murder, but it never came off because the ballad form was inadequate, was too facile. The action of ballad is self-contained, but this action (the murder) is not explained; it must be interpreted. To try to "put the story in a ballad / Would be like shoveling a peck of red-hot coals / In a croker sack to tote them down the road / To start the fire in a neighbor's fireplace" (31). The metaphor suggests simultaneously the inadequacy of the form to communicate the reality and the desire, or need, to communicate, to start a fire in a neighbor's fireplace. The metaphor suggests that the poet sees poetry, potentially at least, as a *place*, a kind of region, in the sense that it is a ground for relationship between author and audience. The difficulty even of explaining the problems of composition is once again suggested through the irony that in stating the inadequacy of the folk style R.P.W. uses folk expressions such as "croker sack" and "tote."

Responding to R.P.W.'s metaphor, Jefferson says, "There is no form to hold / Reality and its insufferable intransigence" (31). But Jefferson himself goes on pressing for an adequate form even as he recounts the inadequacy of the form his knowledge had taken:

I know, for I once thought to contrive
A form to hold the purity of man's hope.
But only dumped hot coals in that croker sack.
The fire burns through, the blood bleeds through, the bowels,
And not of compassion, are pierced, and foulness
Flows forth upon — no, I'll revert to the former metaphor:
If then I had known what I now know,
I had thought it exquisitely better,
Given the courage, which perhaps I lacked,
To seize the hot coals of the human definition
In my bare hands, and scream, and run what steps
I could before I fell, and the white
Articulation of hand-bone trellised through
Fire-black flesh. (31–32)

Such a speech makes quite clear how uninterested Warren was in transcribing the documented Jefferson into his poem. Such an irrational vaunt, in fact, makes this Jefferson akin to the Warren fanatic. Yet here he is participating in the basic linguistic problem of the poem, the dubious relation of fact to symbol or language. The absolute solution he seeks is to break beyond language to symbolic action — action that simultaneously dramatizes the glory and the agony of articulation — even as his words make clear that language is all that is available to him. He has discovered the basic truth about poetry that Warren asserts in "Pure and Impure Poetry": that a poet who strains nature out of nature to write a "pure" poem is a false poet. Jefferson's particular trope here, the purity of form fouled by human waste, reflects the intensity of his disgust and also echoes the central drama of the poem by paralleling the foulness that the monstrous Lilburne Lewis represents for Jefferson's dream of human perfectibility. He has to "revert to the former metaphor." He had, and has, in common with the poet, the strong desire to communicate his vision but wants a form as pure as the vision — which, as the analogy reveals, results in self-mutilation or death. Metaphor or martyrdom is all we are allowed, but metaphor, the poem finally suggests, can signify the validity of the heart's action.

The debate between Jefferson and R.P.W. seems to reveal this function of literary art as they analyze even the function of irony in their collaborative creation. Not knowing what dog dug up the remains of the murdered slave, they agree that making it Lilburne's hound would create a symbol "most sardonically apt" (45). They are engaged in *forming* the story, but this time, rather than simply following the usual pattern of assertion and revision, their very tone implies a criticism of their speech. Their complacency, their satisfaction with the irony, is the failure here, for the sardonic stance creates a distance similar to that which had been the second problem with the ballad form for R.P.W: the pleasure of folk simplicity is a snobbish pleasure (43). It is only when R.P.W. brings the irony around again and finds that if it is symbolically apt that Lilburne's hound betrayed him, it is similarly apt that Lilburne, of Jefferson's own blood, betrayed Jefferson. At least in the logic of this poem (a logic that makes it possible for Lucy to feel she failed because she died), it can take its place in the complex and sophisticated vision the composing process drives toward (43). It is this nonsardonic irony of inwardness, or irony with a different heart, that can overcome finally the naturalism and historical complacency which make the crime settle into distant consciences.

Perhaps one can understand this even further by considering what R.P.W. says of Aunt Cat's motivation for helping Laetitia escape her husband, Lilburne. The passage appears in this form only in the 1953 version, but the idea it expresses remains pervasive in the revised version:

> every act is Janus-faced and double,
> And every act to become an act must resolve
> The essential polarity of possibility.
> Thus though the act is life and without action
> There is no life, yet action is a constant withering

Of possibility, and hence of life.
So by the act we live, and in action die.

No, that's not the thought I had meant to follow.
I had meant to say that if the act resolves
The essential polarity of possibility,
It yet will carry that polarity,
As deep in the inner flesh of autumn fruit
We trace the frail configuration of spring's flower.
But that image, with its sense of beauty and delight,
Is scarcely appropriate for my notion, and my own line
Has a sort of conventional euphony and sweetness. (55)

A meditation on the "if" theme so pervasive in Warren, the passage provides yet another instance of the poem's reflexivity, as twice the poet is betrayed by language and twice he revises his statements and even critiques his poetry. Conventional form proves "all wrong" for his notion, for such forms fail to reflect the inwardness, the double motive, of Aunt Cat or any human. But R.P.W. is not ready to say with the cynical Jefferson that there is no form to contain reality; the poem in which the debate over form is carried out is a sign that there is. It is also a sign of Warren's special sense of both irony and symbol as necessary forms of communication. Poetry is the paradoxical effort in language to break through the frozen meaning that words themselves create and to return us to meaning's "living surge."

The language and structure of Brother to Dragons have elicited some interesting critical comments. Leslie Fiedler's judgment that the language of the poem is "Bombast" — "a straining of language and tone toward a scream which can no longer be heard, the absolute cry of bafflement and pain" (210) — is perhaps an approximate description of Warren's rhetoric. But as Calvin Bedient has countered, the poem is "too morally earnest to suggest a scream"; however, Bedient also says that "these characters cannot redeem what has happened; they can only talk" (84). That statement characterizes the

common critical confusion over the poem's form. In the first place
the judgment ironically exemplifies the modern dilemma that Warren was so interested in vivisecting in the poem: a contemporary distrust of language. All *any* poem can do is "talk." Such a judgment
also seems to stem from an attempt to lock the poem into, or at least
to judge it by, a traditional form — tragedy. The poem does indeed
bear a strong resemblance to the middle drama of the Oedipus
trilogy, *Oedipus at Colonus*, in which the young seek the disgraced
and self-betrayed father among the Furies. But in the end *Brother to
Dragons*, as if by lifting layers of cover, unfolds historical developments in a dramatic form. It moves toward drama's core, its origin. It
is, in short, a form of ritual, as if Warren would work his way back
through tragedy to an earlier, more primitive form of communal regeneration. In relation to tragedy, it is perhaps best thought of as an
expansive exodus. The voices are choral voices that replay the action
and find the meaning of that action through spiritual restoration.
Dennis M. Dooley points to R.P.W.'s three long digressions, which
provide his own spiritual history and parallel the spiritual history of
Jefferson; Dooley sees the digressions as similar to the interpolated
stories of the earlier novels, only they are frames here rather than the
contained exemplum (101, 111). This structural device suggests the
internalization process we have seen Warren using in works subsequent to the original version of *Brother to Dragons*. As R.P.W. says,
the form must both contain us and be contained by us. The struggle
is for a poetic form that approximates, albeit imperfectly, that naturalistic adjustment captured in the condition of the catfish in the Mississippi, the Mississippi in the catfish. Yet even as it approaches that,
the rhetoric constantly reminds us of our separateness, of our differing condition.

Unlike *Brother to Dragons* and "Mortmain," *Jefferson Davis* has little
of anything like anguish in its tone, yet it shares with these other
works a deep concern over the relations between individual con-

sciousness, language, and interpretation. It seems that Warren must establish his method before he can ask, twenty-six pages into the book, "Who was this Jefferson Davis?" The question comes as the formalization of the childhood vagueness of feeling, interestingly articulated still as a question, a sign of the adult problem.

In the comparison of Davis with Lincoln and in such anecdotes as the one concerning the sorrowful end brought on Davis's daughter by her father's refusal to allow her to marry the Syracuse lawyer she loved, Warren attempts to separate Davis from the polarized symbolism that obscured his image after the Civil War. For the North he was largely a cowardly criminal; for the South, an emblem of the "eternal City of the Soul." Such approaches to the problems that the figure of Davis presents seem parts of an overall Wordsworthian attempt to clarify for the poet himself what that image of Davis, coming out of the old wordless flow of childhood, means. For Warren's way *out* of history, so to speak, is personal, too. He concludes *Jefferson Davis* by a method that had already become common in his longer works: leaving the past to describe an event in the present which takes place on the same ground. Variations of the method appear in *Brother to Dragons* and *Chief Joseph of the Nez Perce*, and Warren employs it in two of his novels by writing objective, statistical descriptions of modern Kentucky near the end of *World Enough and Time* and of modern Tennessee at the end of *Meet Me in the Green Glen*. Such endings perform a dual task, the one cathartic, distancing readers from the tragic lives of the characters, the other fusil—yet one more attempt by the author to find the effective form for carrying the coals of truth to light the fires of his neighbors.

Jefferson Davis ends with a lengthy account of the celebration of the restoration of Davis's citizenship, conducted from May 31 through June 3, 1979, at his birthplace in Todd County, Kentucky. In recounting the community drama commemorating the major events in Davis's life and the square dance following its second performance, Warren emphasizes the crowd's apathy, despite the ostensible motive for the gathering. His purpose, however, is not simply to portray the citizens of Todd County as apathetic and ignorant hicks; in fact, he applauds their efforts and writes of several who are anything but apathetic or ignorant. But his descriptions of the square dancers for whom Jefferson Davis is just a name, "if that" (101), and of a twenty-year-old who, caught in the rain delay on the third night of the celebration, is miserable without his TV and beer are comically distant from the historical and heroic events he has already narrated. The emphasis on the gross sensation and complacency toward the past of modern Americans seems to corroborate what Warren argued in *Legacy* and again here in *Jefferson Davis*, that the lives of the men of the Civil War were different in their struggle for moral awareness and inwardness from the lives lived in a society whose uniformity and complacency are a result of movements that began during that war.

The description of the official celebration is more functionally comic than mean, finally. No mere piece of contemporary local-color writing, the scene demonstrates Warren's sense that the citizen cut off from poetry in the age of technocracy and the fluid self is similarly cut off from the past. Though acknowledged as a communal celebration, the event offers little respite for the profound human loneliness that haunts Warren. The form of this biography emphasizes that the only way to make a healing connection is through a poetic sensibility. The celebration episode is functionally juxtaposed with another involving Warren's private visit to the site of Davis's monument during a trip with his brother. At the end of *Brother to Dragons*, R.P.W. records his visit with his father to the home of the Lewises, and in *Chief Joseph* the poet writes of his visit to the battle-field with friends, riding in a Honda — a fact that strikes him as another comic juxtaposition.

The point of these transhistorical pairings seems to be to illustrate that one must confront history alone, and the last few pages of *Jefferson Davis* are a description of this process which flings us back on the first twenty-five pages of autobiography that introduced the book. In language that evokes the mood of ritual, the opening of the section seems to set the process for understanding in motion: "It is a rainy morning in late August. I want to stand before the monument to see it rear, as years before, blank and lonely against the sky. There is no person in sight—none near the towering obelisk. And there is nobody beneath that structure." But the way by which Warren came to this spot where a region has commemorated its hero is once again personal, just as his desire to stand before the monument has arisen out of his personal past. "That morning, last August, I had already stood beside occupied graves, some miles southward of Fairview. My brother and I—wordless, as usual on such occasions—had observed the graves of our parents, then of his first wife, and then of one of the two persons who had been my closest friends in boyhood, the one who had been my tutor in boyish woodcraft and who, through short years of greatness and long years of failure, had remained a friend" (108).

The wordlessness of the poet and his brother may indicate many things, but one thing it suggests is that the *return* is more than physical: it brings the poet back to the silence of the preverbal stage of inquiry he wrote of at the beginning of the book. He is also standing before the graves of people who have been the subjects of some of his most powerful poems: his parents and Kent Greenfield, the lifelong friend from Guthrie who for a brief time had been a major-league pitcher. Over the course of the book the poet has moved out of the silence of childhood, through language, back to a meditative and ritualistic silence.

Yet this is only a part of the process one witnesses here. The next step in that process is to turn from the familial and personal past to the communal past or, rather, to extend the personal into the communal. Warren and his brother "discover" Old Jeff Davis, a figure from boyhood times in Guthrie who for a while was confused in the boy Warren's mind with the region's hero. The description of the graves of Old Jeff and his wife in "the potter's field" is a passage important to the meaning to be taken from the experience, for it suggests the process by which, after adult growth of reason brought awareness of the distinction between the two Jeff Davises—after there is a more mature grasp of language, that is—imagination rejoins them. Old Jeff, of course, has long ceased to be confused with Jefferson Davis, yet there is a need to know him as well as the great man. Warren humanizes the image of Old Jeff to make him more than a static image in his memory. By the process of historical synthesis, Warren's vision of their common human suffering, Old Jeff and Jefferson Davis become linked again. The wife's tombstone was "the handiwork of the bereaved, twisted old husband, the town's feckless jack-of-all-trades, whose grief-stricken masterpiece was scarcely a masterpiece. He had obviously first made a wooden box, some twenty inches by thirty, and about five inches deep, then filled it with cement, probably bracing it with scraps of chickenwire. At last, before the cement had really hardened, he had, with some blunt blade, scratched on an epitaph" (109).

Though this may seem a lavish and sentimental passage at first, it illustrates Warren's propensity for imaginatively creating a scene through minute detail. And the irony of the limits of language—the awareness of the provisional nature of the imaginative creation—is captured in a statement that at once affirms and denies: the "masterpiece was scarcely a masterpiece." But the metonymic phrase "grief-stricken masterpiece" is important here. It associates the man with his work and clarifies that the "grief" which drove him to the work reflects the depth of feeling associated with masterwork even if technically it is not a masterpiece.

For emphasis, Warren contrasts the homemade tombstone of the wife with the "commercial-made" marker on Old Jeff's own grave. Warren's purpose becomes even clearer when, after humanizing and distinguishing Old Jeff and linking him to Jefferson Davis through the human need, at any level, to monumentalize life, he discovers and emphasizes the significance of another link between the jack-of-all-trades and the president of the Confederacy: "Beside the crank-sided slab was a neater little stone, commercial-made—the kind a grateful government sets up to commemorate its penniless veteran. From it I learned that Old Jeff, too, had served his country, at the time of the Spanish-American War and a little thereafter. In heroism or in quaking fear — it is not recorded" (109–10).

Warren's writing is full of Old Jeffs, virtually anonymous figures whose lives take on significance through the process of imaginative knowing that makes them mirrors of the great. The interpolated stories of Willie Proudfit, Ashby Wyndam, and Munn Short in *Night Rider, At Heaven's Gate,* and *World Enough and Time* are examples of such mirroring. There is also the participation of the "nameless" in the poem "Founding Fathers, Early-Nineteenth-Century Style, Southeast U.S.A.":

> Or take those, the nameless, of whom no portraits remain,
> No locket or seal ring, though somewhere, broken and rusted,
> In attic or earth, the long Decherd, stock rotten, has lain;
> Or the mold-yellow Bible, God's Word, in which in their strength they
> also trusted. (*New and Selected Poems* 282)

These too are a part of "the old story," like Sam Houston, Jim Bowie, and others who are named in the poem and in the history books and who own signet rings and have their portraits painted.

What is difficult to decipher, perhaps, is the relation of these nameless to the great men of history. It does not seem to me, finally, that Warren saw history as *made* by great men, though Ruppersburg calls that sense of history "one of the most anachronistic qualities of [Warren's] perspective." Ruppersburg is more accurate when he goes on to say that Warren's "work evinces a deep concern with the common citizens of the nation . . . who embody the same American essences as the Great Men" (2). Although he certainly distrusted the masses and criticized America's celebration of the "common" man, Warren did not see the ordinary as inherently lesser beings than the great; he attempted to penetrate the surface of anonymity and find human constants. His writings, in fact — his alternative scenarios, for example — indicate his understanding that accident plays an important role in distinguishing the great from the ordinary, the success from the failure. In "Founding Fathers" he finds the "monument" to each life, though he has to imagine the monuments of the anonymous, and what the great and the unknown have in common is that they are all our parents: "For we are their children in the light of humanness, and under the shadow of God's closing hand." This last line of the poem, through the familiar pattern of light and dark contrasts, suggests both human passion and inherent human limitation. This fusion, like that of Old Jeff and Jefferson Davis, is the product of imaginative knowing.

But Warren was not finished with his process of imaginative synthesis after the Old Jeff material, or with criticizing modern society. He goes on to speculate that Davis would have rejected the citizenship that was restored to him in 1979, for his sense of honor would not have allowed him to accept anything that looked like pardon. (Recall Warren's argument fifty years earlier that John Brown's sense of himself made it impossible for him to plead insanity, even to save his own life.) Davis might have refused the citizenship for another reason as well, just as Lincoln or Grant might have refused citizenship in a society "that sometimes seems technologically and philosophically devoted to the depersonalization of men." Warren goes on to write, "In a way, in their irrefrangible personal identity, Lincoln and Grant were almost as old-fashioned as Jefferson Davis" (*Jefferson Davis* 113). Thus Warren brings together in a vision of wholeness the poles of a traditional man like Davis and of the "new" man, represented in different ways by Lincoln and Grant.

But how does this bear on us? Warren ends *Jefferson Davis* by quoting Herodotus on his purpose in writing history: " . . . that the great deeds of men may not be forgotten . . . whether Greek or foreigner; and especially the causes of their wars" (114). Warren's book, not despite but through its personal nature and its inwardness, is directed by a similar public purpose. The biography is much more than a monument like the one erected in Todd County. It reflects the process of remembering more than the hollowness of a name. It is a book directed by the historian's view, but it depicts a consciousness emerging from the innocence of youth, moving away from the subject and then coming back to it—informed and with imaginative power—as an adult trying to make "lying words" work. In its structure the book resembles many of Warren's poems, and it has in common with the later poems an emphasis on the knower as well as the known. That is, the process by which the ostensible subject of the work comes to be known is finally just as important a subject for the work's total meaning. *Jefferson Davis Gets His Citizenship Back* is thus separated from *John Brown: The Making of a Martyr* by more than the fifty years between the dates of their composition. It is the work of a consciousness that seeks finally to communicate through difficult, slippery language with an audience with whom the author shares a heritage of guilt and the attempt to avoid responsibility but also the possibility of a meaningful understanding of the past.

And here we may consider another dimension of the wanderer figure as he evolves in Warren. "Old Nigger on One-Mule Cart," *Brother to Dragons*, and *Jefferson Davis Gets His Citizenship Back* are all perhaps to some degree what *Segregation* decidedly is: one man's attempt to fight the impulse to withdraw within himself. As the work points out the inherent dangers of abstract thinking about social issues—which include the loss of self and the destructive movement back and forth between complacency and panic—it serves as a warning to Pharisees and would-be Pharisees who need the example.

The wanderer figure puts Warren in the tradition of American writers who define or draw on a "representative" American—Benjamin Franklin, Frederick Douglass, Henry David Thoreau, Walt Whitman and others. In each case it is in the writing itself that perspective and the meaning of the figure are discovered, creating a model. What Warren would show through his figure, however, is a representative situation or dilemma more than a representative or model man. The transcendence of time and space in America's self-making, self-singing traditions is evoked for reconsideration as time and space come rushing back in the wanderer's consciousness with potentially crushing force. Franklin's entry into Philadelphia after kicking the prohibitive dust of Boston off his heels, Douglass's apostrophe to the freedom-symbolizing ships in Chesapeake Bay, Thoreau's eternity reflected in the depths of Walden Pond, Whitman's aggregate self skirting sierras and resting his elbows in sea gaps—all such images of the unrestrained, transcendent self, prospective or realized, seem implicated in Warren's characteristic images of the self's identity in the world. But Warren's images for confirmation in nature tend to be much more complex in their suggestions of the possibility of selfhood, as in R.P.W.'s apostrophe to the river late in *Brother to Dragons*:

> River, who have on your broad bosom borne
> Man and man's movement, and endured the oar,
> Keel-pole and paddle, sweep and paddle-wheel.
> And suffered the disturbance of the screw's bronze blade,
> And tissued over that perpetual scarification
> With instant sweetness and confident flow—
> You who have suffered filth and the waste
> Of the human establishment,
> Ordure of Louisville and the slick of oil,
> The drowned cow, swollen, from the mountain cove,
> And junk jammed on the sand bar in the sun—
> I take you as an image
> Of that deep flood that is our history,
> And the flood that makes each new day possible
> And bears us westward to the new land.
> I take you as image and confirmation
> Of some faith past our consistent failure,
> And the filth we strew. (130)

In *Jefferson Davis* the ambiguous monument is revisited, and with it the ambiguous self as it seemed then. The *return* is the significant movement to reclaim the significance of the detritus of history, to pick up the Old Jeffs stranded on the sandbars of personal consciousness, to drag the river of our national consciousness, but no more to disprove the Romantic self than to challenge the modern cynicism Warren encodes in his Jefferson: "Oh, what's one nigger more / In the economy of pain?" Or one more maniac such as Lilburne Lewis or one more "corruptible simpleton" such as Isham (83). What they are, finally, is humanized through a language that is simultaneously "lying" and symbolic of the poetic effort to arrive at the "living truth," which because it is living is, like the river, shifting. Poetry, in the broadest sense, is the formal effort to create a ritual that captures both that shifting truth and the constants necessary even to begin to speak of the human.

CHAPTER FIVE

Regionalism, Nationalism, Modernism

The Exile's Place to Come To

He was a "liberated Mississippian" who had just joined New York's burgeoning and implacable Southern expatriot community; he was the first of many Mississippi "exiles" I would see in the Big Cave — for, in truth, as I would come to understand, Mississippi may have been the only state in the Union (or certainly one of a half dozen in the South) which had produced a genuine set of exiles, almost in the European sense: alienated from home yet forever drawn back to it, seeking some form of personal liberty elsewhere, yet obsessed with the texture and the complexity of the place from which they had departed as few Americans from other states could ever be.

WILLIE MORRIS, *North Toward Home*

◆ In his introduction to the 1994 collection of essays *Regionalism Reconsidered*, David Jordan takes an unusually approving look back at the Vanderbilt Agrarians. Singling out Davidson, Ransom, and Warren in particular, he lists their collective accomplishments: they "freed regionalism from the constraints of naive [Howellsian] realism; they repudiated common assumptions about a homogeneous national identity; and they suggested that a harmonious interaction between a human community and the environment it inhabits need not be an anachronism, even in developed industrial societies" (xv). Although admitting the customary charge that the Agrarians were politically "regressive," Jordan claims them as precursors of the regionalist theorists who write in *Regionalism Reconsidered* from deconstructionist, bioregionalist, multiple-world semanticist, and feminist points of view. "Donald Davidson," says Jordan, "presaged deconstruction by half a century when he revealed the hidden ideology underlying Howell's realism" (xii).

Having drawn such penetrating conclusions, however, Jordan adds that the "advent of the new criticism diverted the agrarians' attention from regional concerns before they had pursued the implications of their important insights" (xiv). By expressing the all too typical assumption that New Criticism took its adherents out of the social world into the detached realm of poetry, he is able to make the large claim that fifty years passed before "regionalism would once again offer significant contributions to urgent cultural debates" (xv).

To make such a claim, one must either work with a very narrow definition of regionalism or ignore the post-Vanderbilt careers of several of the Agrarians, most particularly Warren's after 1950. Or one must do both. The essays in Jordan's volume do show that several regionalist theorists have significantly narrowed their working definitions of *regionalism* by tying the concept to one of several social, political, or linguistic theories — environmentalism, feminism, multiple-world semantics. Marjorie Pryse, for instance, applies the term almost exclusively to a group of American women fiction writers from 1850 to 1910. Bioregionalist Michael Kowalewski sees nonfictional prose as the dominant genre of regionalist writing and Thoreau the prototype for contemporaries such as Barry Lopez. Including Jordan's in his introduction, there are only two mentions of Warren in the volume: references to his essays "Not Local Color" and "Some Don'ts for Literary Regionalists," published in 1932 and 1936 respectively. In other words, Warren is considered only by his association with the Agrarian movement.

Such picking and choosing is not uncommon, for one may properly say that Warren is a neglected figure only in the area of his influence in shaping American literature in the twentieth century. Ernest Suarez has convincingly argued that Warren's place (and James Dickey's) in Southern and contemporary poetry has been neglected by literary historians because his accomplishment is not easily contained within the narrow ideological confines that recent historians have depended on to group poets. Warren breaks the mold of too many regionalist and contemporary schools (183–84).

The paradoxical diversity of narrow approaches represented in recent regionalist criticism notwithstanding, one may extract from it certain common traits that come back quite logically to Davidson's critique of the Eastern literary establishment in *The Attack on Leviathan*. Beyond the obvious fact that regionalism has to do with a vital relation between a work of literature and a specific place, regionalist writing by theoretical definition concerns itself with three additional functions. First, a typical regionalist text tends to *emphasize* its difference, both in subject and in approach to its subject, from "nationalist," "universalist," or "local-color" literature. Second, a typical regionalist text tends to approach the issue of region on a small scale, to examine human relations to a specific topography or ecosystem within a larger region. Third, a regionalist text may have a pedagogical intent: that is, a self-conscious strategy to teach readers how to read it by resisting or breaking down the conventional expectations of fiction, and of fiction's relation to culture, fostered by a dominant group. If these are the common traits of a regional literature, I would argue that a significant part of the fifty-year hole that Jordan sees would be filled by a more accurate assessment of the literary concerns and accomplishments of Robert Penn Warren. If informed by Warren's post-Agrarian career, particularly his work after 1950, regionalist theory as it has begun to be accepted in academic circles would be substantially modified. Although it might be aligned with feminist, Native American, and African American critiques of nationalist literature, it would also be understood as a body of literature that resists poststructuralist tendencies to deconstruct the self as the goal of its critique.

In chapter 1 I contrasted Brad Tolliver's analysis of Southern loneliness in *Flood* to the Southern identity expressed by the hero and heroine of George Washington Cable's *John March, Southerner*. If Brad Tolliver is one incarnation of the Southern exile, the moment when he explains Southern loneliness to Yasha Jones is extended in *A Place to Come To*: incarnated as Jed Tewksbury now, the exile seems, by tying consciousness to landscape, to critique the sentiment toward the South exemplified by Cable's lovers:

> I had never been west before, and it was a new kind of loneliness. This new kind, I decided, comes because the distance is fleeing away from you, bleeding away from you, in all directions, and if you can't stop the process you'll be nothing left except a dry, transparent husk, like a cicada's, with the ferocious sunlight blazing through it. So people out there just huddle together like cattle before a storm, but the storm is not of the sky and the elements. Indeed, it is felt most dangerously on the stillest day when the visible fleeing horizon shivers in the brightness of distance. The storm is a purely metaphysical twister that sucks up the self and carries it away. No, I'll go back to the other metaphor: a constant, slow bleeding away into the four quarters of distance.
>
> In any case, this loneliness was, for me, a new kind. For unlike the bleeding away of the self into distance, the kind of loneliness I had known so well—the Southern, not the Western kind—is a bleeding inward of the self, away from all the world around, into an internal infinitude, like a pit. This was the kind I had been bred up to, and I had taken full advantage of my opportunities. I was the original, gold-plated, thirty-third-degree loneliness artist, the champion of Alabama. (93–94)

The tenor of Warren's conceit here of course is the development of consciousness, but the vehicle is more than a clever mechanism. The Southern or, for that matter, any regionalist sensibility *is* a matter of geography, of landscape, as well as a matter of history and community. Though his relation to the South is ambivalent, Brad Tolliver's anxiety is at least in part the result of the same problem of communication faced by Barbara Garnet and John March. If there is no "South," as Brad Tolliver says to Yasha Jones, there is nevertheless a Fiddlersburg, which is what Tolliver tells Jones he himself believes in: a matrix of event, kin, swamp, hill, and subsections in which individual being exists and *knows*—a concrete microregion with a specific terrain and history that shapes the consciousness of its inhabitants and its exiles.

The very form of Warren's novels of the 1960s and early 1970s also bears out his regionalist concerns. Neil Nakadate has explained that with the publication of *Flood* in 1964 a change began to be noticeable. In Warren's later fiction his "chief concern is less with self knowledge per se—the need for it is not discovered here, but assumed—than with the manner and mood of man's conscious pursuit of understanding and verification of the meaning of life" (175). This difference parallels a similar change in Warren's poetry. In the wandering-son poems and in the sometimes overlapping "bird poetry"—*Audubon*, "Evening Hawk," "Red Tail Hawk and Pyre of Youth"—an ontological crisis is the starting point in consciousness, not just the condition discovered. In thematic terms, at least, this is not a great difference from what Warren was doing earlier but a subtle one, and in the end the two questions that seem most significant for Warren's characters—"Who am I?" and "How can I live?"—may actually call for the same answer, or answers. Warren, in his later fiction, is still a writer "given . . . to the interplay of excess, the dramatic clash of opposites conceived and drawn in large outline" (Justus 53). Illusion and fact remain the poles between which his characters struggle in a dialectical process. And his major theme is still the self and its dependence on a sense of continuity and responsibility. A change at the level of thematic realization may be that more and more the possibility for individual fulfillment emerges from the conflict of the "terrible division."

Critics have tended to see a weakening of Warren's powers in the later novels. Calvin Bedient goes so far as to argue that the fiction was a waste of Warren's talent, delaying his creative fulfillment in poetry

(17). His most admiring critics generally favor the work of that period which Jordan defines as a distraction from the cultural implications of the earlier Agrarian years. James Justus perhaps represents this point of view best when he writes that the later fiction "suffers as its worlds grow less political." The contexts of the later novels, compared to the resonances of the political contexts of the first three novels," are "thin." But the differences, as Justus is careful to point out, disappoint our "conventional expectations" (162). The novels from *The Cave* through *Meet Me in the Green Glen* are, indeed, markedly different in their contextual focuses, in their rendered worlds, from Warren's first five novels. Protagonists in *The Cave, Flood,* and *Meet Me in the Green Glen,* are no longer defined, or ill defined, by their willing or reluctant embroilment in political organizations. Instead, their uneasy relationship to a specific place figures significantly in their motivations. Place, of course, is significant in virtually any fiction; in the work of a writer such as Warren, whose genius thrives on the functional description of the minutest details of interiors and landscapes, it is especially important. In *The Cave, Flood, Meet Me in the Green Glen,* and *A Place to Come To,* place rises to special significance in relation to the author's technique as a philosophical novelist: it is place that strives to rise to the level of a massive living symbol.

Warren's treatment of place in the later novels seems very close to the thinking of a number of regionalist theorists. As the concept of *home* is devalued and then reenvisioned by his protagonists, their relation to home becomes their most telling definer. Johnstown (*The Cave*), Fiddlersburg (*Flood*), and Dugton (*A Place to Come To*) are places that become closely associated with the primal being of the protagonists. They are places, moreover, to flee from and return to in compulsory action. Spottwood Valley (*Meet Me in the Green Glen*) becomes for a time a place out of time, like the spot beneath the trees in "Bearded Oaks" where lovers may learn to "practice for eternity."

Furthermore, small-town life in these late novels offers an opportunity for a more direct impingement of one character upon another

and, simultaneously, for less dependence on problematic connections—such as, say, the purely metaphysical brotherhood between
Tiny Duffy and Jack Burden near the end of *All the King's Men*—
to make thematic suggestions. Warren exploits the modest size of his
communities by employing a multiple point of view that both in-
creases readers' awareness of the existential separateness of his characters and somewhat paradoxically creates the possibility for a wider
dispersion of each novel's central vision. *The Cave*, for example,
has no clear single protagonist, but a number of characters come
to a state of reconciliation with their fates through knowledge. Similar multiple "redemptions" occur in *Flood* and *Meet Me in the
Green Glen*.

These three novels, in fact, may be best classified as regionalist
domestic novels, a genre that has developed along several lines in
British and American literature. In England the novels of Jane Aus-
ten, George Eliot, and Thomas Hardy testify to the flexibility of
the form, given various authorial turns of mind. In America the genre
offered rich possibilities for development by nineteenth-century
American women regionalists, as Judith Fetterley and Marjorie Pryse
have taught us to recognize in the important 1992 anthology *American Women Regionalists, 1850–1910*. Their dual emphasis on regional landscape and topography in relation to community *and* do-
mesticity, especially evident in New England (but also in the South
and Southwest), culminated in Sarah Orne Jewett's masterpiece, *The
Country of the Pointed Firs*. In the twentieth century, Ellen Glasgow's
Barren Ground and Welty's *Delta Wedding* and *Losing Battles* are
evidence of the genre's continuing viability. Works in this regionalist
tradition tend to emphasize isolation without resorting to the extreme
remoteness usually associated with the Gothic. Nor as a rule do they
devolve into the fiction of caricature practiced so well by Flannery
O'Connor and so poorly by so many others.

Like many writers in this tradition, Warren narrows his fictional
scope to the close examination of three or four families related to a
specific place in his novels from 1959 to 1972. Examining these nov-

els in the light of this tradition and in the light of the other work he was engaged in during that long decade might force a reconsideration of the terms of critical disappointment with them. Here, however, my discussion of them is necessarily brief to pave the way for a deeper discussion of Warren's most ambitious fictional treatment of the Southern exile, *A Place to Come To.*

Certainly these late novels, with their multiple points of view, bear the stamp of the author of *Brother to Dragons, Segregation,* and *Who Speaks for the Negro?* They show an author continuing his search for a form that would reflect the complexity of experience through the compilation of parallels. The most obvious structural change from the early novels is the absence of the exemplum, the interpolated story. Instead, Warren relies on repetitions of experience within the individual life or a unity-in-diversity realized through the several experiences of central characters. Often the pattern suggests a cyclical movement akin to Yeatsian mythic theory. Nick Pappy of *The Cave,* for example, is a repetitive failure, spiraling downward geographically and spiritually.

In the same novel the guitar of Jack Harrick, which becomes something of an Orphean lyre as Monty Harrick plays it and sings before the mouth of the cave in which his brother Jasper is trapped, is the symbol of a ritualistic transference of power. The guitar, called in the idiom of the hill folk the "box" (a regional figure of speech that suggests emptiness but also the mysterious *gift* that reappears in Warren's poetry), is passed from Jack to Jasper to Monty. But what the father, Jack Harrick, discovers is that not all men are like him: "Every man's got to make his own kind, his own kind of song" (*Cave* 401). With the realization that the boy Monty has gone into the ground to be with his dead brother, Jack begins to play the guitar and sing the same song Monty had improvised earlier at the mouth of the cave. Inheritance flows backward from son to father. The repetition of a pattern here creates an imaginative still place in time.

The plot of *Flood* is based on a repetition of action similar to the ritualistic repetition Yeats employed in his verse drama. Brad Tolliver had brought the young engineer Alfred O. Tuttle to the old Fiddler house where Tuttle either raped or seduced Brad's sister Maggie. Maggie's husband, the physician Calvin Fiddler, killed Tuttle, but only after he was goaded by the talk of the townspeople. Now, with the government reservoir about to flood it, Fiddlersburg is almost absolute in its stasis, so the whole place becomes in outward respects what it had become for Brad already. In other words, it is in microcosm a dark version of what Warren said the whole South had been in his young imagination, a land unchanging. In the nearby penitentiary Calvin Fiddler looks like a boy gone gray, and living in the old Fiddler house, where she takes care of Calvin's mother, Maggie feels like a girl gone gray. The events in time present are essentially repeats of the events of twenty years earlier. Brad returns to Fiddlersburg with the filmmaker Yasha Jones, who, after listening to Maggie's compulsive, Ancient Mariner–like telling of the family's story, falls in love with her. Calvin Fiddler escapes from the penitentiary (the escape itself is a repeated act) and arrives at the old Fiddler house to kill Yasha Jones. This time, Brad —who during the earlier Dionysian episode that he was largely responsible for creating had passed out after brutalizing his wife, Lettice — prevents the murder and in the process gets shot by Calvin Fiddler, who immediately takes steps to save Brad's life.

These two acts of responsible selflessness initiate both men back into life. Calvin Fiddler returns to prison, where he becomes an active physician. Yasha Jones and Maggie Fiddler marry, have a child, and move to Greece to make Yasha's new film. Brad Tolliver, in the novel's final scenes, returns again to the penitentiary to visit Calvin Fiddler and then attends a final church service held to bid a communal farewell to Fiddlersburg. He cannot understand the tears that flood his eyes at the novel's end, but the reader sees his weeping as yet another repetition in the novel: Brad's swamp-rat father, during times of oppressive loneliness, had returned to the swamp to get drunk and weep. There is no Jack Burden to synthesize and articulate the meaning of all this experience. The meaning lies more in the ritualized repetition of a pattern such as Brad's weeping (or the son's lifted hand in "Covered Bridge") than in analysis. Warren seems to depend increasingly on a representative situation rather than on representative men. It would be overstating the case to say that he finally rejected history in his fiction—as Walter Sullivan argues (106)—but in less absolute terms one might say that an important development in Warren's technique was a deemphasis of history and an emerging emphasis on knowledge through myth. It is myth as a complement of history, however—as L. Hugh Moore has said, an accommodation of history to man (20).

This change in narrative method is closely associated with the evolution of Warren's use of place in fiction. Fiddlersburg is dead long before the floodwaters come. As Maggie Fiddler says, it is a place where, when something falls down, no one bothers to pick it up again (46). A communal listlessness makes the town an image of impotence much like Camelot after the betrayal. The only change in Fiddlersburg is the slow change of decay, and it becomes associated in Brad Tolliver's mind, as home often does for Warren's protagonists, with a repulsive paternity. Yet it is simultaneously associated with a primal unity to which Brad longs to return. Place becomes a metaphor for self, but, paradoxically, only after one accepts the place of origin can he transcend it in any way to achieve a spiritual vision. To deny one's origin is a flaw fatal to selfhood.

Nevertheless, that denial seems necessary to American success. Warren's exile figure is almost always an American success, through whom he creates a psychic split akin to the one W. E. B. Du Bois identified in the American black or a dual perspective somewhat like what Peter Caccavari has identified in the carpetbaggers of the Reconstruction fiction of Algernon Tourgee. Warren's interest, however, is in the reconstruction of the individual.

Warren's most extensive treatment of the link between the Southern exile and American success would be through Jed Tewksbury in *A*

Place to Come To. Just as in his late poetry the flight of wild birds comes to be an emblem of identification with achieved selfhood, in Warren's final novel the concept of home becomes an idea associated with the self's relation to the world. It is not a new concept but a reaffirmation and new exploration of an idea Warren pondered as early as "Original Sin" and "The Ballad of Billie Potts." The place one comes from leaves an indelible impression on self, and it may be, as Victor Strandberg has argued, associated with a sense of the primal self which is recoverable "only through the medium of the remembered image, or poetry" ("Poet of Youth" 92). Warren's definition of home, however, as "not a place" but "a state of spirit . . . of feeling, . . . of mind, a proper relationship to a world" (Watkins and Hiers 102) is inwardly shouted by Brad Tolliver at the end of *Flood:* "There is no country but the heart" (440). Warren indicates his preference for Romantic individualism or the plurality of "a world" in his definition of reality, as opposed to a neoclassical or naturalistic singular, "the world." But taking it in context, one can see that he presses that idea in full knowledge of the dangers of solipsism. Conscious of irony, insisting on it, in fact, he neither purifies self-identity nor deconstructs it.

Coming home is synonymous with coming to a point of vision, for one does not truly come home until there is an imaginative integration of the past associated with home — be it a past of mental anguish or of nostalgic comfort — with the present. In this sense one *achieves* "home." One does not go home again; one, in a sense, remakes home. In the context of Warren's late novels, especially the last one, home *is* a "place to come to." In certain respects *A Place to Come To* brings the Warren reader full circle back to some of his earliest writing.

The return is still an important pattern in the last novel, and as always it involves a coming to terms with the past. As Justus writes, "The pattern of return, both literal and imagined, is the most frequent structural device for the protagonist as exile, and that struggle with one's physical home — its values, its lingering capacity to reward and punish, its ability to assert its own numinous identity—is often an aesthetic analogue for the greater struggle for self-definition on which one's very psychic health depends" (304). Warren's final fictional protagonist is still, in one sense, the same wanderer/son first introduced in the early poetry, and there has been general agreement that Warren revisits most of his old themes here. Joseph Blotner writes, "The novel's concerns have been clearly perceived [by critics]: the problem of the deracinated individual seeking a secure set of values in a civilization in decline, the search for identity, and the acceptance of the past" (437–38). Given all this, however, the novel's main concern is the split within the man who seeks the plasticity and anonymity requisite for success in the twentieth century yet is too haunted by reality to pull off the great psychic con on himself. In this case the wanderer tells the story of his life into middle age. As always the emphasis is on finding a way to live, so the place to come to is not the grave, as Richard Howard suggests (73). The place is "home," the poise of mind one might achieve before the grave.

Warren named *A Place to Come To* along with *All the King's Men* and *World Enough and Time* as his most satisfying novels, though he had named *Flood* as the third before he wrote *A Place to Come To* (Blotner 438, 357). Many of his most admiring critics have disagreed, attributing Warren's enthusiasm to the artist's tendency to think his most recent work his best. But we may understand Warren's assessment better by thinking of *A Place to Come To* not as the last word he would write on the subject but as a major fictional capstone for the exile motif we have now seen him building over the course of his career. I indicated in chapter 1 something of this novel's large scope. In many ways it is broader in scope than the first five novels and certainly much broader than those that immediately preceded it. Furthermore, compared with the rendering of events in the individual lives of characters in some of the other late novels, Jed Tewksbury's experience is revealed with far more fullness and immediacy. Jed speaks directly to the reader with the secret-sharer intimacy of a Jack Burden, though Jed's is a more ponderous voice.

Another critical tendency has been to read the novel as part of the drift in late Warren to throw off provincial narrowness for a refreshing and even cosmopolitan view of experience (Bohner 154). Certainly its world is broader and inhabited by more sophisticated characters than the fictional worlds of *The Cave, Flood,* and *Meet Me in the Green Glen.* Nevertheless, *A Place to Come To* is Warren's most regionally minded novel. Everywhere Jed goes he reflects on his South. The Chicago he lives in is, despite the presence of Dr. Stahlmann, the same Chicago as that of Walker Percy's *The Moviegoer,* a place where the Midwestern sky "is the nakedest loneliest sky in America" (203). Ripley City, South Dakota, the home of Jed's first wife, Agnes—where the two of them are married and where, relatively soon after, she is buried—is, despite its own provincialism, no more a *place* for Jed than Chicago. Although he is accepted as family by the people there, he can only for a short time believe that the spot of ground beside Agnes is his place to come to. For some reason Jed cannot have the peaceful life represented by his first wife and Ripley City. Eventually, the spot where Agnes is buried becomes the place in darkness, under a blanket of snow, where his loved one lies. It assumes otherworldly qualities.

In Europe, as a soldier and later as a scholar, Jed is directly confronted by the problem of "home." The Italian partisans he fights with are fighting for their *terra* rather than for their country. The problem Jed faces in knowing his own history is made clear by his difficulty in finding the English equivalent of *terra.* Even the Nashville that Warren writes about in this novel is not Southern—or rather it is somewhat officially, hence artificially, Southern; its chief representative, Lawford Carrington, "Mr. Nashville," seems almost stereotypically sculpted for the role of Southern hero, given his lineage and the fact that he is "so goddamned Greekly handsome" (131). Yet he must undergo all the failures and diminishment that the hero cut in that mold faces in the modern world: vital action is replaced by sport—swimming and tennis; a sense of community, by parties; and the sense of self and tradition, by an inferiority complex as large as the barn he converts into his home.

Warren makes much of the fact that this renovated stone barn is unusual for that section, unlike the converted barn Warren himself lived in with his family in Fairfield, Connecticut, after 1952 (Blotner 282). Carrington is imposing his will on the landscape with unusual, borrowed, or imported architectural symbols. His art, too, comes in for a critique as less than indigenous, for it means nothing to him if it cannot pass New York standards. As his wife, "Rose" Hardcastle Carrington is both an inspiration for his art and one of the accoutrements of his heavily stylized life.

With the individual power of neither, Carrington has the flair of a Jay Gatsby or a Thomas Sutpen in his attempt to impose his will on others and the natural world; and despite the fact that as an insider he should have more substantial relations to a community than either of them, he has all their emptiness, finally. The people that complete the Carringtons' social circle — except for the Cudworths, Mrs. Jones-Talbot, and the McInnises — play very hard at being cosmopolites, enchanted with trendy foreignness. Through the converted barn men and women come and go talking of mystic poetry, exotic sexual positions, massage techniques, and the comic exoticism of the strange South — the last provided largely by Jed himself.

For Jed the whole experience seems detached from reality, and the detachment and fragmentation of the Nashville episode are emphasized by his narrative method in presenting it: he recalls individuated scenes as though (his analogy) he were turning over greeting cards with pictures on them. Narrative, here and elsewhere, gives way to sequencing similar to the kind Warren came to rely on in his poetry, and here again the purpose seems to be to achieve a certain psychological distance from the object. Other examples of official or documentary distancing in the novel include Jed's recollection of the scenes during the aftermath of his father's death. They are scenes not related to him but rather like "a picture seen in one of those books of photographs of the South published during the Depression years when the region was dubbed the nation's Economic Problem Number One" (7–8). These instances of "symbolic memory" must be connected to a larger pattern of "narrative memory" in order to be made real and vital. But Jed, like the wandering son of the poetry, avoids this process at times by relying on the standard interpretations. His stay in Nashville, like his travels through all the places of the novel, is an attempt to escape the contamination of Dugton. The contamination of home is signified for Jed — as it is for Cy Grinder in *Meet Me in the Green Glen* and Brad Tolliver in *Flood* — by an embarrassing paternity. The story of *A Place to Come To* is the story of Jed Tewksbury's acceptance of and return to Dugton as a corollary to his acceptance of his own fate and his own responsibility in that fate.

In Jed, Warren dramatizes universal separation through a local, Southern milieu, continuing to work in a fiction of extremes. The extreme is suggested by the novel's opening paragraph, one of the most interesting in contemporary fiction and significant enough to quote again here:

> I was the only boy, or girl either, in the public school of the town of Dugton, Claxford County, Alabama, whose father had ever got killed in the middle of the night standing up on the front of his wagon to piss on the hindquarters of one of a span of mules, and being drunk, pitching forward on his head, still hanging on to his dong, and hitting the pike in such a position and condition that both the left front and the left rear wheels of the wagon rolled, with perfect precision, over his unconscious neck, his having passed out being, no doubt, the reason he took the fatal plunge in the first place. Throughout, he was still holding on to his dong. (3)

Again, the novel's opening suggests that Jed has reached something akin to a stand-up comic's distance from his source material. He escapes the stain of being Southern by assuming the role of official Southerner, becoming, as it were, an ethnic comedian, "looting Erskine Caldwell" for material when he finds his Chicago colleagues interested in things Southern: poverty, fascism, literature (22). Thus Warren gives us the figure for whom there is always an undercurrent of reality beneath a smooth, official surface. It is easier to live among

the uninitiated if one gives them the clichés they expect, what Warren in *Segregation* called the "cliché of fear" and the "cliché of hate"
(9, 11). But the novel also foregrounds the issue of Southernness in
this way, becoming an exposé of the exposés by writers such as Caldwell and photographers such as Walker Evans. Warren shows that the
"official" literary vision of the South has created an atmosphere of
epistemological comfort and moral complacency in regard to the
South among northern intellectuals and the Southerners who become interlopers in that atmosphere.

One suggestion of the undercurrent of reality in Jed's experience
occurs in one of the Cudworth episodes and offers much insight into
the subconscious of Jed Tewksbury as well as further evidence of Warren's regionalist concerns in the novel. Visiting the farm Cud urges
him to buy, Jed encounters a tenant whose figure seems to resonate
in several directions.

> As I stand there, I become aware that the man in the patched and
> faded overalls, the tenant of the farm, is covertly watching me. He is
> a man in his fifties, once robust and handsome, but now stooped and
> with muscles thinning on the big bones, and long ragged mustaches,
> once black but now gray-streaked, and the gray stained yellow with to-
> bacco juice, and under the shadow of the low-pulled brim of the old
> worn-out black felt hat, the eyes, bloodshot and defeated, glare in out-
> rage at me. He reminds me, in that moment, of the pictures by Brady,
> and other such photographers, of Confederate prisoners captured in
> late, disastrous battles of the war. As he spies at me from under the
> shadow of the low-pulled brim, he is, I see, secretly chewing at the long,
> ragged mustaches. (177–78)

In addition to being a fine example of Warren's skill in suggesting tensions through surface description, this photographic portrayal reso-
nates with connections to Jed's father, who would have been about
the age of this man and who bore some resemblance to him in his
features. Through the shadow imagery the outraged glare takes on

implications other than those of economic deprival and class separation. The connection is deepened by the allusion to Confederate prisoners, as one of Buck's favorite drunken pastimes had been to pretend he was a Confederate soldier. Jed undergoes an unacknowledged Hamlet-like visitation of the ghost of his father here, and the visitation plays no small part in his refusing to buy the farm.

The photographic nature of the image, furthermore, connects it with others that form a "poor white" motif in the tapestry of the novel's structure, studded as it is by a sequential method of "scenes" that often breaks down the larger chronological frame. In this way the novel reveals the influence of Warren's development as a poet — the interconnectedness of all his work, really, as he turned more and more to personal subjects. Memories projected as scenes and connected by similarity of detail contribute to the mirror effect and theme. But with the collection of scenes of rural poverty as well as a number of direct allusions, Warren actually puts the story in the context of a literary interpretation of the rural South. He evokes names such as James Agee, Caldwell, and Evans not simply as a gloss but as a kind of official view of the South, a view that proves inadequate to the inner needs of the exile, although, like most of the nation, he would like to adopt it.

The novel's implicit argument with the documentarians is carried out with little defensiveness, however, for by aligning himself with these forces Jed participates in the communion of Pharisees as an ironic observer — an interloper, as he says — finding in the documentary mode of the 1930s a proper distance from his own childhood which passes for scientific objectivity. And in "looting Erskine Caldwell" he finds a way to pacify his Northern colleagues' anthropological curiosity about the South by playing the role of a Southerner (22). To live with the past he must, like Faulkner's Quentin Compson, refashion and order it. Jed's particular way, to repeat, is to adopt the attitude of the stand-up comic who mines his personal past for material and turns his pain into social and economic triumph. But he is too self-conscious to get by with the game. It is when he plays the role of the Southerner in Nashville that meaning seems most difficult to brush aside, as in the case of his relations with Maria McInnis and again in the photographic essay on the tenant. The danger of meaningfulness is the great threat to the psychic balance Jed holds through cynicism.

Another part of the undercurrent of reality for Jed takes shape in the force of his mother's life. Though she is a proud woman determined both to survive the indignity dealt her by her uproarious husband and to give her son an opportunity for a better life, the extremities of poverty and hardship in Elvira Tewksbury's life have made her an extremist in certain ways herself. During scenes of Buck Tewksbury's wildest actions she sits with a blankness of being that reminds readers of Faulkner's abused Mrs. Henry Armstid in the "The Peasants" section of *The Hamlet* (298). Yet when she sees history repeating itself as Jed begins drinking and whoring, Elvira physically attacks him in his bed and breaks his nose with a shoe. Eventually she insists that Jed leave Dugton and never return.

On the surface it may appear that such extreme action as Buck Tewksbury's carousing and death and Elvira Tewksbury's beating of her son actually reinforces the "strange South" syndrome that Northern and Southern "liberals" had taken for gospel from Caldwell and others. But as Elvira's character unfolds over the course of the novel through her letters, readers begin to understand that her life is invested with the kind of reality that works against the atrophied, official version. Her letters are marvelously funny, but not merely as examples of traditional dialect humor. They are funny because, rather than a caricature, she is a fully realized human being with a sense of humor. Her letters reveal the love she finds with Perk Simms and the contempt she always feels for "Miss Pritty-Pants," Rozelle Hardcastle. She is a woman of both pride and self-humor, qualities illustrated when she encloses with one of the letters a photograph showing her new teeth. And she is a woman with a strong sexual nature, illustrated when she recalls for Jed with some relish what a forceful and handsome man his father had been. But she is also a woman wounded.

She longs to see her grandson but will not relent and ask Jed to bring him to her. She is among the strongest and most fully realized women characters in the Warren canon, even though she appears for the most part only through her letters. But these letters function as documents that counter the documentaries Jed alternately relies on and critiques as "official" exposés of the South.

James Justus has argued that Warren's linking of poverty and spiritual dislocation distinguishes him from most of the other Agrarians (313). Yet although Warren pulls no punches in depicting Southern poverty and its effects, he does challenge the documentary school of Southern letters on epistemological grounds. In *Segregation* he acknowledges the factuality underlying the "cliché of fear" and the "cliché of hate" which were standard fare for the documentarians, but he goes on to reveal an unsettling pluralism that constitutes not so much a rhetorical apology for the South as a challenge to the documentarians to examine their own motives as they draw their conclusions. As Warren has Jed Tewksbury evoke images from Caldwell, Evans, and others, he accomplishes something quite similar. One effect of the official literary and mass media treatments of the South is that they offer a refuge for the Southern exile, an acceptable point of view to adopt. A long passage early in the novel reveals a great deal about Warren's perspective on the psychology of the Southern exile and illustrates how he characteristically locates that perspective in relation to those of other Southerners. The scene occurs in Chicago at the apartment of Dauphine Finkel, Jed's fellow graduate student and lover, after Jed has reenacted the death of his father. He writes of himself in the third person, suggesting the shame he later feels over the incident but also the detachment customary for the exile:

> Inflamed by adulation, he began to play the role of Southerner to the hilt. He carefully improved his diction (with some unhappy side-effects on his study of Romance languages), tried to recall folksy locutions, and looted the works of Erskine Caldwell, an especially juicy Southern writer of that period, for material to use in constructing his own family

history. He even invented certain episodes, and one of them won special acclaim: his father, returning late at night and plum-tuckered from a lynching over in the next county, didn't forget to leave a little keepsake on the tyke's pillow—carefully wrapped in a piece of waxed paper, a really-truly nigger ear to dry and carry as a luck charm. This episode was, of course, set back in the earlier years of the tyke's childhood, before drink had begun seriously to corrode the natural tenderness of the father's nature as well as family relations on the Tewksbury farmstead. (22)

Although other passages in the novel acknowledge the validity of fact captured by some of the documentarians, here, by having Jed imitate them with wild success, Warren suggests the voracious appetite for the strange South among readers which the documentarians satisfy. But the strain of wearing such a mask is enormous and cannot, in Jed's case, be maintained for very long. Asked to perform again a few nights later he angrily assumes his cracker voice and blows his cover: "You know, I jest wonders why ain't none of you folks ever told me how any of yore fucken fathers died" (22).

Perhaps the difference between the extreme action in Warren's tenth novel and in the regional domestic novels that preceded it and the extreme action in a Southern Grotesque, Southern Gothic, or Southern documentary novel is not so much in the action itself as in the emotional content invested in that action, the heart's engagement with it. The parallel personal and regional dimensions of Warren's writing may be considered, again, intertextually. The local/cosmopolitan and past/present conflicts explored through dream visions at the personal level in the wandering-son poems seem to require a modification of form when Warren explores them from a more obviously communal perspective. The result in one instance is a poem that represents Warren's only experiment with a form we have come to classify as magic realism, "Dragon Country."

Part of the function of extraordinary action and condition may be suggested by Warren's symbolism in this poem, whose appearance alongside the other personal poems about his children and his past in *Promises* suggests that the poet's going back into his regional past was part of that reconciliation process of which James Perkins has written. The elusive dragon in the poem ravages the Todd County, Kentucky, countryside, but the initial terror gives way to denial as Northern papers and even Southern big city papers make fun of official efforts to deal with the problem: for calling out the national guard the governor is branded St. George of Kentucky. Meanwhile, the dragon continues to drain the life of the place, as Warren's allusion to the historical mass migration from the South indicates:

> If a man disappears—well, the fact is something to hide.
> The family says, gone to Akron, or up to Ford, in Detroit.
> When we found Jebb Johnson's boot, with the leg, what was left,
> inside,
> His mother said, no, it's not his. So we took it out to destroy it. (*New and Selected Poems* 276)

The dragon may represent those forces — economic, social, psychological — that have depleted the human resources of the South in this century. As the symbolism suggests, only parts of men are to be found, and the land becomes a wasteland:

> Land values are falling, no longer do lovers in moonlight go.
> The rabbit, thoughtless of air gun, in the nearest pasture cavorts.
> Now certain fields go untended, the local birth rate goes low.
> The coon dips his little black paw in the riffle where he nightly
> resorts. (276)

But later the dragon's kinship with the Theban Sphinx becomes clear: it is the force that makes wisdom a necessity. It is the "Necessity of truth" which treads the land and brings the pain that paradoxically makes joy possible, for without it "life might dwindle again / To the ennui, the pleasure, and the night sweat, known in the time before" (276). The complacency of the Thebans who too easily forgot their murdered king in the peace brought to the city by the human wisdom of Oedipus seems to be invoked here. Whatever its universal implications, the local and immediate referent of the Dragon is that consciousness of Southernness, or perhaps of conditions in the South, which made it necessary to refuse the comfort of the Great Alibi. But the psychological effect could cut two ways, denial and partial humanity being one result.

The poem might well function as an epigraph for much of Warren's late fiction. The conditions it describes could be applied to Claxford County, Alabama, as well as to Todd County, Kentucky, conditions that provide a background for understanding the psychological makeup of a Jed Tewksbury. As long as his past is something he denies, he is a partial man, as even his mother can see when at last she cries out that the accolades of the world will do him no good when the lonesome time comes (398). The legend of Buck Tewksbury is, perhaps, the personal dragon he must come to grips with, but Buck represents a cultural as well as a familial dragon. Without these local meanings, without locating them in relation to their specific significance in his past, Jed cannot understand the human constants that the tragedy of Buck Tewksbury's life comes at last to represent for him. Warren, in fact, does use the kind of extraordinary action associated with Romance in the novel, but the official snicker is just that, official, and the exile is afforded an opportunity to bypass participation in the official snicker. It is a means of his success. What the novel finally reveals is that the extreme action is the result of extreme human emotion and desire; Elvira and Buck are invested with a humanity with which the comedian and technocrat Jed Tewksbury must come to terms. The process of his learning is not on the typical bildungsroman pattern. His growth is measurable through the course of his familial, amorous, and professional relationships; intertwining, these bind, release, and return to him complexly at various points in the novel.

In the last glimpse Jed has of his mother she has been drinking and having sex — ironically, the combination of offenses on her son's part that had earlier led her to break his nose. Like Jack Burden before him, Jed is disturbed by the discovery of his mother's identity as a sexual being, and he leaves her house without speaking to her, assuming a superiority over her apparent hypocrisies. Elvira's sexuality is, of course, a humanizing factor, and her experience is connected to a larger series of sexual acts that make sexuality a major theme of the novel. Jed's sexual adventuring is, in fact, one way to chart his career in exile, and he experiences enough of it to make us think of him as a traditional rogue. But placing too much emphasis on that interpretation risks overshadowing a major subtheme Warren develops involving the sexuality of women. In the Dugton of Jed's youth the female sex was divided between "poontang" and untouchables like Rozelle Hardcastle, whose last name suggests both the chastity and the value she represents for the town. Rozelle is the beauty queen of Dugton, and Warren evokes the tradition of heroic narrative which his own narrative undermines by making her, as the "law of nature" dictates, the betrothed of Chester Burton, the richest boy in town. When Rozelle violates the pattern and shows an interest in Jed, the poor white, the full effect of his bitterness at his class and family bars any union the two might have enjoyed. He abandons Rozelle at a high school dance, behavior reminiscent of Cy Grinder's abandonment of Cassie Spottwood in a hospital in *Meet Me in the Green Glen* for the same reason — self-hatred.

Cy Grinder tries subsequently to transform himself from poor white into technocrat by taking a correspondence course in engineering. Failing at that, he succumbs not to his fate so much as to fatalism and marries the poor Gladys Peegrum, thinking of the marriage as the crowning glory of his white-trash existence. Jed, as part of the logical process of his own transformation program, enters the new worlds of ancient languages and eventually a famous Midwestern university. Later, having returned to Chicago after World War II, he meets and marries fellow graduate student Agnes Andresen from Ripley City, South Dakota. The marriage occasions one of Jed's first comparative studies of place as he learns the difference between Western and Southern loneliness, a difference he emphasizes in the passage quoted early in this chapter. In that passage his shifting back and forth between metaphors — distance bleeding away from the self, and a metaphysical storm — to describe Western loneliness is a good example of Jed's tendency to use and revise metaphors in a fashion similar to the process we saw earlier in *Brother to Dragons*: testing language as a test of experience. The passage also suggests that loneliness, the novel's major theme, is a human condition but one that must be examined in its different manifestations to be understood. Western loneliness is a loneliness of landscape, and despite Jed's unflattering comparison of Westerners to cattle, community offers a kind of defense against it. But Jed's more intimate knowledge of Southern loneliness as a bleeding inward of the self makes him conscious of a loneliness of history as well as of landscape, of a people stranded in time without even the belief in the power of reenactment to connect them to their past. Buck Tewksbury's drunken reenactments of Civil War battles and Lawford Carrington's near parodic imitations of the heroic past are examples of the futility. But according to Jed it is this very loneliness that accounts for his own success. The bleeding inward, rather than the bleeding away, necessitates a negative self-reliance — negative because it depends on a surface reality that is radically different from the inner reality. The Alabama loneliness artist is a special breed of the American confidence man.

To understand the significance of this fact we can pursue the significance of one apparent source for Warren's development of Jed's early adult career, particularly the episodes concerning his relationship with Agnes. The source, it seems reasonable to speculate, was that historical South-hater, humorist, and self-styled con artist Sam Clemens — or, more specifically, Clemens's marriage to Olivia Langdon. Warren did considerable work on Twain in the 1970s, both critically and creatively: first for *American Literature: The Makers and the Making* (edited with Cleanth Brooks and R. W. B. Lewis) and for the essay "Mark Twain" (*New and Selected Essays*), published in the *Southern Review* in 1972; later on, closer to the publication of *A Place to Come To*, in "Last Laugh." In that poem Warren locates the origin of Sam Clemens's humor in a nihilism born after seeing his father's autopsied body: "It's not every night / You can see God butchered in such learned dismemberments" (*Now and Then* 57). That Clemens's "joke," the death of God, gradually destroyed the faith of his wife was a point Warren had emphasized in his essay on Twain earlier. In the poem Livy dies staring up at a comfortless sky, her death resembling the death of Agnes Andreson Tewksbury, whose own Christian faith had eroded during her marriage to Jed.

Before he marries Agnes, Jed has twice seen a father figure *exposed*. Even before the embarrassment of his father's death, the boy saw him fall drunk against the hearth and lay himself out "like a stunned beef," an analogy that recalls the butchering metaphor of "Last Laugh." "When I was little," Jed writes, "I'd see the body lying over there cool-cocked drunk, and [my mother] sitting across from it, not close, and staring at it, and it was like holding your breath until your head swam and something was about to explode" (4–5). Later, Jed discovers the body of his mentor, Heinrich Stahlmann, who has committed suicide in the shower:

> Then I saw the bare feet sticking out from under the curtain of the little box shower.
> There he was.
> He was sitting on the floor, wearing his underwear shorts. His head was bowed forward on his chest. The legs, stuck out straight before him, looked very thin and white, as though long submerged in water, with the veins large, slightly varicose, and blue. The old Luger was on the cement bottom of the cubicle. The hole was neatly over the heart. (77)

These moments of exposure of "father" are associated with discovery, or at least expectancy. If the exposed body of the "cool-cocked" (pun not only intended but practically shameful) Buck Tewksbury brings the boy Jed to the verge of an awful discovery, the exposure of the dead Stahlmann is associated with a less encompassing knowledge yet evoked through a similar image of disempowerment. Jed enlists immediately after Stahlmann's funeral. "In case of a landslide," he explains in an allusion to the theory of history that Stahlman developed after watching a hare being crushed by a landslide, "I had discovered that I'd rather be a boulder than a rabbit" (77).

Jed's marriage to Agnes is based on common professional interests, order, and security; it is a "little floating island, cut off from the world" (99). But like Twain in his marriage to Olivia, Jed is subject simultaneously to contradictory sexual or antisocial forces and to his need for the respectability and calm Agnes can provide. He breaks the protocol of the civilization she represents by substituting bourbon for sherry and initiating rather rough sex at unaccustomed times. Agnes's desire is for the comfort associated with the Western hospitality of Ripley City, the desire "to add one more chunk of human warmth to the therapeutic huddle" (94). But for Jed the marriage is a refuge from the personal past, the same source of anguish Warren saw in the "loneliness artist" Twain. Jed can therefore not achieve the level of intimacy that Agnes expects to warm the domestic hearth.

She is quite naturally shocked when he tells her why he will never take her to Alabama to meet his mother:

> My mother . . . is a woman of great strength of character, and many remarkable qualities, including a trenchant, sardonic humor, but she is of minimal education and no talent for handling abstractions, and you and she would find few ideas to exchange. To characterize her further, she must have been very good-looking in her girlhood, but as is usual among pore white trash—the class to which we, though my mother would hotly deny it, may be said to belong—whatever beauty she had has long since been ravaged. But one more detail. Though she is a rather small-built woman, with small hands, hard work long ago toughened them to the texture of cast iron. And, oh yes, this reminds me that, in her letter, she said I should tell you how I got this broke-nose look. (98)

Jed's dispassionate honesty leaves Agnes and readers reeling, but it is possible only because of his clinical detachment, marked by his classroom diction—"few ideas to exchange"—and his textbook use of transitions: "To characterize her further," "But one more detail." It is familiar to Warren readers, of course, as the kind of professional detachment adopted by the son in such poems as "Natural History." The same tone of detachment is associated with Jed's professional success, which surges with Agnes's death. Jed's informing her in this way that there are places in his psyche where she cannot go initiates what becomes a widening breach between the two, culminating in Agnes's irrationally (and momentarily) blaming him for her development of uterine cancer and Jed's partial displacement at her bedside by her former and still faithful beau, who also blames Jed for what is happening to Agnes. In his Twain-like guilt, compounded by the fact that he has destroyed her faith (she tells him on her deathbed that he was right, there is no God), her physical condition becomes associated for Jed with the spiritual death he feels he has caused her. To escape the grief and guilt, irrational but of course real feelings, he plunges into the detached process of composing "Dante and the Metaphysics of Death"—the essay that "makes him," professionally speaking.

The God-bereft deathbed, with Jed having consciously to remind himself that Agnes's spasms are merely soulless mechanical twitches, seems both to recall and to counter their first episode of lovemaking: at the moment of orgasm Jed had broken out in laughter, shocking and insulting Agnes. And when he tried to comfort her by comparing his feeling to the religious ecstasy of Holy Rollers or other Pentecostals, he made matters even worse.

That equation of physical and religious ecstasy is later displaced by a purer, and safer, mechanical explanation of feeling. During his affair with Rozelle Hardcastle Carrington in Nashville, his metaphor for orgasm demonstrates the further development of his characteristic way of depersonalizing experience: "the orgasm was like the 'black hole' . . . a devouring negativity into which all the nags and positives of life may simply disappear like dirty water when the plug is pulled at the bottom of the sink. It was the death in life-beyond-Time without which life-in-Time might not be endurable, or even possible" (220–21).

The pun in this instance is such low comedy that it is hard to take

beside the philosophical sentiment with which the passage concludes, but the low comedy is par for Jed's view of his existence as a
man of pure action during this period. Nothing makes it clearer that
he adopts the language of mythology and the language of technology,
and sometimes combines the two, in a strategy of self-negation than
his description of sex with Rozelle. In his hands, literally, she is transformed from the beauty queen of Dugton (or in the less reverent
language of Jed's mother, "Miss Pritty-Pants") and from Mrs. Lawford
Carrington (Rose), into the "archetypal ass." Jed's floral language
ironically designates the rose she represents for him. In the following
passage he narrates what happens after he pulls her crotch against his
thigh and feels a stabbing sensation at the spot where the two touch:

> Bemused in that sensation, I held the body pressed against my thigh,
> then, suddenly, pushed it from me, and looked down. First at that spot
> on my leg where the stab was and where dampness gleamed, then at
> what I supported in my hands, the thighs that, slowly and whitely, had
> fallen further apart to present, in the midst of the lush yet brambly-
> looking pubic corona of damp-curling, bronze-gold hair, the orchida-
> ceous swell of the waiting sex. Staring down at it, what I was aware of
> was not the poetry of the yearning, anonymous wound with the faint
> gleam of light caught there to give some hint of the roseate inwardness,
> but for the first time in my life, of the true, archetypal ass, the unbolted
> breech so simplistically and brutally designed for its blankly abstract
> function and the plunge into depersonalized, and depersonalizing,
> darkness. (197)

Jed even perverts Cartesian law by half comically assuming as his
motto *debatuo ergo sum*, which he translates as "I fuck, therefore I
am" (218). Rozelle, too, participates in making sex a druglike escape,
commanding Jed at moments of her deepest anguish, "Fuck me. . . .
For God's sake, quick" (204).

With the "black hole," he and Rozelle make another island cut off
from the world, a very different kind of island from the one initiated

by the orgasm of the Holy Laugh with Agnes. The deluging of this island, however, is foreshadowed by two distinct pieces of evidence of meaningful connection to the outer world. One is Jed's growing jealousy of Rozelle's husband, Lawford Carrington. The other is the behavior of Maria McInnis, who might have become Jed's lover had things gone differently. Her mother's long suffering from a psychotic condition has been a source of pain for Maria, just as Jed's father has been a source of pain for him. Maria says that Jed's story of his father's death saved her by making it possible for her to face the reality of her family's condition. The past is not a joke, then, but a force. Even the Southern experience is less a joke than most of these characters seem to think. And Jed comes to see that "the world survives all contempt, even that of lovers" (209), a statement that applies as well to the lovers in *Meet Me in the Green Glen*, whose affair closely resembles Jed and Rozelle's. What Jed must confront again is that there *are* meaning and interconnection in the world, and that he is an agent of them.

Jed's third significant relationship with a woman occurs back in Chicago (after the year in Nashville), where he attempts to live by a new set of vows to join the human race. Civic responsibilities and matrimony become the external signs of a new order. He registers as a Chicago Democrat, joins a Neighborhood Defense Association, and rings doorbells for worthy causes (335). He marries Dauphine Finkel, whom he had known intimately during his first sojourn in Chicago. An intelligent progressive leftist who had introduced him to the "ideas that were going to redeem the world," she had also "been able to forget to say something instructive and curl up silently into [his] arms" while he, feeling her heartbeat, "could become fleetingly aware of a nameless truth deeper than any ironclad opinion [they] might learn to share" (336–37). During that prewar love affair with Dauphine, Jed finally got himself kicked out of her apartment by calling attention to the political inconsistencies in "her passionate defense of Adolf Hitler's virtues and the beauty of his friendship with Stalin" and observing that "for a Chicago Jewess, no matter how rich or insulated from reality and logic, to take up with that cruddy little house painter–turned–mass murderer smacked of a deficiency of racial self-respect" (24). Warren compounds experiences here. Quite capable of pointing out "reality and logic" on these points to Dauphine, Jed is deeply disturbed by but unable intellectually to cope with similar inconsistencies in himself. Dauphine, who had apparently enjoyed the successful displays of ethnic comedy on Jed's part at the earlier party, did not realize the irony in her calling him a "redneck Southern fascist" after he employed the same persona to insult her friends.

By the time they meet again and marry in Chicago, both are professionally successful, and the marriage initially works out well. They respect each other's work, attend functions and parties together, and make the "beast-with-two-backs." But there is also a return of the chance for spiritual fulfillment with Dauphine, as when Jed describes her face "straining to enter into the truth of the truthless music" at concerts they attend together (337). More than anything else, the son born of their union, Ephraim, gives rise to a whole new experience of love for Jed:

> The little character . . . was the joy of my heart. I loved the nights when, after he was abed, my wife and I sat together and a less shadowy music, for a period anyway, flowed over her face. But—dare I be honest enough to say—I loved most the nights when, because of the pressure of my work, real or pretended, I was alone with him while my wife went out—to "keep fences built," as she put it. I could hold him on my lap to my heart's content. I could bathe him, and in the process investigate every little gleaming and flowery part of him. I could feed him, in the early time of bottle and later by the little curved-handled silver spoon from which his mother had once fed, enraptured to have a hand in the sacred process by which life went on, interrupting myself with such a flow and flood of nonsense that even now I blush to remember them. (338)

It isn't ordinary baby talk but long, improvised conversations on Sophocles, the Old Testament, Shakespeare, and other literary figures, which prove embarrassing later. We may also note how the language of "sacred process," the investigation of "every little gleaming and flowery part of him," undeniably recalls the language describing the sexual episode with Rozelle. Here, however, the physique of the son is associated with heart's content, with poetry and sacredness, rather than with brutal function.

Yet within two pages Jed records the end of the bliss of several years and the shocking thought: "How much simpler things would be if [Ephraim] did not exist!" Daupine's unhappiness in their marriage seems to be revealed to him suddenly and wholly one Sunday morning, but his reaction suggests that he was somehow prepared for it. He reflects on those evenings with Ephraim and on his own past but realizes that all along he had fled from the past to those evenings, to his civic responsibilities, and to his high-profile marriage. For all his intellect and education he is like Bobbie Ann Mason's disabled truck driver Leroy Moffitt in "Shiloh," who has left the insides out of marriage and history and whose Popsicle-stick and Lincoln-Log models correspond to Jed's laurels and stack of three-by-five note cards as emblems of distance from reality.

Intimations of what is missing from the marriage are suggested for Jed by occasional "weakness" when, staring down at the sleeping Ephraim, he wonders if there had been a time when Buck, before alcohol eroded his feelings, had similarly looked down upon him. Thus Jed imaginatively reenvisions the "story" he had entertained Dauphine's friends with earlier, but like all incarnations of Warren's wanderer before him he flees from such imaginative connections between his past and present by immersing himself in work—even though the work has become "less and less compelling" (340). The sudden reversal, textually at least, in his attitude toward his son is not really as sudden as it seems. The undercurrent of reality has been present all along.

The significance of this second marriage to the overall story of Jed's development is also suggested by the brevity of its narrative space, taking up, as it does, only a fraction of the time devoted to the single year in Nashville. Such a brief treatment seems out of joint perhaps, until we realize that the marriage is in some ways a reoccurrence of the Nashville episode, although certainly not reducible to just that. The marriage ends after Dauphine explains to Jed that she has recently had an affair to try to generate some feelings in herself but in fact failed to generate any feeling at all, even guilt. Jed's clinical response to the whole matter—he plays the role of an understanding friend steeped in contemporary psychology—indicates the very emptiness she has experienced: it was like trying to feel guilty, she said, for "going to the toilet!" (344). Her adultery is another meaningless black hole.

In drawing his parallels Warren makes much of both reversals—the shoe is on the other foot as Jed is the cuckold now—and repetitions. The thoroughly domestic Christian Agnes Andresen had lost her belief in God during her marriage to Jed; the atheist/activist Dauphine loses her sense of meaning in anything. "Oh, we tried so hard . . . to do everything right," she says of her experience with her lover. "But nothing means anything" (344). As Agnes Andresen's death had been the paradoxical birth of love, here the affair is paradoxically meaningless because the marriage it would violate seems meaningless. The only solution is divorce—"very rational, very friendly, even shot through with mutual respect" (344).

Far more than simple roguish adventures, the coupling and uncoupling depicted in the novel constitute a major subtrope in support of the primary symbolism of place. Analysis of the major episodes dealing with Jed's sexual relations reveals just how much they correspond to and indeed go a long way toward revealing the psyche of the exile who detaches himself from the past in order to create himself anew. Imagery of islands and black holes indicates the various degrees or kinds of existential loneliness that Jed's marriages and affairs, despite his genuine feelings of love for the women he is involved with, paradoxically represent.

That Warren intends some such symbolic function of Jed's loves is suggested in the counterpoint developed by several fulfilling love relationships in the novel. There is, notably, the fulfillment that his mother finds back in Dugton in her marriage to Perk Simms. Yet a closer consideration reveals rather striking similarities between Elvira Tewksbury Simms and the "Miss Pritty-Pants" she so reviles. For one thing, her relation to Simms begins in adultery, and Jed's "discovery" of her affair foreshadows the shadowy afternoons of his adulterous affair with Rozelle. For another, she has in common with Rozelle what Jed calls the "art of the mystic promise" that Southern girls master, the ability to make a man feel that they have with him "some deeply significant, if unspecifiable, background in common" (149). It is an illusion, Jed says, to be enjoyed as an illusion, yet it seems to reinstate some value in the kind of mystic sense of identity played out between Barbara Garnet and John March in Cable's novel. After Elvira's death Perk Simms tells Jed that his mother "had the gift. . . . She had the sleight. . . . To make a man always feel like a man. She could stop anything she was doing . . . and just for a second give you a look that made you feel you and her had a wonderful secret" (393).

Rozelle's later marriage to the "swami," who turns out to have been a Southern black man all along, and the marriage of the Cudworths (discussed in chapter 1) offer significant contrasts as well. But some interesting parallels between Cud Cudworth's professional career and Jed's make the example they offer even more resonant. Before becoming a Tennessee horse breeder, Cud had been associated with an important law firm in the North after attending Yale Law School. He was, as he says, "out for blood" in the world of law, a figure of speech that connects him with such characters as Willie Proudfit and Private Porsum, foils who drew literal blood in earlier novels. Then, like other Warren characters who seek to make a name for themselves by public deeds, Cud discovers a certain emptiness or blankness in professional success or the heroic action; he finds that he is not in the picture of his life at all, as Warren phrased the problem in "Billie Potts." After winning an important case, he awakened the next morning with ambiguous feelings toward his profession. He resigned from the firm, admitting that the enticement of a promotion almost caused him to stay simply because of the kindness of his boss, who misunderstood his motives for quitting: "But I didn't stay. . . . I walked out of the Old Man's office, and in that very split instant I felt real" (174). Cud's self-authenticating act of separating himself from "the father" (the Old Man) is the act Jed Tewksbury is trying simultaneously to duplicate and to avoid. He transforms himself, trying to leave the stain of his past behind; he attaches himself to a profession about which he has his own ambiguous feelings; he resigns posts and moves from place to place. But he never takes the self-authenticating step that would actually place him in the human community in the way the Cudworths have done. He cannot, as Cud urges him to do, buy the neighboring farm, marry the socialite Maria McInnis, and mimic the agrarian ideal because of the duality they represent — or, rather, because of his inability to comprehend the manner in which the Cudworths face that duality: "I had felt, now and then a sense of unreality in their world, but now . . . the awareness struck me that I had clung to the notion of the unreality of their world simply because I could not face the painful reality of their joy. The joy sprang from their willed and full embracement of the process of their life in time, and I, God help me, was in flight from Time. I could not stand the reproach of the sight they provided" (254).

This reproach is one instance of Jed's seeing through his own situation, an isolation that is tolerable as long as he can believe it is based on an accurate and destructive view of reality. The seductive idea of human communion represented by the Cudworths must be fought off by the rigorous defensive intellect, for flight from Time is the psychic flight from felt reality. What makes Cud feel *real* must be converted into unreality for the cynical Jed, but the paradoxical Romantic impulse that lingers through his cynicism, which is in fact the initiator of cynicism, remains susceptible to an image of what home might be.

The language in this passage also recalls the language of Jed's meditation on the orgasm as the "death in life-beyond-Time," and through such connections one begins to see how much Jed's plight resembles the condition of other Southern fictional wanderers.

Welty's Bowman, for example, whose career as a traveling salesman is symbolic of his own "flight from time," feels rebuked by the fertility and pride he discovers in poor and ignorant tenant farmers who have something so simple as a fertile marriage. For him as for Jed, profession is equated with identity, and both works implicitly criticize the abstract nature of work in modern times and thereby echo a concern expressed in *I'll Take My Stand.*

Warren's use of Cud's story is a return to the story within the story, the interpolated exemplum case that was a significant structural feature of his earlier novels. The Cudworths' life of stability and fertility does offer a significant contrast in this novel, yet the exemplum does not offer a simple agrarianism as a corrective for modern dissolution; the reader never feels that Jed's failure is in not imitating the life he feels reproached by. Still, there is an implied criticism of modern attitudes toward work in the way Cud's career as a lawyer reflects on Jed's. At least one critic believes that Jed might just as well have been a businessman as a scholar (Snipes 154). This would seem to be precisely the point.

CHAPTER SIX

The Scholarly Gypsy

Profession as the Neutral State

We live in time so little time
And we learn all so painfully,
That we may spare this hour's term
To practice for eternity.

ROBERT PENN WARREN, "Bearded Oaks"

◆ One can hardly overlook the parallels in A Place to Come To between Cud Cudworth's former career as a lawyer and Jed's career as a scholar. Jed sets about his career with some of the same ruthlessness and cunning. After the death of his mentor, Dr. Stahlmann, and his own experiences in the war, the scholarship which had earlier seemed to open the door to a cleaner world is corrupted, and Jed echoes Macbeth by calling it "a trick performed by an idiot for the edification of fools, or vice versa." But there is also the Faustian fun of "having it taken seriously—and getting paid for it" (99–100). Jed becomes a brilliant technician, and although at least one critic has praised Warren for avoiding the academic novel (Justus 303), the book is at times as devastating an attack on the pretensions of the scholarly profession as any written in the next twenty years, when both the academic novel and its parodies flourished. Take Jed's account of his work on his dissertation:

> With great cunning, I began to plot my brilliant career. I had a firm
> start, I realized, in a dissertation that involved not a single idea. My

next step was to cultivate my supervisor, Dr. Alesbury Sweetzer, who had originally, with furrowed and suffering brow and out of (truly) great learning, proposed my topic. In my earnest search for knowledge, I devised complicated and idiotic questions (which I, by a careful study of his more obscure articles, knew that he could answer), and with a worried expression, took them to him and apologetically begged for help. Soon I heard that my supervisor (who had always hated Dr. Stahlmann with a passion) had fallen into the habit (in spite of my earlier connection with Dr. Stahlmann) of referring to me as a very promising young scholar. So I branched out, cautiously of course, and tried the same tactic on the Chadworth Professor of Medieval History, who also happened to be a Division Chairman. (100)

Twice before, Warren had explored such manipulative relationships between professor and pupil—in the short stories "The Life and Work of Professor Roy Millen" and "The Unvexed Isles." In each case an aging professor distanced from his own poor rural past (both are versions of the exile) becomes jealous of a gifted and economically privileged student. Each professor also lacks the powers of self-analysis to understand his own motives for betraying the student. Jed, as a student, is an expert at manipulating such types. Yet it is a sign of his mature humanity that once he is himself a professor, teaching is the activity he takes most seriously, trying constantly to "come down hard" on his students.

Jed's detached cunning during his second period of graduate study has its more mystic parallel in the composition of "Dante and the Metaphysics of Death," the essay Jed writes as Agnes lies dying. Leaving Agnes in the hospital after her operation, Jed has a night at home that is very similar in some details to those we have seen the insomniac poet go through:

> I took a stiff drink and went to bed. In a bed that was both strange and familiar. In the dark I ran my hands over my own body, back and forth, as she had done over hers. I wondered what truth was lurking in the dark, pulsing inwardness that was body. Body is body,

> I thought. How silly, how absurd to give any particular body a name.
> I could not sleep.
>   So I got up, went to my desk, and found the fool dissertation. My
> eyes simply would not focus on the words. I had the feeling, all at once,
> of total entrapment. It was as though I had come to the desk as to a last
> hoped-for exit. But masonry, quite fresh, had been erected across the
> aperture. I had been betrayed.
>   I felt that I was going to vomit. (104)

Several things are going on here. First, this passage is one of a
number of verbal explorations of *body* in the novel. Here incarnation
is associated with absurdity; during sexual relations with Rozelle the
body becomes associated with blank mechanistic function; with the
babe Ephraim an exploration of the boy's body becomes associated
with miracle. Second, the passage associates *words* with escape from
physical existence and the pain of limitation imposed by physical
existence; they are the "last . . . exit," now closed. The scholarship
has been Jed's way out of himself; now he has been sealed in with the
ramifications of *body*, at this point his own, Agnes's diseased one,
Buck Tewksbury's permanently "cool-cocked" one.

The absurdity of body and the absurdity of name are actually
saving notions, however. Such a view negates the painful reality of
physical/familial identity. If all body is fused absurdly or mechanisti-
cally, Jed is not the son of Buck Tewksbury, the husband of the dying
Agnes, the adulterous lover of Rozelle. The specific details of this
passage—the arbitrariness of name, the moment when clean profes-
sionalism will no longer still the soul—recall the dilemma of the persona in the son poems. And just as in "I Am Dreaming" the son leaves
off the old text—the vision of the mother and father he is creating—
for the Otherwhere of the New England woods, Jed finds a new and
mystic relation to a text:

> At last my hand reached out, and with a painful dubiety picked up
> and arranged before me a sheet of paper. I stared at the blank whiteness.

I swear to you that my mind was as blank as the paper. With wonderment, I watched my right hand pick up a pen and begin to write. Each letter, as it took shape on the whiteness, seemed a mysterious achievement, each word a self-generating miracle. I waited with intense interest for what the words might say. The words were in a line across the top of the sheet. Each word began with a capital. When the words were finished, the hand drew a firm black line under them. They said:

Dante And The Metaphysics of Death.

The hand kept on writing until 4 A.M. (104)

Even the emblematic contrast between white and black will be familiar to readers of the poems. And Jed's description of the process of watching it all as if someone or something else were doing the writing is one more example of the split in the exile, which Jed identifies as the split between Jediah Tewksbury the investigator and Jediah Tewksbury the subject of the investigation.

Jed is not a fiend, of course, but he does bear some similarity to Hawthorne's Faustian monomaniac Ethan Brand in the way he begins to take pleasure in his ability to manipulate others. It is, in fact, at this point in the novel that he begins to overlay his story with allusions to Faust. But when he internalizes the process, as he does in his meditation on his split self, he raises questions germane to reading his own life and the texts of his profession: "In what ways . . . might the heart pangs and tears of J.T. — *subject* be modified by his awareness of the clinical eye of J.T. — *investigator*? As I sat by [Agnes's deathbed], I yearned for purity of feeling, for a sense of meaning in my experience, but when feeling gushed up in my heart, I caught myself asking if the yearning itself might not be the mother of self-deceit. Or, even, asking if the awareness of the clinical eye might provoke the enactment desired" (107). In this Hawthornesque dilemma, Jed is his own most interesting subject. He feels deeply, but his intellect distrusts the feeling.

There is an interesting split among readers of the novel regarding the value of Jed's profession. Some, often academics themselves, have seen it as his means of salvation, perhaps because they need to believe that his is a profession which by its nature proves resistant to the ordinary nags and pitfalls of worldly life. Others (and this seems a more accurate reading) have emphasized how little impact his scholarship has on his spiritual development. Jed's ambivalence toward his profession is reflected most often through the most significant myth he weaves about his own life: that his success, rather than something achieved by his own power and agency, is the result of a "bargain with the Prince of This World" — or, as he puts it in other contexts, an "identity with fate." In this condition of the subsumed will, the mind participates in what appears to be life as an observer, without resistance, like the mind of Isham in *Brother to Dragons*, the common mind of the crowd and the mind of Jack Burden in *All the King's Men*, and the mind of nearly every character at one time or another in *Meet Me in the Green Glen*. The mind does not recognize itself outside the darkness of naturalistic forces or the forces of fate, but it is paradoxically detached from those forces by feelings of invulnerability derived from the sense of meaninglessness. For Jed the invulnerability is the link between two ways of speaking, making the naturalism of his "identity with fate" virtually synonymous with the mythology of his "bargain with the Prince of This World." He discovers what both Amantha Starr and Issac Sumpter come to think of as the "inner logic" of the world, a mysterious and dangerous force (actually a dangerous illusion as revealed in each case) which seems to make events conform to the individual's will without the individual's effort.

As his career goes on, Jed more and more views his work simply as a way to anesthetize himself. Warren uses the humanities as an arena wherein high hopes are broken by a recalcitrant world and personal vanity, much as Arthur Miller and David Mamet use the business world in their dramas. He has written about academic life with a perceptiveness and irony to make any scholar wince. Yet debunking the study of literature as a means of knowledge is no more his ultimate purpose than destroying the purity of Adam Rosenzweig's dream of freedom in *Wilderness* is undertaken merely for the sake of debunking the Northern cause in the Civil War. Though Jed has learned to wear his profession as an adopted coat of arms, he does in the end recognize that it treats of human communion. What he must do is what Adam Rosenzweig must do, not perform a different set of actions, necessarily, but perform all with a different heart.

There is, in short, something more substantial in Warren's ironic view of the scholarly profession than debunking. For Jed to embrace his profession as he at first conceives of it, as a means of self-transformation, would mean that ultimately he would have to accept Dr. Stahlmann's dream of the *imperium intellectūs*. Stahlmann dreamed "of a world not of nations. Of a timeless and placeless, sunlit lawn, like that of Dante's vision, where the poets and philosophers and sages sit, and where we who are none of those things may come to make obeisance and listen. We may even, if a little grace is vouchsafed, report something of what we have heard. That others may come" (69). Stahlmann dreams of a future utopia based on Renaissance and neoclassical views of the distant past, even as Adam Stanton dreams of the good society based on his vision of the Southern patriarchy: "the idea that there was a time a long time back when everything was run by high-minded handsome men wearing knee breeches and silver buckles or Continental blue or frock coats, or even buckskin and coonskin caps, as the case may be . . . who sat around a table and candidly debated the good of the public thing" (*All the King's Men* 262). The trouble with both dreams is that the dreamer takes them outside the world, outside time and place and the corruption that both entail.

Jed had begun to pursue his own language-focused conversion dream when he discovered that the Latin taught to him by Mary McClarty at Dugton High could be a transformative window to another world, that a new name for a thing changed not merely the name but the thing itself, and that with enough new names one could make an entirely new world (26). This is an ironic use of the phrase "new world" and a foreshadowing of Dr. Stahlmann's failed attempt to adjust to American life, since it depends in this case on the discovery of the "dead" language of an ancient world. Significantly, the first word Jed learns to translate from Latin is *agricola*, and the textbook illustration of "farmer" looks nothing like the image of the word formed from Jed's Dugton experience. The dream of translation is attractive and corresponds to Jed's emerging and finally more mature sense of transformation from Southernness when he comes to Chicago, where the university becomes his "Harvard Yard" and the *imperium intellectūs* a "fondled axiom." But it is a dream that takes responsibility for knowledge away from the individual, that does not recognize the joint reality of knower and known.

It is significant that Stahlmann speaks of his dream only in the past tense. The cruelty of the Nazis and his own failures in the face of what happens to his homeland, coupled with his guilt over his Jewish wife's death, lead him to suicide. Ironically, he cannot create a new world in the New World, an irony I return to in greater detail later. If anything in the novel suggests the invalidity of the *imperium intellectūs*, however, it is Jed's wartime killing of an SS officer who in civilian life happened to be a classical scholar—hardly the way for one member of an elite intellectual group to treat another, hardly firm evidence that intellectual cultivation alone transforms souls. The killing represents the end of Jed's youth and, even more, his own kinship with the destructive forces of men—represented by fascism and the cruelties of his own group of partisans—and of nature, represented literally and symbolically by Stahlmann's story of the hare killed in a landslide. The intellect cannot by itself heal the problem of man's separate state. Jed killed the SS officer for pragmatic reasons, to gain the respect of his men, and out of some fairly horrible selfishness: he envies the young officer's courage and composure. Readers might well come away from these sections of the novel with the understanding that if Stahlmann's dream were applied to an actual political world, it might look very similar to the Nazi nightmare.

Jed treats his own accomplishments with aloofness, not so much because of his modesty as because he sees through the laurels. The result is that Warren has written a fictional American spiritual auto-biography that undermines the rags-to-riches motif with Faustian themes. His story is marked by many of the commonplace sacrifices and hardships of youth that go back at least to Franklin's *Autobiography*. The hungry Franklin upon his arrival in Philadelphia assures readers of his humility: "I had made many a meal on bread." Jed actually starves himself sick when he first arrives in Chicago, only to feel later that his scholarly success is the paradoxical result of the death of his first wife Agnes. He feels not that he has earned success but that he has sold his soul.

It might be tempting to reduce all of this to Warren's old-fashioned point of view—to say, that is, that Jed's interpretation of his success is the author's blind promotion of a myth by which a Western patri-archal system is perpetuated, obscuring the fact that Jed is able to make his way out of poverty because he is a white male who finds open to him certain arenas that are denied to members of other so-cial and racial groups and to women. Jed, after all, begins his rise in the world by attaching himself to a man who is in some ways the very figure of Western male authority. Having achieved his success, he can then write the appropriate account of it, complete with the transcendental bent that cautions against too much concern with ma-terial acquisition.

Such a reading, however, misses Jed's primary motivations (and Warren's, which may be different ones) for his appropriations from American and Old World myth. For Warren does not simply counter the documentarians with his mythic method. Jed's aloofness and de-nial of self are achieved by both tricks—social science and mythic allusion—for much of the novel. Further, such a reading misses what is perhaps most significant about Warren's own exile. He is a repre-sentative figure and perhaps even a model, though I have no illusion that Warren would agree with that assessment. To whatever extent he functions as a model, however, he is a model of self-consciousness, a major revision of the older heroic narrative pattern.

For Jed, who like Jack Burden is a student of history, history is the blind force that rushes men along. But over and over Warren has insisted on the necessity for man to proclaim himself through an assertion of his will. The idea expressed in *All the King's Men* holds true again here: "History is blind, but man is not" (462). Jed explains the tenuous relationship between man and history in the following way: "Something is going on and will not stop. You are outside the going on, and you are, at the same time, inside the going on. In fact, the going on is what you are. Until you can understand that these things are different but are the same, you know nothing about the nature of life. I proclaim this" (5). That Jed is the most "postmodern" protagonist in the Warren canon, as some believe, would seem to be evidenced here in a passage about the expanding universe and the inconclusiveness of history and the effects of the apprehension of this condition on human epistemology. But an expanding universe is not for Warren a meaningless one, any more than a "lying" language is a meaningless language. Strong evidence that Jed is arriving at the knowledge of meaning and interconnection in the "something" that is "going on" comes after his mother's death. By this time he has long been divorced from his second wife, Dauphine; his son, Ephraim, whom he loves dearly, has grown; and he has developed the first friendship of his life with Stephan Mostoski, the boy's maternal uncle.

It is during this period that Jed encounters still more anonymous characters who become mirror images. He attempts to rescue an elderly woman being attacked by two youths on a Chicago street. Despite his efforts, the woman is fatally wounded. Jed himself receives a stab wound and is briefly suspected by the police of being the woman's attacker. Later, sitting by the dying woman's hospital bed (a repetition of what he had gone through with Agnes); he pretends to be the son for whom she is calling in her delirium. The entire episode is replete with the kind of meaningful associations we have learned to recognize in Warren. At one level it is obviously intended to represent Jed's acceptance of responsibility for his own mother through a surrogate. A less positive interpretation would say that it is his way of alleviating his guilt for not being by the bedside of his own mother when she died. But one is also reminded of Jack Burden's declaration that "each of us is the son of a million fathers" and of his assumption of responsibility for the dying Ellis Burden after discovering that Ellis was not his biological father (*All the King's Men* 462). However complex his motivations, Jed does assume responsibility, which constitutes an act of moral awareness. He may have aided the woman automatically during the attack, but he makes a conscious decision to assume some responsibility for her afterward.

The theme of the union of all flesh is emphasized by the simultaneous linking of the old woman with both Agnes and Elvira and by the confusions over Jed's identity: first the police suppose that he is the mugger; then for a time the hospital staff assumes that he is the old woman's son; and finally the delusional old woman believes that he actually is her son as he sits at her bedside. Jed seems to become aware of the fusion of all life in a different way, however. Whereas earlier "body [was] body" and it seemed "absurd to give any particular body a name," here there is less cynicism as he actually asserts identity by a willful participation in the one flesh. His telling the old woman that he is her son is yet another instance in Warren of the Conradian "true lie."

An even stronger suggestion of Jed's acknowledgment of kinship with others is revealed in his description of the young mugger who stabs him:

> Then I was lying on the pavement, and my last vision, before fading out, just at the moment when traffic was halted by a light ahead, was of the taller of the two assailants—a youth of, say fourteen or fifteen—as he leaped, rather as he seemed to drift with ineffable, slow, floating godlike grace—godlike, truly, it seemed—to the hood of the nearest halted automobile, to stand beautifully balanced there with the purse—like Medusa's head hanging from the hand of Cellini's Perseus in Florence—but his pale yellow face lifted to the high stars, his lips open in a wildly beautiful, lyric, birdlike cry of triumph, an angelic, gratuitous and beautiful cry to the stars.

I remember thinking how beautiful, how redemptive, all seemed. It
was as though I loved him. I thought how beautifully he had moved,
like Ephraim, like a hawk in sunset flight. I thought how all the world
was justified in that moment. (387)

The staring up at the stars, the comparison with the hawk in sunset
flight, and the godlike grace in the youth's movement—these details
link this passage with similar moments of vision in the poetry. The
comparison to Perseus, or to a statue of Perseus, suggests the process
of mythmaking by imaginative connection. The discovery of beauty
in the mugger is similar to the Ancient Mariner's discovery of the
beauty of the sea snakes—and is the allusion to Medusa's head intended to suggest such a thematic connection? The comparison with
Jed's son establishes a connection between the youth and Jed. In the
world of continuity and interconnection, man is not only the son of
a million fathers; he is the father of a million sons, a link in the
"something" that is "going on." What Jed undergoes here—in a state
of grogginess to be sure—is a "momentary eternity" like that in the
imagined scenario at the end of *Chief Joseph*: a "stranger" might
pause as a traffic light turns green

> and thus miss
> His own mob's rush to go when the light
> Says go, and . . . may look,
> Not into a deepening shade of canyon,
> Nor, head now up, toward ice peak in moonlight white,
> But, standing paralyzed in his momentary eternity, into
> His own heart look while he asks
> From what undefinable distance, years, and direction,
> Eyes of fathers are suddenly fixed on him. To know. (64)

What is needed is not a vision that takes one out of time but paradoxically a momentary eternity that fixes one in time. Jed's profession
and his sexual relations, even his marriages, have in some ways been

his means of keeping up with his "own mob's rush." But this late in the novel his vision is a doubling of the old woman's belief that he is her son. The old woman, however, is sustained by delusions at the moment of death; Jed, like the imagined motorist in *Chief Joseph*, must return to the world of action to test his vision.

Jed's physical wound parallels and compounds his spiritual ones, and in a state of exhaustion he pleads guilty to sonhood. This acknowledgment is the beginning of his acceptance of his own particular *terra*. He returns to Dugton, a move that is actually the last of a series of returns (to Chicago, to Italy) during the second half of the novel, reversing the pattern of his earlier wanderings. In Dugton he meets the humble Perk Simms, the man who had given Jed's mother love for so many years and who seems eager to extend that love to her son. When Jed enters the house of his boyhood, objects seem "to glow with a special assertion of [their] being" and of his own, reminding readers of the special assertion of objects in the room of the past in "I Am Dreaming of a White Christmas." It seems as though he is returning to a "final self, long lost" (390). Later, in the graveyard where, perhaps as another act of reconciliation with the past, his mother has at her own request been buried next to the long-dead Buck Tewksbury, Jed remembers what Dr. Stahlmann had told him: that out of his anger and innocence he might write something worthy. The anger is still the anger at being Jed Tewksbury of Dugton, Alabama, but the innocence has been changed:

> The mysterious anger was there, and unannealed, God knew. But my *simplicitas* was not *sancta*. My *simplicitas* had lost the blessèdness of knowing that men were real, and brothers in their reality. And all I had in place of that was a vast number of cards that measured three by five inches, with notes in my large and legible script. But could not a man pray?
>
> Was all too late? Was all too late, after all?
>
> I had a wild impulse to lie on the earth between the two graves, the old and the new, and stretch out a hand to each. I thought that if I

could do that, I might be able to weep, and if I could weep, something warm and blessèd might happen. But I did not lie down. The trouble was, I was afraid that nothing might happen, and I was afraid to take the risk. (399)

Jed convicts himself here of the Faustian sin, but the unpardonability of that sin is not as certain for him as for Hawthorne's Ethan Brand or for Faustus. The very urgency of his questioning asserts hope. Still among the living, Jed cannot hope for the perfect peace of his dead parents, and he is still in a world where the idea of nothingness is frightening. Yet his fantasy to move to a preverbal state of consciousness is not dissimilar to what Warren does at the grave of his own parents in *Jefferson Davis*; that he refrains from attempting a mystic union with the parents is perhaps a mark of Warren's fearful wisdom. Jed's physical return to and reconciliation with the past, however, suggests a knowledge of the common pain of human experience (he is able at last even to say, "Poor Buck"). He understands that Buck, too, had suffered because he had never been able to adjust himself to his own time. He had resorted to drink, to sexual exploits, and to a dream of the glory of 1861–65 in much the same way Jed has tried to escape his own time by his immersions in sex, social and professional respectability, and classical and medieval literature. Jed has made a connection between his own life and the life of his father. Because he realizes his own failures—killing the SS officer out of envy for his composure, deflecting from his own will the responsibility for his successes and his failures—he comes to see that his father's life was tragic. He has had that vision which initiates the only real transformation in Warren, a transformation of the heart through the apprehension of universal tragic experience.

From examples such as the Cudworth episodes, the photographic description of the tenant farmer, the interrogation and killing of the SS officer, and finally the mugging and the hospital scenes in Chicago, one begins to see how much the novel depends for its meaning on the technique of doubling. William Bedford Clark has written of "secret sharers" in Warren's late fiction, "black characters who function as emblems of guilt or as shadowy *alter egos* for more prominent white characters" ("Secret Sharers" 66). Citing "Old Nigger on One-Mule Cart" as evidence, Clark concludes that one explanation for the prominence of these African American doubles may be personal. Clark's insight into Warren's use of the black alter ego points us toward an even larger tendency in Warren's later work: a tendency to identify his protagonists and personae through juxtaposition with one or more particular types of outsiders. Some are African Americans, but Jews, Germans, Greeks, Native Americans, and occasionally tramps are also used to tell the tale of a central homeless character, usually the displaced Southerner struggling against the encroachment of his past.

It was such a person who provided the germ of *A Place to Come To*: Warren's friend from Vanderbilt who had left for Chicago, where "big things were happening." Twenty-five years later (it is worth repeating from chapter 1), as Warren found himself listening to the man's story over a drink in his hotel room, the old friend documented his success, repeatedly stated that he had been right to leave the South, and then, "in the middle of this self-congratulation . . . suddenly said, 'I'm lonelier than God.'" For Warren this man exemplified the type who hated the South or felt inferior because of it and fled but—never finding an alternative world in which to live—became placeless (Watkins, Hiers, and Weaks 328–29).

Warren seems to have had this type in mind also in the mid-1960s when he wrote in *Who Speaks for the Negro?* of Southerners and American blacks who shared certain traits: "Some Negroes and white Southerners, in self-hatred—sometimes self-hatred disguised as liberalism—or in self-seeking, accept [the melting pot]; they 'pass'" (427). Even earlier, in *Segregation*, he had written of the complacent

Southerner transplanted to Northern soil away from the turmoil of the South where he might "eat the bread of the Pharisee" and feel relief from the reality he had been born to (51–52).

In all of Warren's writing (perhaps in all of Southern literature) there is hardly a more vivid example of a placeless white Southerner seeking to pass and choking down the bread of the Pharisee than Jed Tewksbury, and to tell the story of his "passing" Warren mirrors Jed's exile experience with the similar experiences of others. Heinrich Stahlmann, "the swami," and Stephan Mostoski are Jed's major secret sharers in displacement, their varied representational experiences appropriated as a vehicle for the novel's major themes. As foils, these characters seem as important to an understanding of the novel as Jed's relation to his childhood home, his relations with women, his Faustian intellectual development, or his profession as a scholar. In fact, the parallelism of the exiles' careers provides a structural unity whereby Warren comments on Jed's condition and on his development, often in ways of which Jed himself seems unaware. The repetition of patterns in the late novels, discussed in the first part of chapter 5, carries thematic burdens in a similar way, but much closer to the kind of mirroring one finds in A Place to Come To is the triangular relationship of Adam Rosenzweig, Mose Talbutt, and Jedeen Hawksworth in Wilderness. That earlier use of interracial and international doubling may well shed some light on Warren's use of the technique in his last novel.

Excluding Meet Me in the Green Glen, in which Angelo Passeto shares the position with several others, Wilderness is the only one of Warren's ten novels in which the protagonist is not a Southerner. A Bavarian Jew coming to America to fight for the slaves' freedom during the Civil War, Adam Rosenzweig is, potentially at least, part of the supply of immigrant manpower that Grant could depend on for the "swap system" he employed against Lee. To that extent, the character of Adam seems to have been suggested by historical reality. No mercenary, he is drawn from the figure of the nineteenth-century Byronic Romantic who burns to put his ideals into action. There are other good reasons, however, for making the novel's protagonist an outsider. For one, Adam brings no regional baggage with him that could cloud the issue for which he wants to fight. Neither the Cause nor Unionism figures in his estimation of the right side. He views American slavery not in its context but as an abstract violation of human freedom, which he can conceive of only as an absolute virtue. Adam's tendency to think in absolutes, a habit of mind common among Warren's nineteenth-century protagonists, and the fact that he has never seen a black man before coming to America to fight for the slaves' freedom suggest the gap between his dream and the reality of the war's context — a context from which he is even more removed than a Northern liberal such as Tobias Sears or the firebrand Seth Parton in *Band of Angels*. Jed Tewksbury is just as distant from the local concerns of the partisans he fights with in his own war, but his is the distance of the technician rather than the distance of the idealist.

As much as Adam is a Byronic figure seeking action to match his ideals, however, he is a self-exile fleeing family, homeland, and Jewish tradition. He thinks his father a traitor to the pure cause of freedom after the dying man renounces his own heroic past as a freedom fighter and accepts, at his orthodox brother's insistence, the definition ascribed to him through Jewish traditions — undergoing, as it were, a return. Yet throughout his adventures in America, Adam carries with him the physical reminders of that tradition: phylacteries, *talith*, and *seddur*. These seem just so much excess baggage until, near the novel's end, he discovers that their true significance for him lies in the possibility of human communion that they represent. After arriving in the midst of the New York conscription riots of 1863, and nearly losing his life, he makes his way to the home of Aaron Blaustein, where a servant girl restores his damaged prayer book. He thanks her dispassionately, but by the end of his experiences in the novel "he wishe[s] he had opened the book before her eyes and praised her. Why hadn't he done it? It would have been so easy" (305).

Adam's distance from Judaism is the clean break he makes with the past in order to pursue his dream. His ignorance of political and social life in America also suggests the more significant gap between his dream and himself, and like several other Warren protagonists — Jeremiah Beaumont most notably, perhaps — his longing to define himself in clean action is undermined by competing impulses and limitations. He finds in America a literal and a figurative *wilderness* totally alien to his preconceptions, an environment that absorbs the dreams of men until they are bitter or empty. But, as always in Warren, the failure of the individual's dream is not merely the result of the crushing and massive contingencies of experience; it is partly an inner failure. It is perhaps obvious by now that Adam's experience is essentially the experience of Warren's Southern exile. If his internal failings are symbolized, as some have argued, by his club foot (another Byronic echo), which keeps him out of the army and makes a sutler of him instead of a soldier, it is a system of symbolic events associated with his failure that suggests Adam's ultimate achievement of a vision of life's interconnection, unifying his dream and the reality he discovers.

Part of that system of symbolic meaning involves teaming Adam with Jedeen Hawksworth and Mose Talbutt. Warren uses these two foils in polar juxtaposition, but their lives (like the lives of Adam Stanton and Willie Stark before them) move relentlessly toward a point of violent intersection — the moment when Talbutt, the former slave and army deserter turned sutler, will kill Hawksworth, the Southern exile in this novel, who was forced to flee the South after speaking in open court in defense of a black man. Each tries to deny his past. Hawksworth calls Mose a "black son of a bitch" and speaks cynically of Adam's romantic notions of freedom. Talbutt tries to learn to read and, after the revelation that he is a deserter, pleads with Adam to believe that the scars on his back were caused by a slaver's whip rather than a cruel Union officer's discipline. Each man is a victim of experience that has made him cynical and solipsistic.

Both Hawksworth and Talbutt are important in the novel's exploration of the self's relation to the individual's beliefs about the nature of freedom. Jedeen, on the one hand, grows angry at Adam for saying that blacks should be free. Aware of the irony of freedom because of his own experience, he asks the young Romantic, "Do you think anybody is — is free?" (180). He offers an example of the irony of a man who can in one lifetime stand for a principle *and* seem by his own words to deny the validity of that principle. Mose too clouds the idea of freedom for Adam. The central act of Mose's pulling Adam onto a cellar shelf as the cellar is flooded by rioters who are attacking the blacks hiding there must be interpreted and reinterpreted by Adam to find its meaning. Mose tells Adam that there had been no nobility or humanity in the act; he had pulled him out of the water to keep Adam from thrashing about and thus attracting the attention of the mob.

This revelation is one of several that instills a sense of devaluation in Adam. For instance, when he broke from the *Elmyra* — the ship on which he took passage to America to fight in the war and on which he was going to be forced to return because an accident at sea had revealed his deformity — freedom was suddenly devalued because no one pursued him. No one cared where he went, so freedom became synonymous with alienation. Similar feelings overwhelm him as he thinks of what Mose has told him about his reasons for saving him.

His sadness enveloped him. He felt again, as he had felt on his unhindered flight from the *Elmyra*, and upon learning of the death of Aaron Blaustein, devalued. He felt his identity draining away. Was no man, in his simple humanity, more to any other man than a stir or voice, a sloshing in the dark?

Then he thought that that nameless man on the shelf, reaching out in the dark to that sound, had had after all, a choice. He could more easily, and safely, have slipped a knife into a throat than drawn a man up to safety.

With that thought, Adam Rosenzweig felt better. He felt, somehow, restored, however little, to hope.

Then he thought that for himself drawn up in the blind lottery of that cellar to the shelf others had not been drawn up.

He closed his eyes and he saw again, as in the dawn light in the

backyard when he had crept from the house in New York, the bodies of
those who had not been drawn up. It was all a blind lottery. Like your
life. He lay there and thought of the price of his life. Others had paid
the price of his life. Then he told himself that that was not logical. It
was completely illogical. (224–25)

There is a similarity here to other passages in Warren's poetry and
fiction which reveal the exile's anguishing need to know what meaning there is in the seeming illogic of experience. Along this line of
thinking, Adam eventually develops the idea that Mose Talbutt is representative of existential man because he is the man who can be completely himself, outside history; Mose has conquered history (225–
26). In *Who Speaks for the Negro?* Warren speculates that the black
American *is* such an existential man, but here he seems to suggest
that Adam is wrong. Mose cannot conquer that part of history which
is his personal past, anyway. Mose murders Jedeen Hawksworth, even
though it is Adam this time who calls him a "black son of a bitch."
The fact that Mose rises at night to kill Jedeen instead of Adam can
be logically explained by the fact that he steals Jedeen's large money
belt, but Adam connects the two incidents and sees Mose's motivation to kill Jedeen as a fusion of characters. And the fact that Mose
takes not only the money belt but the cards on which Adam has written the alphabet to help Mose learn to read leads Adam to imagine
Mose "crouching in some shadowy undefined spot . . . while his big
hand gripped a pencil and copied a letter from a card." It is an image
that reveals the complexity of Mose's character and implicitly evokes
the self-making motif of many American slave narratives, with its emphasis on reading as a clandestine act for the American black. For
Adam, however, it is an image "too complicated, too terrible, for him
to give a name to" (231–32).

The complexity is further suggested by the revelation that Mose
Talbutt's real name is Mose Crawfurd, and Mose is thereafter thought
of in Adam's consciousness as "Mose Talbutt–Mose Crawfurd" as if
he were two men. Complexity is also emphasized by the circum-

stances in which Mose saves Adam's life (or at least keeps him from definite harm) for the second time, during a scene of cruelty that closely parallels Warren's interpretation of the inwardness of the war in *The Legacy of the Civil War*. This is in the flour-tub scene, during which Union soldiers stage a game by having blacks root for money with their mouths through a tub of flour. Simms Purdew, the gamecock hero of the regiment, adds to the sport by grasping the heels of one black man and holding him head down in the flour. It is one of the many instances in which Adam must face the cruelty of *man*, not simply the cruelty of the foe who would deny freedom to a race. The irony lies in the fact that the cruelty is performed by a Union soldier — a hero, no less — and in what is revealed of Mose Talbutt's character when he stops Adam from going to the aid of the man in Simms Purdew's grip. The interplay between Adam and Mose is central, for it reveals the complexity of motivation and the irony of self. Mose, to save the white man, keeps the white man from helping a black man. Adam, in trying to free himself to save one black man, is forced in his enthusiasm to strike the black man who is trying to save *him*. The scene is not simply an attempt to debunk Northern heroism; it is a demonstration that no human impulse is ever simple.

Complexity of motivation is further revealed through Jedeen Hawksworth, the Southern exile, whose experience closely resembles Adam's. Jedeen's seemingly self-contradictory action of telling Mose to get his "black sonofabitching" hands off the dead Carolinian in the Gettysburg grave springs from his recognition, as he later explains to Adam, that it could have been himself lying there (a statement that foreshadows Adam's situation among the dead soldiers at the novel's end). Even more complex is Jedeen's motivation for defending a black man and getting himself run out of North Carolina in the first place: he did it because he was ashamed of his father, though he does not understand this until later. His father had publicly lauded Colonel Johnston F. Harris, who owned the accused slave, in a display that revealed the older Hawksworth's "ass kissin'" nature. When his father asked the crowd before the courthouse to cheer the public-minded Johnston for refusing remuneration for his loss of property, some didn't, and what made Jedeen go inside the courthouse and speak in the black man's defense was "knowing that them as didn't cheer, just couldn't because they was too ashamed. To see my pa. See him do it in public. . . . I hated them for being ashamed for my pa. . . . And because I hated my pa for making me ashamed of him" (160).

This shame of the father strikes at Adam's own experience, for he felt betrayed by *his* father's deathbed admission that he had sinned in leaving God and home to fight for freedom. Jedeen's ironic interpretation of what he has learned of life has relevance for Adam as well, for it shows how one man is influenced by the actions of another in the spiderweb world: "You live yore years and time it looks like you never know who to thank. . . . It was them not cheering kept me from laying back yonder on that hill, tonight. Dead in the ground. I might of been kilt charging up that hill with Pettigrew" (161).

The theme of human connection through patterns of repetition and complexities of motivation extends and deepens as the narrative continues through Adam's encounter with the murderous Confederate draft dodger Monmorancy Pugh, a darker version of Jedeen Hawksworth. But for a significant portion of the novel Warren has placed the burden of his themes on the discordant union of a Jewish immigrant, a former slave with a dual identity, and a bitter Southern exile. In an imaginative reconfiguration, he links virtually the same types again in *Flood* and *The Cave*.

In *A Place to Come To* he comes even closer to suggesting, as he had in *Wilderness*, that exile is a necessary step for a real understanding of sacramental vision because the exile has to face his own very particular kind of separateness. Like the greatest regionalists Warren is interested not merely in the documentation of life in *a place* but in exploring the significance, the psychic necessity, of *place* in life. From Dugton, Jed plunges simultaneously into worldliness and the clean world of the scholar, yet the worlds in this novel reveal themselves to be duplications of Dugton. Readers often grasp this fact before Jed himself does because of Warren's use of doubles. The first of the novel's three major doubles is Heinrich Stahlmann, Jed's mentor in classics at the University of Chicago and a German emigré who impresses students not only with his knowledge but also with his aristocratic bearing. Stahlmann seems drawn from that group of German exiles who after January 30, 1933, as Siegfried Mews has written, "began to conceive of themselves as representatives of the 'other,' better Germany whose traditions had been perverted by the Nazis" (103). This state of mind is analogous to Warren's assertion that there was an "old America" whose traditions and values had been lost to an impersonal technocracy and the deflection of difficult social issues into codified, two-party politics. He found the two worlds exemplified in the differences between Senator Sam Ervin and the "plastic" men of Watergate (*Who Speaks?* 12; Blotner 412). The distinctions between the perversions of older worlds are, of course, important, but Warren nevertheless registers the parallels between exiles from the flawed older worlds as human responses to cataclysmic changes of "home." Are there options, he asks, other than exile or becoming what Michael Kreyling calls "the hero as extraneous man" (154)? Warren draws parallels, albeit ironic ones, between Jed's relation to Dugton, Alabama, and Stahlmann's to Germany. In doing so he gives the relationship between the two a fraternal dimension that perhaps does not so much undermine the paternal one as throw it into a sharper light.

Jed comes to associate Stahlmann with his own program of self-transformation long before he actually meets him, in much the same way that Jeremiah Beaumont in *World Enough and Time* comes to see protecting Rachael Jordan as his destiny well before he even knows her, or that Adam Rosenzweig sees fighting for the freedom of the American slave as his destiny. Each of these young men makes abstractions of human beings to plug them into an idea. In *A Place to Come To* Warren initiates the theme of the exile's loneliness even as Jed waits to see the great man for the first time. Jed compares his own loneliness with that of Odysseus, whose loneliness for Ithaca, "a craggy sea-mark—good for nothing but breeding boys" (55), is a lone-liness for something, whereas his own is a loneliness "for nothing" (56). When Jed wonders if Dugton was even good for breeding boys and then responds to his own question by stating, "It had bred me" (56), the thought leads to a seizure of laughter and a sense of existential freedom from the past.

His connection to the place he believes he has excised from his consciousness is almost immediately reestablished, however, in one of the book's seriocomic episodes. When Jed, after shyly stalking Stahlmann for some time, is suddenly confronted by the imposing man and ordered to account for himself, he spasmodically begins reciting the opening of the *Aeneid*. Stahlmann listens for a full five minutes and then says, "Enough. . . . Your pronunciation is vile. You must be from the South" (59). Though no cruelty is apparently intended, the response could hardly be more crushing, for the connection between "vile" and "South" can only confirm Jed's sense of inferiority. He responds by plunging into a recitation of "the great chorus from *Oedipus at Colonus* that welcomes the stranger to the land famed for the glory of horses and horsemen, where the nightingales sweetest sing—the chorus now probably being uttered with an even more vile accent" (59). It is the only way he *can* respond, because a "new" language is necessary to translate Jed Tewksbury out of Dugton into the ostensibly different world of the university and Dr. Stahlmann, into an esoteric "classicism." The discovery that language is all has the paradoxical effect of empowering the exile.

The surrogate father–son relationship that develops between the two men is certainly familiar to readers of Warren's earlier novels. Despite the vast differences between Stahlmann's social sophistication and immersion in a nineteenth-century gentility and Jed's sometimes calculated social crudity and lowly Dugton origin, there are important similarities in their familial experiences. Certain details in Jed's description of the library in Stahlmann's home link the two men. On Stahlmann's wall hangs the saber that his father "as a captain of the hussars had wielded, in a charge at Sedan" (61). In the

Tewksbury home in rural Alabama there had been a saber, too, one reputedly used by Jed's great-grandfather to fight Yankees. In an earlier scene Buck Tewksbury took it from above the fireplace and, in drunken fury, swung it wildly until he "took a header onto the stone hearth and successfully laid himself out like a stunned beef" (4). After Buck's later fatal header from his wagon, Jed's mother threw the saber into a creek and quieted Jed's protest by explaining that Buck had bought it at an auction for fifty cents—forty-nine cents more than it had ever been worth, in her estimation (13).

Dr. Stahlmann, as a master fencer, can carry on the tradition inherited from his father at least symbolically. Jed carries on his inherited tradition with comic pantomimes of his father's death, reenacting Buck's final act of, in Jed's irreverent phrase, "holding on to his dong," the sword of sorts that had been his real claim to fame. Though it is Jed who supplies these details, he himself does not draw these connections overtly. As Randolph P. Runyon has noted, "There is a great deal going on in the novel of which Jed is unaware" (*Taciturn Text* 229). But readers should not miss the irony achieved through this juxtaposition, or fail to see how the normal pattern of parody is reversed, is turned inward, for the more comic version of paternal legacy cannot fully undermine the more noble one. The issue of paternal legacy cannot be denied simply because it is grotesque or subject to parody.

Circumstances sometimes make it necessary for Jed to face the parallels in their experience more directly, particularly when Stahlmann's analytical and inquisitive nature asserts itself. During the dinner the two share on their last night together, their exile experiences are linked symbolically through food. Meals in Stahlmann's home consist of traditional German dishes, reminders for the professor of an older way of life. Reflecting on his own loneliness over dinner in ways that make Jed uncomfortable, Stahlmann overtly parallels their experience by saying that Jed too must feel, "gastronomically speaking . . . a stranger in a strange land" (65–66). Jed's response is telling, for it shows how his defensive intellect can be short-circuited by stirred memory. He wants to deny feeling a stranger but is suddenly overcome by the memory of "the taste of collards and corn pone, of fried ham and grits, of sorghum and black-eyed peas," and in the next instant he is "struck with a blind yearning to feel the collards, the corn pone — those substances — in [his] mouth, the texture, the odor, the taste" (66). That so apparently pedestrian a matter as food figures so significantly in this passage may seem at first an indulgence in local color on Warren's part until we realize that being overcome by such a "blind yearning," by such a sensual and emotional relation to the past, is psychologically dangerous: it obstructs the illusion of non-meaning that Jed depends upon to remake himself without the stain of Dugton.

The same episode reveals a similar danger in the matter of citizenship. Stahlmann's relation to America as an immigrant is much like Jed's, for characters in Warren often try to go from a specific place within the geographical borders of America to a more abstract "America." America is, Stahlmann says, a *patria* more abstract than either Germany or Claxford County, and Jed cannot help him learn the "requisite innocence of heart" to be an American citizen, since Claxford County lies as far outside the America they discuss as does Germany (68). Stahlmann needs to learn "innocence" to be an American; Jed, the Southerner who never had this particular innocence, in his own way is seeking it. As Stahlmann sees, it is a "murderous innocence" Americans have (72), a phrase for the quality that from another vantage point would become America's "righteous might." Stahlmann cannot enter into this innocence, cannot "pass," finally, given his guilt about his wife's death and the fate of his homeland under the Nazis. His suicide that very night is not exactly preferable to Americanization, but it is clear that Americanization would be its own kind of annihilation for him rather than a cure for the profound guilt and loneliness that he feels and that reflect on Jed's own condition. He cannot give up himself and just be a good American.

Jed's relationship with Stahlmann establishes a recurring pattern of one exile's experience impinging on another, a very common pattern in Warren. In this novel, however, the pattern becomes more than a major motif for the theme of interconnection. It is actually a dynamic plot device, tracking Jed's gradual recognition that his identity rests in large part on his membership in a paradoxical community of exiles.

The themes of ethnic diet and American citizenship in the passage just discussed foreshadow parallels with Jed's second secret sharer, the swami—actually a Mississippi black who poses as an Indian mystic and poet and mesmerizes the hard-playing set who frequent the Lawford Carringtons' home in Nashville. Long after the Nashville episode Jed learns the swami's true identity from Rozelle, who is now married to him. As Stahlmann's food provides him with "a little piece of *old* Germany" (65; emphasis added) and Jed's "blind yearning" for collards and corn pone tie him to Dugton, the swami's need for a reminder of his origin is evidenced through food. Rozelle tells Jed during their final meeting, "What it amounts to is [wherever we go] I'm supposed to make things taste like a nigger shack in Jackson, Mississippi, and so I do what I can in place of sowbelly, chitlings, collards, corn meal, and sorghum. In other words, I'm what you might call his Ole White Mammy" (366). Recalling the words Jed had flung in defensive anger at the inquisitive Stahlmann—"We were poor as niggers. We ate like niggers" (66)—Jed's account of this conversation is another instance of his telling more than he knows. The common desires of a displaced palate are a concrete suggestion of a deeper connection through spiritual isolation, for the swami apparently, like Jed, protects and promotes himself by protean shifts of identity.

It would be oversimplifying the matter to say that this is the only significance of Rozelle's marriage to the black man. I suggested earlier that the marriage functions as part of Warren's rewriting of the Southern heroic narrative. It also further reveals Rozelle's pathetic nature as she continues to attach herself to men as an ornament, a showpiece, however prized. This time she attaches herself to a drug dealer who has, like Fitzgerald's Gatsby, parlayed his business into an awesome stature that overleaps respectability and whose indirect hand in Lawford Carrington's suicide repeats Carrington's indirect hand in the death of Rozelle's first husband, Michael X. Butler (the middle initial being highly suggestive). Rozelle now informs Jed rather playfully that she intends to commit suicide when she loses her Helen-like power over men, and she has at least enough knowledge of her husband's business to know that there are easy ways to do it. She exists, as Jed does for much of his life, for the derived meaning of playing a joke on a myth—the myth of the beauty and charms of the Southern belle. The joke turns inward, however, as she flees her life long from the role of Southern matron without ever learning the painful yet graceful acceptance of time's reality exhibited by Mrs. Jones-Talbot.

To judge by the food passage I quoted above, however, Rozelle's role in the marriage seems to provide her with restorative returns of her own as she helps her husband create his dreamy return to Jackson. Stahlmann raised an issue that arises again here when he said to Jed that the American black is the "only free man, . . . the perfect existential man" (76). By now we understand how fully Warren has explored and denied the argument that the black American's existence is any more purely existential than the white's, the modern equivalent of the old notion of the well-adjusted "darkie." For that matter, Warren's thinking here sets him apart from Faulkner with his notion of the "enduring" black and the "cursed" white. Warren's own speculation on the black American's existentialism in *Who Speaks for the Negro?* has shifted to a speculation of his most theoretically minded characters, uttered as an envious sigh under the weight of history. With his usual self-irony Jed responds that he believes Claxford County, Alabama, had made the same of him (77).

As Clark points out, both Stahlmann and Jed are wrong ("Secret Sharers" 72). What Jed comes close to articulating here is that he is one of those who, in self-hatred, "pass"—that is, one who attempts to wash himself clean of the past for a new identity. (The phrase that would become fashionable in the 1960s, "liberated Southerner," was unavailable to Jed in the early 1940s.) Though both the swami and Jed seem to thrive at times on their extraneous condition, the idea of "perfect existentialism"—like the novel's numerous other idealities: the *imperium intellectūs*, the "black hole" of orgasm, Marxist utopia, and Yankee virtue—turns out to be an illusion. And the illusion that the past and experience do not matter is the main trick Jed and his black secret sharer have in common. Their connection is emphasized by an incident one evening at the Carringtons:

> The swami was just in the act of reading aloud, in the original Hindi, of course, one of his own poems, and when he had finished the original text, he gave an English translation, in verse, too. After the coos of awe and rapture were over, he began another original composition and drove through to the bitter end. At this point his gaze found me. "Ah, dear Professor," he said, "you can tell our friends how much is lost in any translation, how the vital pulse of language is diminished, and this newer composition I must, I humbly apologize, render somewhat freely and pray to offer a more adequate translation in the future."
>
> But now he plunged in, with an effect much like a melange of R. Tagore, Lawrence Hope, E. B. Browning and Felicia Hemans, not to forget considerable allusion to some handbook of the exotic positions practiced in his native land. Having quickly had enough of such rich fare, I rose as quietly as possible and began to thread my way through female forms seated on cushions, meanwhile murmuring my apologies, and I swear to God that, as my eyes momentarily engaged those of the swami, he almost winked— or maybe did wink— and gave some sort of complex smile that seemed to be full of ironical dimensions involving, among other things, camaraderie, amiable contempt and brotherly knowingness—as though he were just trying to indicate that if I didn't mess with his racket, he wouldn't mess with mine. (253–54)

Both these Southerners adopt exotic identities and win social success with exotic acts. But the brotherly wink, which readers will recognize from *All the King's Men*, is only a part of the communication here. By addressing Jed first verbally and then with his wink, if he does wink, the swami reverts to the African American tradition of *signifying*. What is most interesting about the case is that he simultaneously signifies *on* Jed and signifies *to* Jed. That Jed is at once the person signified on and the only person in the room who feels that the swami is signifying suggests the complex relations of outsiders which Warren is trying to define. What Jed obviously feels is the identification in falseness he has in common with the swami, not only in partaking of the blandishments of the home of his cuckold but in his whole life, for Jed is the con man who cons himself.

The extent of the parallel is much greater than Jed articulates, even after he learns more about him. The swami is, like Jed, another Southerner seeking to "pass"; he has learned to talk like someone who is not "really a nigger after all" (366), making his way in the world just as Jed has by learning a new language. Having gone AWOL in India, he learned Hindi well enough to compose poems in that language, but perhaps his more amazing feat was learning to speak English with an Oxford accent. Jed learns Latin, Greek, and Italian in pursuit of a new world to live in, but the biggest self-transformation he makes through language is learning to speak a Chicago standard English — except for those times when it suits his purpose to resort to Dugtonese.

The swami does not impinge on Jed's consciousness as heavily as Dr. Stahlmann. Jed is obviously made uncomfortable by this foil — it is, indeed, as if he were looking into a mirror — but readers see much more of their twinness than ever intrudes on Jed's consciousness. By the time he makes what he calls his first true friend in Stephan Mostoski, Dauphine's uncle and the last of Jed's major doubles in the novel, his consciousness has grown to the point that he is ready to analyze his relation to home with less anger and defensiveness than he displayed earlier. Although he declares that he and Stephan have nothing in common but solitude, there are actually several parallels in their histories. Both fought in World War II, on opposite fronts, and each now lives in what is essentially a countryless condition. It

is, in fact, through Stephan Mostoski even more than Stahlmann or
the swami that Warren raises Jed's exile experience to a universal level
and simultaneously suggests its modernity. With Mostoski, Jed does
not create postures or fall into defensive down-home talk. He con-
fesses openly the hatred for the South which had caused him to flee
it. But he also tells Mostoski he had found nowhere to flee to: "I had
tried to buy my way out of solitude by supporting the causes of virtue,
but I felt isolated even from that virtue, an interloper, one might say
into Yankee virtue" (347–48).

Part of the friendship between the two rests in the fact that their
experiences have made each the perfect auditor for the other. A
Polish Jew, Mostoski had fought against the Russians until, after being captured in 1941, he agreed to fight the Germans, "being about
as happy to kill Krauts as Russians." He had, he said, "a 'delectable
war,' all enemies, no friends" (347). Jed's case was not so extreme, but
he too suffered a certain detachment even from the Italian partisans
alongside whom he fought. Like the swami and, symbolically at least,
like Jed, Mostoski had also for a time gone incognito. Having been
mistakenly classified as deceased by Russian officials, he assumed a
gentile identity until he reached America, where he resumed his Jewish name and his career as a professor of physics.

It is Mostoski's vision of the future, though, as he speaks of a
"countryless world to come," which draws the parallelism of exiles
into something of a coherent design. "We are merely feeling," he
tells Jed, "the first pangs of modernity, . . . the death of the self
which has become placeless. We are to become enormously efficient and emotionless mechanisms, that will know — if 'know' is not
too old-fashioned a word to use in this context — how to breed even
more efficient and more emotionless mechanisms. Let us take another drink and drink to Perfection, and to laughter" (348). In some
ways Mostoski's postwar vision is a naturalistic slant on Brad Tolliver's mental declaration at the end of *Flood*: "There is no country
but the heart." Closer to its textual home, however, it is an ironic
inversion of Dr. Stahlmann's vision of the *imperium intellectūs*. The

vision here is a horrific blend of Huxleyan efficiency and Hawthornean self-consciousness. But it is qualified by what readers actually see happening—Mostoski establishing a human relationship with Jed Tewksbury.

Warren has framed much of Jed's adult experience between Stahlmann's humanistic utopia, a high modern shoring-up against the ruin of civilization, and Mostoski's mechanistic one, a reluctant embracing of the deconstruction of the self. And he has done so suggestively, for it falls to Jed to make his meaning in the space between such extremes. Warren's doubling in A *Place to Come To* and elsewhere implies that Southern white identity may be understood to some extent by an ethnic analogy, as a number of social historians have argued. Ironically, the Southern exile, who is a revision of the Southern hero of an earlier period, finds himself brother to the outcasts of his father's and grandfather's generations, and in more than the metaphysical sense: brother to them in the more tangible sense of *experience in kind*, the sort of experience associated with the meaning of *home*.

It is fair to ask to what extent this ethnic analogy, as it tends toward a universalization of experience, masks very real political and social differences between Southern WASPs, blacks, and Jews. I suspect the answer is to whatever extent an individual's critical biases tell him or her that literature tends to mask such divisions. To my mind, Warren's novel builds the question into its structure as part of the overall ironic effect it moves toward. Difference *is* the issue, *is* the irresolvable truth. The novel, if novels ever do this sort of thing, challenges the Derridian notion not that language tends toward polarities but rather that in making our own political or discipline-specific arguments we can complacently conclude that one polarity tends to be privileged over the other.

In the apparent new order, Mostoski's professional edge as a physicist is that the discipline he deals in "is a study of the vastness of solitude—infinite motion in infinite solitude." Jed, on the other hand, "suffer[s] the disadvantage that sometimes [his] professional subject matter, however much [he] and other scholars might bleach it, treat[s] of moments of human communion, however delusive, and of human community, however imperfect" (348). The "disadvantage" lies in the persistent "stain" that meaning always is in Warren, the stain that refuses to be bleached away. Jed has tried to bleach of meaning not only the literature he studies but the life he lives. Sexual love is emblematized as a "devouring negativity," and scholarship in the humanities becomes technical work (Jed believes in being a good technician). The largest stain, of course, is Claxford County and his paternity, which he tries to bleach with sardonic humor. If he could maintain the fiction that experience is meaningless, then the pain of his isolation might be decreased, but there are too many signifiers of meaning in his life—in the literature he studies, as he says, but also in the experiences of his fellow sojourners in exile, as he often fails to note. Yet those experiences offer still another kind of signifying text in the novel. Jed must finally make his peace with Dugton in order to *be*.

Clark rightly concludes that the effect of Warren's handling of his black "secret sharers" is the universalizing of the problem of selfhood, the central human experience for Warren ("Secret Sharers" 74). To this I would add that Warren makes a similar use of the fallout of modern history, in particular of various displaced groups to which his fiction gives individuation. In one sense he repeats the step taken by Thomas Nelson Page, James Lane Allen, and other Southern writers of the Reconstruction era who appropriated the experience of former slaves (their most immediate Others) to reconfigure the Southern hero in such stories as "Marse Chan" and "Two Gentlemen of Kentucky." The terms of Warren's appropriation, if it is that, are quite different, of course. For Warren, the Southern exile replaces the Southern hero as the central figure through which we might learn something about what Michael Kreyling calls "the ongoing cultural, literary, and political wrangle over the nature of the southern mind and heart" (1). The South is better understood by the figure of estrangement than by the figure of representation. Or finally, perhaps, the figure of estrangement emerges *as* the figure of representation. The phrase "community of exiles" might seem too ironic, but the human communion possible in Warren is based on a recognition of universal estrangement and an acceptance of what Hawthorne called the magnetic chain of humanity and Warren, in a more encompassing vision, the osmosis of being. By appropriating the experience of diverse exiles to tell the story of one, he creates a chain that contextualizes and enlarges that one story to fuller philosophical, historical, and perhaps finally religious dimensions, for it is the novel's readers in the end who participate in a larger communion by participating imaginatively in the art Warren has made.

Conclusion

What poet ever knows what another generation wants?
A great alibi, anyway.

ROBERT PENN WARREN, letter to the author

◆ Certainly I have not exhausted the implications of Warren's exile figure, nor would even a comprehensive examination of the
figure account for Warren's massive accomplishment as a writer. I
have, I trust, revealed more deeply how significant the exile is in the
complex configuration of subject and technique in Warren's work.
Those texts generally regarded as his masterpieces—*All the King's
Men, World Enough and Time, Brother to Dragons, Audubon: A Vision*—share with the exile literature a common artistic vision, epistemological and ontological theories, and a regionalist resistance to
the depersonalizing forces of "new" America that make Warren's a
significant twentieth-century voice in some old and new debates. His
almost single-minded devotion to literature as a mode of achieving
the meaningful self and approaching thorny social problems makes
him a model for any age.

At the end of Warren's final novel, Jed Tewksbury believes neither
in the *imperium intellectūs* nor in an "identity with fate," this novel's
equivalents of Jack Burden's Brassbound Idealism and Great Twitch.
He is, instead, a man whose lost will is regained and who is at last,
like Jack Burden, ready to enter the human community. His hard-
won selfhood is suggested by his return to Dugton, his acceptance of

responsibility for the old woman in Chicago, his Ancient Mariner–like recognition of the beauty of the young mugger, and finally, the letter he sends to Dauphine asking her to rejoin him. "It is not that I cannot stand solitude," he writes. "I ask for your company for what blessèdness it is" (400–401). A *Place to Come To* ends with the vision in which Jed understands the continuity that bridges time and understands, too, his place within the framework of the world as a son and a father: "I fell into the fantasy that someday—perhaps on the mission to put the ashes of Pore Ole Perk in the ground, unmarked, but not too unhandy to the spot where Ma lay [as Perk Simms had shyly requested]—I would be accompanied by Ephraim, and I could point out to him all the spots that I had dreamed of pointing out to him" (401).

Jed's longing to connect his son with that part of his life that he had vehemently denied to his first wife, Agnes, signifies his achievement of "home." By imaginatively reversing the program of deracination he had designed for himself, he has, like some of Warren's divided characters before him, discovered that the past always matters and that his *terra* —which is best defined as all experience impinging on the individual's consciousness of self—must be accepted and respected. He has learned that the past has its influence on identity, and without a sense of the past's reality individuals cannot have a sense of the future. He has discovered that men must live in time, because the illusion of no-Time is the death of identity. Finally, he has recognized that a life of awareness is a dialectical process in which abstractions such as the *imperium intellectūs* must be weighed against experience for validity, but a process that requires the moral courage not to submit to its antithesis, an "identity with fate."

The "Place" Jed Tewksbury comes to is a vision that acknowledges his own limitations, his own separation from an original innocence, but also a vision that he is not alone and that even within the great complicity of the human community love is possible. His search leads him to a valid, hard-won way to live by knowledge and acceptance of the great conflict between the idea and the fact. He has selfhood, that sense of inner unity which parallels the order in an outside world and makes life possible.

Percy Munn, the protagonist of Warren's first published novel, *Night Rider*, was a character born for the role of the traditional Southern hero who through his own inner blankness, a blankness that matches the great blackness of the world, destroys himself by ever more desperate attempts to identify himself extrinsically. Warren's final novel takes as its subject the moral achievement of a poor white Southern American moving through and beyond the usual signifiers of accomplishment to learn to live with himself without "passing"— a triumph in history. The stories told in the two novels suggest Warren's movement from a high modern theme of the hollow and cultureless man to a more personal and Romantic vision of history and the possibilities of a fulfilled life—the author's own triumph.

The exile figure in Warren's fiction, nonfiction, and poetry places his work directly in the tradition of the self-making theme in American literature. Its significance in relation to that tradition, however, lies in the particular irony of inwardness with which Warren questions the tradition and reasserts it. As an image of the fluidity of selves, the wanderer signifies a postmodern freedom from the past and from a culturally imposed identity, yet such freedom is the same sort of unshackling necessary for both the traditional American success story and the story that only appears to be its antithesis—the common American-drifter theme. Despite this assertion of freedom, Warren's exile, like Southern literary exiles generally, is haunted by a regional past that asserts its reality in his consciousness as a psychological and philosophical problem, treated often as a textual problem, a problem of reading.

The consciousness of Warren's exile is consequently laden with *ifs* that stand in the way of his absolute freedom. The fuller significance of Warren's exile and his "if" theme might be better seen in the context of the "if" theme of American idealism identified by Martha Banta in *Failure and Success in America*. Analyzing the idealism of Josiah Royce, Banta identifies a tradition in which both the ideal and the real are held to be true and calls this duality the essential American tradition: the necessity of the ideal in order for life to be meaningful and the equal necessity of the ideal's inclusion of reality. There is for Royce a reality that is defined by an *if*, a possibility that could come true (Royce 376). This conception of the "what if" gives rise to a "dissatisfaction with *is* as purposeless circumstances" (Banta 24). Warren's concern with a dissatisfaction with "purposeless circumstances" is revealed throughout the body of his work. In *Wilderness*, for example, Adam Rosenzweig's initial fervent idealism is devalued by circumstances that appear to make life nothing but a "blind lottery." Royce's *if*, the one Banta calls the essential American condition, is always prospective and offers yet another conception of America as all future. Perhaps the characteristic stance is most evident in Whitman, whose *I* seems always awaiting fulfillment, always beginning, and yet always confident of its own *I*-ness.

Or, again, there are Thoreau's mornings, which bring back the heroic ages and, perhaps paradoxically, new possibilities that are free from the contingencies of the past (*Walden* 80). It was Thoreau, of course, who voted for an absolute freedom which absolved the individual of social responsibility, as long as he made sure he wasn't standing on another's shoulders ("Civil Disobedience" 642). The racial context in which Thoreau made his claim in "Civil Disobedience" might lead us to read something like Warren's "The Briar Patch" in part as a youthful attempt to absolve himself *personally* of responsibility for social conditions. Warren discovered, as the body of his subsequent work reveals, that such absolution is available only to the exile willing to eat the bread of the Pharisee while passing. Further, he discovered, as again the body of his writing is evidence, that not being party to oppression is the work of a lifetime rather than the almost casual first step toward the grand fulfillment of a godlike self. It is so because the self exists only in relation to others, not in grand isolation from them.

Such possibilities, however, seem to be contained in Royce's American *if*. Banta notes Thoreau's belief that America was the place where the "crucial gap" between God's will and man's could be closed, "and the efforts required to arrive at cosmic success simultaneously satisfy men's craving for personal triumph." The words could just as easily describe Adam Rosenzweig's motivation for coming to America, or Jed Tewksbury's for leaving Dugton. Banta goes on to write, "If all these things could come about, what a difference it would make in the country's literature! It would be transformed from a bitter history of contention and failure to a joyous account of reconciliation and success. It would be transformed from the agonistic to the irenic—from the less-than-perfect form to the best of all possible shapes. But so far we have an *if* which in no way matches the *is*. As a result, we also have Thoreau's *Walden*" (182).

Through archness Banta perhaps reveals the irony of the blessed cost of living outside the *imperium intellectūs*. One might add that we also have Warren's *Wilderness*, which may stand for the body of his work as an account of a necessary failure in which he sets on its head the kind of *if* Banta is writing about. There is, however, one instance of the Roycean *if* in *Wilderness*. It appears in the first three lines of a poem composed by Adam's father, Leopold: "If I could only be worthy of that mountain I love, / If I could only be worthy of sun-glitter on snow, / If man could only be worthy of what he loves" (5). In these "if" clauses the subjunctive future suggests a condition not fulfilled and perhaps a condition that cannot be fulfilled. It is perhaps the human condition that man cannot be worthy of what he loves. On the other hand, most of the *ifs* in the novel take place in Adam's consciousness and rationalize his sequence of failures; they take the past perfect *had* and are retrospective rather than prospective.

It is characteristic of Warren to be so concerned with the past. Like Hawthorne and Faulkner he was drawn to the past almost magnetically as a source of truth. But his *if* theme is not without significance for the future; as a way to ingest the truth of the past it can lead to a more realistic vision of the future. Before any *if* of the future can be realistically imagined, to Warren's way of thinking, the *if* or *ifs* of the past must be considered, in a process not of deflection but of ingestion. Thus *Wilderness* addresses the philosophical problem posed by the American experience as an experience in the wilderness not so much with a solution as with a reconception of the problem and a reformulation of the *if* that has been previously used to face it. The tangled wilderness destroys the absolute ideal, but Warren's version of an ideal that includes the real—which is inductive in nature rather than a priori—can sustain moral identity in America. What must be reshaped is not experience (which is what Adam tried to do with most of his *ifs*) but the idealist's heart. It would be a heart less hardened by the affronts of experience because its desire would begin with experience, with the near rather than with distant absolutes. Freedom, particularly, would be not an abstraction to be gained for others in a gleaming moment of identity but an ongoing existential problem; it would include the social and moral problem of slavery, or segregation, and make it possible to see such an aberration as a reflection of the human condition to be fought against, rather than as an extrinsic evil to be wiped off the face of the earth by an alien force—which, as it turns out, is yourself. Such a spiritual transformation lies at the moral center of Warren's work and gives it something of the irenic quality Banta writes of. But the irenic is possible only *through* the agonistic; the pain of the past in its pastness must be converted into the future tense of joy, as Warren puts the case in "I Am Dreaming."

Warren's writing about the exile also reveals how thin the line is between idealism and mechanism; how easily the transcendentalist's values are adopted by the capitalist, the Darwinist, and even the nihilist; how closely an extreme individualism and absolute personal freedom resemble nothingness. The imperfect fit of regional identity in his exile counters the drive toward a universal adoption of the ad man's values and epistemological free play. This second significance of the exile figure is captured by the unsettled part of identity that Warren habitually refers to as *you*. Warren made much of the habitual display of Emersonian epigrams on the walls of the Captains of Industry/Robber Barons of the Gilded Age. In our own age, when Emersonian epigrams—"Whoso would be a man must be a nonconformist" and "A foolish consistency is the hobgoblin of little minds"—are used to sell running shoes, when Emerson's own great-granddaughter poses standing on a rock in the middle of a brook as she gazes transcendentally skyward in a slick magazine ad for book bags, when promoters of the Internet advertise it as a *place* where there is no race or gender or physical mark of identity whatsoever but only *ideas* (where the self finds the contemporary equivalent of Emerson's transparent eyeball), when sophisticated journals are filled with jargon-laden prose attacking elitist principles in a language no one outside academe can waste time attempting to comprehend—in such an age it should not be too difficult to grasp the value of Warren's regionalist concerns about the easy confluence of the anti- and ultramaterialist philosophies in the American mind. His appeal for readers who resist the notion that history is *merely* a semantic act lies in his demonstration that arguments for a depersonalized view of history clear the path for the strongest force, allowing propaganda—rather than reasoned argument based on ethical as well as rational and emotional appeals—to determine values. Against the backdrop of such transcendent sham, *you* shudders as the past becomes a metaphorical region for exploration, exploration through revision. For as real as it is in the sense that it has happened, the past is always unpredictable, and its unpredictability is the most consequential signifier of its reality.

The third and related main significance of Warren's exile lies in the relationship of the figure to Warren's development as a literary artist. Driven to find the forms that reveal the implications of exile, he produced a new form with virtually every literary foray after 1950. Turning ever inward and following personal impulses, continuing to press the issues, taking his figure deeper and deeper into the heart of a self confronting the dangerous sham of an abstract national or universal identity, he tore at the roots of America's favorite phantoms: chosenness and exceptionalism. Still, the heroic act held meaning for him, for it was the act of the individual trying to give body to values. In the series of shorter poems that trace the career of a single exile, he moves ever deeper into the consciousness, exhausting the psychological hiding places of the wanderer by short-circuiting his intellect with abrupt shifts of scene and memory. And this figure is related to the more recognizably representative Jefferson, Audubon, and Joseph, each of whom struggles for *place* between individual will and the demands of a common humanity.

In his histories and works of social and literary criticism, Warren cast himself as the exile observer, and that point of view shaped the form of all his nonfiction prose toward genres of discovery, and discovery became not only a mode but a metaphor for the process of self-making. In his late fiction, with the exception of *Wilderness*, he exchanged the historical and the political novel for domestic fiction in which regional claims haunt the assumed selves of the protagonists. And adapting this regional theme in *A Place to Come To*, finally, Warren produced what may be recognized as one of American literature's most significant fictional spiritual autobiographies to cap a career that had produced what is certainly America's greatest political novel, *All the King's Men*.

Traditionally, critics friendly to Warren have tended to emphasize his achievements in the New Critical terms he helped to popularize, or to value his heroic wrestling with a set of large American themes. More recent critics—Ernest Suarez, Anthony Szczesiul, Robert Koppelman, and Fred Thieman among them—have written of Warren as a postmodern answer to deconstructionist principles. In addition to these, Lucy Ferriss has found in Warren's fiction a concern with the question of voice "to the point that we may come to reassess his legacy in terms, not of themes or plots or even characters, but of the ways he pushed the envelope of narrative discourse, not just once but again and again." Ferriss labels Warren "prophetic" for his "disruption of [the Man/Self—Woman/Other perspective] either by admitting female 'selves' or by exposing the Self-Other dialectic as unreliable," thereby demonstrating "his faith in the continuing resilience of interpretation itself" (167).

Because he seizes upon the issues of language and meaning most relevant to the postmodernist, Warren is proving a major figure for those students weary of the more absurd reductionism of contemporary theory. But he is valued not because he is the antithesis of Derrida but because to a certain extent he travels the same road and looks at the world from a similar point of view yet draws very different, reasonable conclusions about the nature and value of human discourse. In making art from his most immediate experience of life, Warren left us a body of work that bridges modern/postmodern distinctions in intellectually and morally instructive ways. His insistence on the value of literary pursuits in finding solutions to human problems of identity and coexistence—values revealed in his career as critic and teacher—is encoded in the collective experiences of his various incarnations of the wanderer.

In *Democracy and Poetry,* Warren argued that poetry could be both *diagnostic* in its revelation of the ills of a society and *therapeutic* as a model for the creative process of healing. The exile in his poetry, fiction, and nonfiction may be a symbol of both functions. The development of that figure rides and drives Warren's artistic development through modernist tendencies to the triumph of his work in more idiosyncratic forms during the last half of his career. In his relentless pursuit of meaning through the privatization of a public trope and the development of his own system of symbols to depict the human dilemma of self, Warren sharply defined what may be one of the most significant representative figures American literature has yet produced.

◇ REFERENCES

Banta, Martha. *Failure and Success in America: A Literary Debate*. Princeton: Princeton UP, 1978.

Bedient, Calvin. *In the Heart's Last Kingdom*. Cambridge: Harvard UP, 1984.

Berger, Thomas. *Little Big Man*. New York: Dial, 1964.

Bloom, Harold. "Sunset Hawk: Warren's Poetry and Tradition." Edgar 59–79.

Blotner, Joseph. *Robert Penn Warren: A Biography*. New York: Random House, 1997.

Bohner, Charles. *Robert Penn Warren*. Boston: Twayne, 1981.

Boorstin, Daniel J. *The Americans: The Democratic Experience*. New York: Random House, 1973.

Brooks, Cleanth. "Robert Penn Warren and American Idealism." Rev. of *Robert Penn Warren and American Idealism*, by John Burt. *Sewannee Review* 97 (Fall 1989): 586–91.

Brooks, Cleanth, R. W. B. Lewis, and Robert Penn Warren, eds. *American Literature: The Makers and the Making*. 2 vols. New York: St. Martin's, 1973.

Burt, John, ed. *The Collected Poems of Robert Penn Warren*. Baton Rouge: Louisiana State UP, 1998.

———. "Reflections on Editing Robert Penn Warren's Poetry." Country Club of Pittsfield, Mass. Aug. 2, 1996.

———. *Robert Penn Warren and American Idealism*. New Haven: Yale UP, 1988.

Cable, George Washington. *John March, Southerner*. 1894. New York: Garrett, 1970.

Caccavari, Peter. "Reconstructing Reconstruction: Region and Nation in the Work of Albion Tourgee." Jordan 119–38.

Caldwell, Erskine. *Tobacco Road*. New York: Modern Library-Random House, 1940.

Cash, W. J. *The Mind of the South*. New York: Knopf, 1941.

Chesnutt, Charles W. *The Conjure Woman*. Ridgewood, NJ: Gregg, 1968.

———. *The House Behind the Cedars*. Ridgewood, NJ: Gregg, 1968.

Clark, William Bedford. *The American Vision of Robert Penn Warren*. Lexington: UP of Kentucky, 1991.

——, ed. *Critical Essays on Robert Penn Warren*. Boston: G. K. Hall, 1981.

——. Foreword. *Segregation: The Inner Conflict in the South*. By Robert Penn Warren. Athens: U of Georgia P, 1994. v–xv.

——. "'Secret Sharers' in Warren's Later Fiction." Grimshaw 665–76.

Cooper, James Fenimore. *The American Democrat: A Treatise on Jacksonian Democracy*. 1838. New York: Funk & Wagnalls, 1969.

Davidson, Donald. *Regionalism and Nationalism in the United States: The Attack on Leviathan*. Published as *The Attack on Leviathan: Regionalism and Nationalism in the United States*, 1938. New Brunswick, NJ: Transaction, 1991.

Dooley, Dennis M. "The Persona R.P.W. in Warren's *Brother to Dragons*." *Robert Penn Warren's* Brother to Dragons: A Discussion. Ed. James A. Grimshaw, Jr. Baton Rouge: Louisiana State UP, 1983. 101–11.

Du Bois, W. E. B. *The Souls of Black Folk: Essays and Sketches*. 14th ed. Chicago: McClurg, 1924.

Edgar, Walter B., ed. *A Southern Renascence Man: Views of Robert Penn Warren*. Baton Rouge: Louisiana State UP, 1984.

Ellison, Ralph. *Invisible Man*. 1952. 30th anniversary ed. New York: Random House, 1982.

Fain, John Tyree, and Thomas Daniel Young, eds. *The Literary Correspondence of Donald Davidson and Allen Tate*. Athens: U of Georgia P, 1974.

Faulkner, William. *The Hamlet*. New York: Vintage, 1931.

——. *Intruder in the Dust*. New York: Random House, 1948.

——. *Light in August*. New York: Modern Library-Random House, 1959.

——. "A Rose for Emily." *Collected Stories of William Faulkner*. New York: Vintage, 1977. 119–30.

——. *The Sound and the Fury*. 1929. New York: Random House, 1956.

Ferriss, Lucy. *Sleeping with the Boss: Female Subjectivity and Narrative Pattern in Robert Penn Warren*. Baton Rouge: Louisiana State UP, 1997.

——. "Sleeping with the Boss: Female Subjectivity in Robert Penn Warren's Fiction." *Mississippi Quarterly* 48.1 (1994–95): 147–67.

Fetterley, Judith, and Marjorie Pryse, eds. *American Women Regionalists, 1850–1910*. New York: Norton, 1992.

Fiedler, Leslie. Seneca in the Meat-House." Rev. of *Brother to Dragons*, by Robert Penn Warren. *Partisan Review* March–April 1954: 208–12.

Grimshaw, James A., ed. *Time's Glory: Original Essays on Robert Penn Warren*. Conway: U of Central Arkansas P, 1986.

Heidegger, Martin. "Remembrance of the Poet." *Existence and Being*. Trans. Douglas Scott. 1949. Chicago: Regnery, 1967. 233–69.

Hendricks, Randy J. "Warren's *Wilderness* and the Defining 'If.'" *Mississippi Quarterly* 48.1 (1994–95): 115–31.

Howard, Richard. "A Technician's Romance." Rev. of *A Place to Come To*, by Robert Penn Warren. *Saturday Review* 19 March 1977: 30–34. Rpt. in Clark, *Critical Essays* 71–73.

Jordan, David, ed. *Regionalism Reconsidered: New Approaches to the Field*. New York: Garland, 1994.

Justus, James H. *The Achievement of Robert Penn Warren*. Baton Rouge: Louisiana State UP, 1981.

Kehl, D. G. "Love's Definition: Dream as Reality in Robert Penn Warren's *Meet Me in the Green Glen*." *Four Quarters* 21.4 (1972): 116–22.

Killian, Lewis M. *White Southerners*. Rev. ed. Amherst: U of Massachusetts P, 1985.

King, Richard. *A Southern Renaissance: The Cultural Awakening of the American South, 1930–1955*. New York: Oxford UP, 1980.

Kirby, Jack Temple. *Rural Words Lost: The American South, 1920–1960*. Baton Rouge: Louisiana State UP, 1987.

Koppelman, Robert S. *Robert Penn Warren's Modernist Spirituality*. Columbia: U of Missouri P, 1995.

Kowalewski, Michael. "Bioregional Perspectives in American Literature." Jordan 29–46.

Kreyling, Michael. *Figures of the Hero in Southern Narrative*. Baton Rouge: Louisiana State UP, 1987.

Landon, Brooks. *Thomas Berger*. Boston: Twayne, 1989.

Lewis, R.W.B. *The American Adam: Innocence, Tragedy, and Tradition in the Nineteenth Century*. Chicago: U of Chicago P, 1955.

Mason, Bobbie Ann. *Shiloh and Other Stories*. New York: Harper & Row, 1982.

Melville, Herman. "Hawthorne and His Mosses." *The Writings of Herman Melville*. Ed. Harrison Hayford et al. 15 vols. Evanston, IL: Northwestern UP/Newberry Library, 1987. 9: 239–53.

———. *White Jacket, or the World in a Man of War*. Vol. 5 of *The Writings of Herman Melville*. Ed. Harrison Hayford et al. 15 vols. Evanston, IL: Northwestern UP/Newberry Library, 1970.

Mews, Siegfried. "Exile Literature and Literary Exile: A Review Essay." *South Atlantic Review* 57.1 (1992): 103–09.

Moore, L. Hugh, Jr. *Robert Penn Warren and History.* The Hague, Neth.: Mouton, 1970.

Morris, Willie. *North toward Home.* New York: Dell, 1967.

Nakadate, Neil, ed. *Robert Penn Warren: Critical Perspectives.* Lexington: UP of Kentucky, 1981.

O'Connor, Flannery. *Flannery O'Connor: The Complete Stories.* New York: Farrar, Straus & Giroux, 1971.

Percy, Walker. *The Moviegoer.* New York: Knopf, 1962.

Perkins, James A. "Racism and the Personal Past in Robert Penn Warren." *Mississippi Quarterly* 48.1 (1994–95): 73–82.

Porter, Katherine Ann. "Old Mortality." *The Collected Stories of Katherine Ann Porter.* San Diego: Harvest, 1979. 173–221.

Pryse, Marjorie. "Reading Regionalism: The 'Difference' It Makes." Jordan 47–63.

Ransom, John Crowe. "Reconstructed but Unregenerate." *I'll Take My Stand: The South and the Agrarian Tradition.* 1930. New York: Harper and Row, 1962.

———. *Selected Poems.* New York: Knopf, 1952.

———. "The Inklings of 'Original Sin.'" *Saturday Review of Literature* 27 (1944): 10–11. Rpt. in Nakadate 207–11.

Reed, John Shelton. *The Enduring South: Subcultural Persistence in Mass Society.* Lexington, MA: Heath, 1972.

Rosenthal, M. L. "Robert Penn Warren's Poetry." *South Atlantic Quarterly* 62 (1963): 499–507.

Royce, Josiah. "The Conception of God." *The Basic Writings of Josiah Royce.* Ed. John J. McDermott. Chicago: U of Chicago P, 1969. 1: 355–84.

Runyon, Randolph Paul. *The Braided Dream: Robert Penn Warren's Later Poetry.* Lexington: UP of Kentucky, 1990.

———. *The Taciturn Text: The Fiction of Robert Penn Warren.* Columbus: Ohio State UP, 1990.

Ruppersburg, Hugh. *Robert Penn Warren and the American Imagination.* Athens: U of Georgia P, 1990.

Simpson, Lewis P. *The Dispossessed Garden: Pastoral and History in Southern Literature.* Mercer University Lamar Memorial Lectures 16. Athens: U of Georgia P, 1975.

Snipes, Katherine. *Robert Penn Warren*. New York: Frederick Ungar, 1983.

Strandberg, Victor. *The Poetic Vision of Robert Penn Warren*. Lexington: UP of Kentucky, 1977.

———. "Poet of Youth: Robert Penn Warren at Eighty." Grimshaw 91–106.

Suarez, Ernest. "Toward a New Southern Poetry: Southern Poetry in Contemporary American Literary History." *Southern Review* 33.1 (1997): 181–96.

Sullivan, Walter. "The Historical Novelist and the Existentialist Peril: Robert Penn Warren's *Band of Angels*." *Southern Literary Journal* 2.2 (1970): 104–16.

Szczesiul, Anthony. "Racial Otherness and Romantic Posturing in Robert Penn Warren's Poetry." Conference of the American Literature Association. May 27, 1995.

Tate, Allen. "The New Provincialism." *Essays of Four Decades*. Chicago: Swallow, 1968. 535–46.

Thieman, Fred R. "Original Sin, Redemption, and Language in Robert Penn Warren's Poetry." *Mississippi Quarterly* 49.1 (1995–96): 311.

Thoreau, Henry David. "Civil Disobedience." *Walden and Other Writings*. New York: Modern Library-Random House, 1950. 635–59.

———. *Walden. Walden and Other Writings*. New York: Modern Library-Random House, 1950. 3–297.

Tucker, Kenneth. "The Pied Piper—A Key to Understanding Robert Penn Warren's 'Blackberry Winter.'" *Studies in Short Fiction* 19 (Fall 1982): 339–42.

Twain, Mark. *Adventures of Huckleberry Finn*. Norton critical ed. New York: Norton, 1962.

Walker, Alice. "Everyday Use." *Everyday Use*. Ed. Barbara T. Christian. New Brunswick, NJ: Rutgers UP, 1994. 23–35.

Walker, Marshall. *Robert Penn Warren: A Vision Earned*. Glasgow: Barnes & Noble, 1979.

Warren, Robert Penn. *All the King's Men*. New York: Harcourt, Brace & World, 1946.

———. *At Heaven's Gate*. New York: Random House, 1943.

———. *Band of Angels*. New York: Random House, 1955.

———. "Blackberry Winter." *The Circus in the Attic and Other Stories*. New York: Harcourt, Brace & World, 1962. 63–87.

———. "'Blackberry Winter': A Recollection." *Understanding Fiction*. Ed.

Cleanth Brooks and Robert Penn Warren. 2nd ed. New York: Appleton-Century-Crofts, 1959. 638–43.

———. "The Briar Patch." *I'll Take My Stand: The South and the Agrarian Tradition.* 1930. New York: Harper and Row, 1962. 246–64.

———. *Brother to Dragons: A Tale in Verse and Voices.* New York: Random House, 1953.

———. *Brother to Dragons: A New Version.* New York: Random House, 1979.

———. *The Cave.* New York: Random House, 1959.

———. *Chief Joseph of the Nez Perce.* New York: Random House, 1983.

———. "A Conversation with Cleanth Brooks." *The Possibilities of Order: Cleanth Brooks and His Work.* Ed. Lewis P. Simpson. Baton Rouge: Louisiana State UP, 1976. 11–24.

———. *Democracy and Poetry.* Cambridge: Harvard UP, 1975.

———. "Episode in the Dime Store." *Southern Review* 30 (1994): 654–57.

———. ed. *Faulkner: A Collection of Critical Essays.* Englewood Cliffs, NJ: Prentice-Hall, 1966.

———. *Flood: A Romance of Our Time.* New York: Random House, 1963.

———. *Homage to Theodore Dreiser.* New York: Random House, 1971.

———. "Irony with a Center." *Katherine Ann Porter: A Collection of Critical Essays.* Ed. Warren. Englewood Cliffs, NJ: Prentice-Hall, 1979. 93–108.

———. *Jefferson Davis Gets His Citizenship Back.* Lexington: UP of Kentucky, 1980.

———. *John Brown: The Making of a Martyr.* New York: Payson & Clarke, 1929.

———. "Knowledge and the Image of Man." *Sewanee Review* 62 (Spring 1955). Rpt. in *Robert Penn Warren: A Collection of Critical Essays.* Ed. John Lewis Longley, Jr. New York: New York UP, 1965. 237–46.

———. *The Legacy of the Civil War.* Cambridge: Harvard UP, 1961.

———. Letter to the author. Jan. 7, 1985.

———. *Meet Me in the Green Glen.* New York: Random House, 1971.

———. *New and Selected Essays.* New York: Random House, 1989.

———. *New and Selected Poems, 1923–1985.* New York: Random House, 1985.

———. *Night Rider.* New York: Random House, 1939.

———. "Not Local Color." *Virginia Quarterly Review* 1 (1932): 153–60.

———. *Now and Then: Poems 1976–1978.* New York: Random House, 1978.

———. *Or Else—Poem/Poems 1968–1974.* New York: Random House, 1974.

———. *A Place to Come To*. New York: Random House, 1977.

———. *Portrait of a Father*. Lexington: UP of Kentucky, 1988.

———. *Rumor Verified: Poems 1979–1980*. New York: Random House, 1981.

———. *Segregation: The Inner Conflict in the South*. New York: Random House, 1956.

———. *Selected Poems, 1923–1975*. New York: Random House, 1976.

———. ed. *Selected Poems of Herman Melville: A Reader's Edition*. New York: Random House, 1970.

———. *Who Speaks for the Negro?* New York: Random House, 1965.

———. *Wilderness: A Tale of the Civil War*. New York: Random House, 1961.

———. *World Enough and Time: A Romantic Novel*. New York: Random House, 1950.

Watkins, Floyd C. *Then and Now: The Personal Past in the Poetry of Robert Penn Warren*. Lexington: UP of Kentucky, 1982.

Watkins, Floyd C., and John T. Hiers, eds. *Robert Penn Warren Talking: Interviews 1950–1978*. New York: Random House, 1980.

Watkins, Floyd C., John T. Hiers, and Mary Louise Weaks, eds. *Talking with Robert Penn Warren*. Athens: U of Georgia P, 1990.

Welty, Eudora. "Death of a Traveling Salesman." *The Collected Stories of Eudora Welty*. San Diego: Harcourt, Brace, 1980. 119–30.

Wilson, Colin. *The Outsider*. Boston: Houghton Mifflin, 1956.

Index